HISTORY OF
THE OCCULT

HISTORY OF
THE OCCULT

T. Wynne Griffon

MALLARD
PRESS

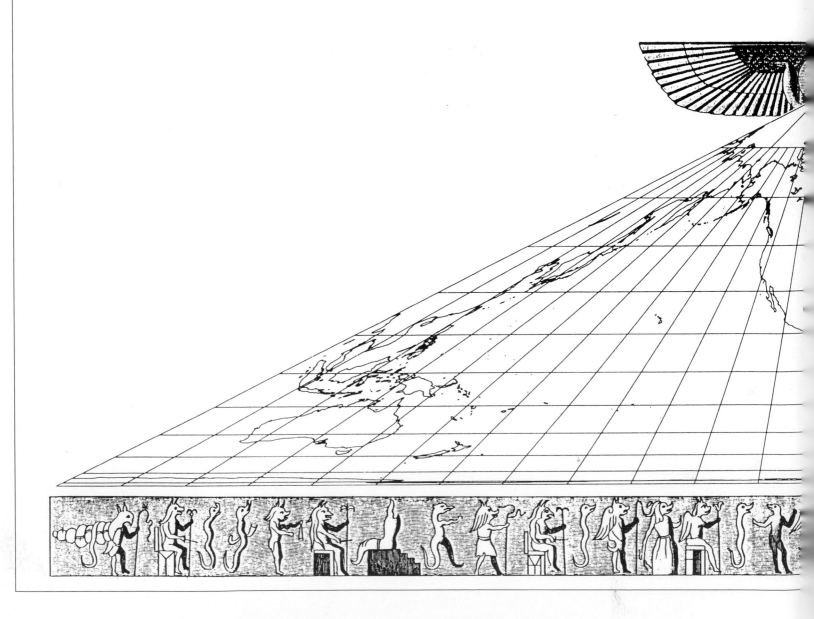

TABLE OF CONTENTS

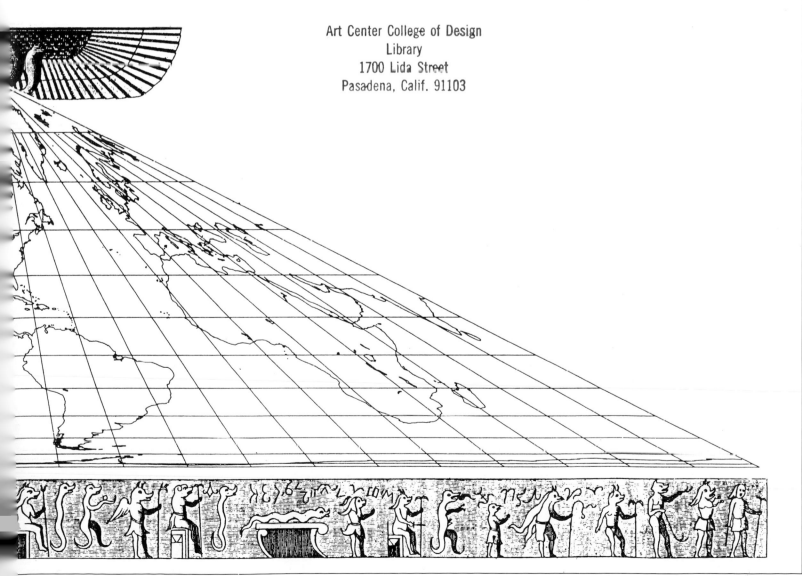

INTRODUCTION

For centuries, the occult has played no small part in the mind of man. In the fifteenth century, belief in astrology was common. Leading universities had professors of the subject on their faculties, and rulers of the era depended upon divinations by court astrologers.

Such ardent belief in astrology seems to have been a natural accompaniment to the pessimistic outlook of the age, as illustrated by this detail from the painting (*opposite page*) by Hieronymus Bosch. The demonic trio points to the corruptness of the clergy, while the fish, the symbol for the astrological sign of Pisces, foretells the imminent coming of the end the world.

Interest in the occult is stronger than ever in the 1990s, as evidenced by New Age shops (*above*), which are found all across the United States and Europe.

ince the dawn of time, people have been fascinated by the world of the occult. Historically, occult lore has been a secret body of knowledge and power that has been passed on by a select group. Though secretive, the occult was very much an accepted part of life. During the Age of Enlightenment in the eighteenth century, however, the occult conflicted with the new world view that was being shaped by science. As science began to exert its influence, the framework that had once explained the mysteries of the world could no longer provide the answers, and occult lore, which had once been regarded as merely secret knowledge, was seen as contrary, even dangerous.

In spite of disapproval and, in the case of witches, outright persecution, people continued to follow the occult arts, planting their crops according to signs of the zodiac or consulting the tarot for guidance. In time, the occult arts of astrology and witchcraft began to lose their hold over the common people, but even as the old traditions faded, a new occultism grew out of the abiding interest in the spirit world.

Modern spiritualism began in 1848, when the Fox sisters of New York claimed to able to communicate with the spirit world. Spiritualism attracted the attention of the well-educated and eventually came under scientific scrutiny, an ironic turn of events considering that less than a century had passed since all things related to the occult had been thoroughly rejected by the scientific point of view. The scientist now reasoned that if psychic events were real then there ought to be a logical, rational explanation for them, just as there was for every other aspect of the universe.

Psychic research began in earnest in 1882 with the formation of the Society for Psychical Research (SPR) in London by Henry Sedgwick, a prominent philosopher. His co-founders included the noted physicists Sir William Barrett, Sir William Crookes and Sir Oliver Lodge, and philosophers Frederic W H Myers and Edmund Gurney—all respected members of the academic community. Their stated goal was to study psychic phenomena and to rationalize them in both religious and scientific terms.

The following year Sedgwick met with William James, the eminent Harvard psychologist and philosopher, who in turn founded the American Society for Psychical Research in 1885. James, along with several other psychologists, focused on studying the spiritualist movement and its mediums—those who claimed to be able to communicate with the spirit world.

Rather than trying to prove the truth of spiritualists and mediums, the ASPR and the SPR sought to understand the paranormal in logical, rational terms. The mem-

Above: Practitioners of black magic gather together to perform their ancient rites.

Above right: Carl G Jung, the noted Swiss psychologist, had been fascinated by the occult since childhood and in fact had been raised to consider the mystical as a normal part of life.

Regarding astrology, Jung once remarked, 'We are born at a given moment, in a given place, and like vintage years of wine, we have the qualities of the year and of the season in which we are born.'

Opposite page: This illustration from 1695 provides a vivid expression of man's belief in the power of the stars.

bers' standing in the scientific community accorded psychic phenomena a new-found respectability. However, the ASPR and SPR were fraught with difficulties almost immediately, as numerous mediums were revealed to be frauds, forcing scientific inquiry to turn away from the séance room.

The spirit world nevertheless remained an area of study, and scientists began to examine haunted houses and poltergeists, the so-called noisy spirits that throw things and 'go bump in the night.' Foremost among the ghost hunters was Harry Price, a former magician who had made a name for himself exposing fraudulent mediums. Price's career spanned 40 years, culminating in a book entitled *The Most Haunted House in England*, which detailed the alleged haunting of the Borley Rectory in Suffolk.

In 1948, some years after Price's death, the SPR launched an investigation of Price's work at Borley Rectory and claimed that many of his findings had been faked. As far as the scientific community was concerned, ghost hunters were now viewed with the same disdain as mediums.

Psychic research entered a new phase in 1927 when Dr J B Rhine established the Parapsychology Laboratory at Duke University in Durham, North Carolina. Investigation into the spirit world and poltergeists was replaced by research that adhered to the more traditional lines of experimental psychology. Rhine's focused on precognition, telepathy and clairvoyance. Operating on the basic premise that these abilities existed in the general population rather than in a select few, Rhine tested thousands of individuals under carefully controlled laboratory conditions. Results were statistically analyzed and Rhine concluded that evidence of telepathy was irrefutable.

Rhine's work came to the attention of eminent Swiss psychologist Carl Jung, who had long been fascinated by psychic phenomena. Jung had even conducted a complex experiment comparing the astrological signs of happily married couples with divorced couples, concluding that couple with the most compatible signs were more likely to have lasting and happy marriages. Jung used these findings to support his theory of synchronicity, or meaningful coincidence. According to the theory of synchronicity, events in the universe may be significantly related in a noncausal fashion. As an example, Jung cited the pendulum clock in the palace of Frederick the Great at Sans Souci, which stopped when the emperor died.

While Jung praised Rhine's work, others decried it, pointing out that Rhine's results were difficult, if not impossible, to duplicate outside the laboratory. Duke's Parapsychology Laboratory closed when Rhine retired in 1965, but psychic research continues elsewhere, particularly at the University of Utrecht in the Netherlands.

Although much of the scientific world remains skeptical about the paranormal, it remains an area of academic study throughout the world and recently gained increased credibility when the American Association of Science admitted the Parapsychology Association as an affiliated member society.

The general public exhibited a renewed interest in occult lore with the advent of the New Age movement in the 1970s and 1980s. The New Age movement grew out of a sense of spiritual emptiness shared by many people, especially baby-boomers who had reached adulthood feeling disillusioned with 'having it all.' These individuals looked inward and began private metaphysical journeys and searched for meaning and harmony through spiritual growth. Drawing from the wealth of spiritual and theological thought from both Eastern and Western religions, the New Age movement also provided a renewal of the ancient occult arts.

Thus, the rich history of the occult remains an area of interest on both the academic and popular fronts and promises to be an integral part of the never-ending quest to understand the world that surrounds us.

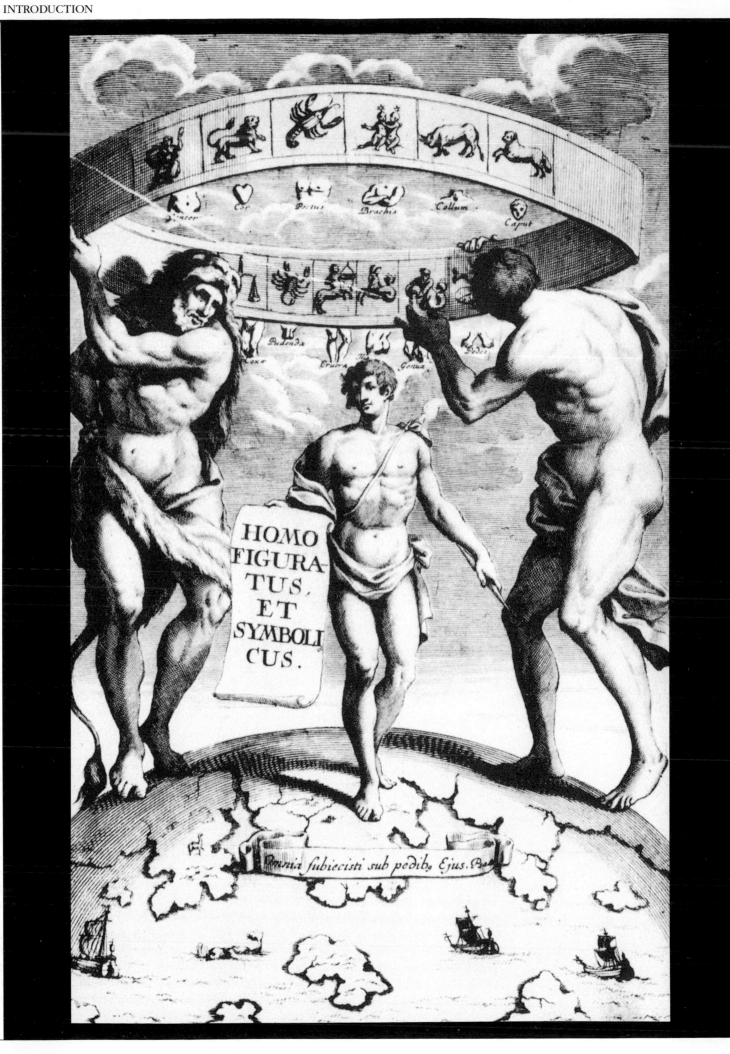

WITCHCRAFT

Opposite page: **An early twentieth-century representation of a somewhat friendly witch and her familiar, a black cat. With her blonde hair and slim figure, this witch is no longer associated with evil or the devil. Instead, along with the glowing jack-o-lantern, she has become a harmless symbol of Halloween.**

he witch has become part of our consciousness through centuries of literature, artistic renderings of literary figures, the papal bull of 1484, the bloody inquisitions of the thirteenth, fifteenth, sixteenth and seventeenth centuries, the Salem witch trials, fairy tales, cartoons and movies. The origins of witchcraft, however, are buried under layers of human evolution and the blending of cultures that naturally occured as people traded, expanded their territories, and conquered their enemies.

British Anthropologist Margaret Murray asserts that witchcraft was a powerful ancient religion of paleolithic cave dwellers. Pennethorne

Hughes, in his historical and eclectic treatment of witchcraft, cites animal cults as an early component of witchcraft. Paleolithic man's totemic relationship with animals is regarded as one of the most evident expressions of early religion. At dances and festivals celebrating a successful hunt, animal skins were worn by the priest-god, who became to the worshippers the incarnate of the totem animal. The priest-god's grunting, dancing, and euphoric manifestation identified him with that animal, and orgiastic coupling with him became part of the religious experience.

The roots of witchcraft can be traced back to the matriarchal religion of the Egyptians, whose settled, agricultural society exported to much of the world art, astrology and a concept of life after death. Since the earliest of times, woman has held the sacred position of hearth mistress, guardian of the sacred fire, giver of life and keeper of life's mysteries.

It was presupposed by most agricultural societies that it should be the women who maintained and used knowledge of herbs, both medicinal or poisonous, for ritual practices, fertility and abortion, and initiation. While Isis remained an important goddess and became the embodiment of the ancient maternal sex-concept, the festivals coincided with witchcraft's celebration of the sowing or reaping of crops.

The mythology of the Ancient Greeks contains references to witchcraft. Hecate was the nocturnal goddess of the moon and a huntress. As goddess of the underworld and mistress of all the black arts and witchcraft, she exercised control over birth, life and death. Her festivals were celebrated at night by torchlight, and her mysterious ceremonies were known to involve the sacrifice of black lambs. Hecate's presence was strongly felt at lonely crossroads, a common meeting place for witches. It was Hecate who was reputed to have instructed the legendary sorceress Medea in her arts.

When Barbarians from the northern

Above: This drawing of a witch provides a striking contrast to the pretty, young witch pictured on the previous page. Note, however, that both witches are portrayed with a black cat, commonly thought of as a witch's familiar. Familiars—minor demons that took the form of a small animal—helped witches cast their spells.

Witches were often thought to be in league with the devil. The drawing *at right* is an artist's rendition of the devil carrying a witch off to hell.

Opposite page: The witches of the late Middle Ages and Renaissance were adherents of pre-Christian, pagan beliefs and participated in Sabbats. In this illustration by Hans Baldung Grien, witches concoct an ointment to be used for flying to the Sabbat.

lands, with their own patriarchal religion, came in contact with the Mediterranean world, they attacked the centers of learning and culture, invading Greece, Crete and entering Asia Minor. The ancient Egyptian religion and its accompanying mysticism was forced underground, something which undoubtedly contributed to the clandestine nature of the cult.

Today, witchcraft is experiencing a reemergence with the Goddess movement, which has its roots in prehistoric pagan religions. Witchcraft is not based on dogma or a strict set of beliefs, but rather finds its inspiration in nature, revering the movements of the sun, moon and stars, the flight of birds, the slow growth of trees and the cycles of the seasons.

THE ELEMENTS OF WITCHCRAFT

For many people today, the term *occult* is synonomous with witchcraft. In that context, withcraft is usually thought of in its traditional sense—as heresy prosecuted first by the Catholic Church and later by Protestant sects. Accordingly, witchcraft came into popular attention in the late Middle Ages in Europe, peaked in Germany in the sixteenth century, lingered on in the rest of the Continent and Great Britain for another century or so, and flared up in America only during the seventeenth century, in New England.

There are two strains of witchcraft commonly referred to as 'white' and 'black.' White witchcraft is usually based on Celtic, Dianic and other pagan fertility beliefs. Black witchcraft or satanism involves devil worship, satanic practices and sometimes perverted sexuality, human sacrifice and murder. Satanism is the worship of Satan as a superior, or preferred, god. Its structure reflects an inversion of the Christian belief system.

Covens of witches are traditionally made up of 13 members, usually of both sexes, and preserve and pass on the knowledge and rituals gained by centuries of practice. They were called *Wicca* or *Wicce*, from the Anglo-Saxon root word meaning 'to bend or shape.' Those who could shape the subtle forces of nature to their will were often the teachers, healers and midwives of every community. Covens are by nature autonomous units, subordinate to no central authority or governing body. There is leadership but no hierarchy, allowing that each initiate might one day become a priest or priestess and lead a ritual or initiate a novice. The coven is a small community of friends. Ancient covens used to gather to exchange information and spells before they were forced underground. The *Book of Shadows* is perhaps the only text that exists which covens would have in common, and it is more poetry than doctrine.

Magic or sorcery has always been an element of witchcraft. Both types of

Above: **The witch as seductress.**

Below: **A scene from a modern witch tale, *The Witches of Eastwick*.**

Opposite page: **This Renaissance depiction of 'spring' presages the more realistic view of witchcraft in the 1990s with the advent of the Goddess Movement.**

witches are known to practice certain arcane spells and to be skilled in magic. Although some practitioners of the black arts claim that their powers were learned or acquired from demonic sources, magic generally is viewed as a combination of abilities, intuition and scientific principles based on mystical knowledge. For that reason, some consider magic as separate from witchcraft.

Magic is accomplished by creating a force field of energy that is channneled by complementary opposites, namely woman and man. This process is known as polarity theory.

Unlike the Chinese yang and yin principle, which illustrates a similar concept but sees the man as the embodiment of the 'positive' qualties of human nature that create energy, and the woman as the embodiment of the 'negative' qualities of human nature that shape or bend the magic, polarity theory in witchcraft sees the male and female forces as the same force flowing in opposite, not opposed directions. In a much diluted analysis, the female represents the life force, while the male represents the death force, each dependent on the other when life and death are seen as moments in a never-ending cycle. The bonding of positive and negative energies through the sexual act has long been mirrored in a traditional wine ritual. During the blessing over the wine the High Priest lowers a ritual blade known as an athame into a chalice of wine held by the High Priestess.

Michelle Delio, one of the founders of the Wiccan Church of Toronto, Canada, offers a contemporary alternative to the traditonal wine blessing in the fall 1990 issue of *Gnosis Magazine*: 'The sun brings forth the beginning. The moon holds it in darkness. As above, so below, for there is no greater magic in all the world than that of people joined together in love.'

In her book, *The Spiral Dance: A Rebirth of the Ancient Religion of the Great Goddess*, practicing witch and author Starhawk demystifies witchcraft and offers a highly engaging and personal approach to the history and rituals of the craft. Based on her own experience, she sees modern covens showing a greater willingness to create rituals that are meaningful to their members by reflecting their needs and insights.

FESTIVALS

Above: An illustration of Satan holding court for newly appointed witches, from Gerard d'Euphrates' *Livre de l'Histoire Cronique*, published in Paris in 1549.

Below: On Halloween, witches mark the coming of their New Year by recalling the dead.

Below right: Hollywood's treatment of Samhain, or New Year.

Opposite page: An early sixteenth-century engraving by Albrecht Dürer of a witch flying to the Sabbat on May Day eve, or *Walpurgisnacht*, a celebration of hope and joy.

Traditionally, witches have celebrated eight great solar festvals, or sabbats, that correspond to the Winter Solstice, Candlemas, Spring Equinox, May Eve, Summer Solstice, 1 August, Fall Equinox and Halloween. The Yule sabbat acknowledges the longest night of the year, and coveners wait for the sun to bring with it the hope and promise of summer. Candlemas occurs on 2 February and is dedicated to Brigid, the goddess of fire and inspiration. Candlemas is a time of initiation.

The Spring Equinox or Eostar ritual occurs on that date when day and night are of equal duration. It announces the return of spring and breaks the chains of winter.

Beltane is another name for May Eve, and coveners dance the dance of life as they weave their hopes around the maypole. They may jump over a bonfire in an act of purification that brings luck.

The Summer Solstice, or Litha, is the festival that acknowledges the longest day of the year and ritually sacrifices the God by throwing a representative figure made of woven sticks with a loaf of bread concealed in the center onto a large bonfire.

Lughnasad is celebrated on 1 August and depicts a time of uncertainty when the grain is ripe in the field but hasn't been harvested yet.

Mabon is a celebration of the autumnal equinox, when day and night are of equal length. It is a time of thanksgiving for the harvest.

Samhain is the witches' New Year and comes on 31 October. It is the time of year when the fields lie fallow and the gates of life and death are open. In Mexico it is traditionally called *Dias de los Muertes* or the Day of the Dead, when families take food and drink, flowers and candles to the graves of their departed relatives and friends and recall their lives and memories.

The origin of word 'sabbat' has undergone considerable debate. Most sources place its origin in the word *s'esbettre*, from 'to fling oneself about,' but Professor Margaret Murray tentatively suggested that it be read 'to frolic.' The sabbat is explained by Professor Murray as 'a very suitable description of the joyous gaiety of the meetings.' Her interpretation is shared by those who see the medieval sabbat as the joyful festival of escapists from a primarily penitential age.

While other explanations have been attempted, etymologists agree on these two points: There is no relation with the Jewish Sabbath or with the number seven.

Many consider witchcraft to be a shamanistic religion because it places high spiritual value on ecstacy which is usually attained through dance. Dancing was frowned upon by the clergy, and St Augustine wrote in the *Speculum Morale* that it was 'an invention of the Devil, the occasion of frequent sin, an insult to God, and a matter of foolish joy.' For the witch,

Above: Bouc de la goetie Basphomet, the goat incarnation of the devil, from a pen drawing in a nineteenth-century French occult manuscript, *La Magie Noire* (Black Magic).

Below: The public burning of Father Urbain Grandier in 1634 for signing a pact with the devil.

Opposite page: Joan of Arc, the French peasant girl, was a clairaudient. The voices she heard inspired her to do battle against the English. Victorious in battle, Joan was a hero to the French, but to the English she was a witch and was burned at the stake.

Ingrid Bergman played the courageous 'Maid of Orleans' in the 1948 RKO production *Joan of Arc*.

however, dancing could certainly have been a religious expression.

Satanism and Witchcraft: A Study in Medieval Superstition by Jules Michelet provides a colorful, period description of the Black Mass. One account hints that in its primary aspect, the witches' sabbat redeems Eve and all women from the curse put upon her by Christianity by her role as priest, altar and consecrated host. At the earliest nocturnal festivals gaiety and back-to-back dancing, as well as food, drink and even drugs, were part of the orgies, or *Jacques*, of the serfs.

Other accounts paint a less romantic portrait of the humiliations women and men endured at these nocturnal celebrations. On 15 February, the date of the Lupercalia of classical witchcraft according to Pennethorne Hughes, goats were sacrificed, women were whipped with straps made from the hides, masks were worn and images and balls were hung in trees.

THE BURNING TIMES

The persecution of witches began slowly. As Christianity spread across Europe little changed among the peasantry who believed in the Mother Goddess who gives birth to a Divine Child who becomes her lover and The Hunter, or Lord of the Grain, who is sacrificed in the autumn and reborn in the spring. As early as the twelfth and thirteenth centuries, a revival in the Old Religion developed momentum as troubadours composed love poems to the Goddess but spoke of Her in terms of the living noble ladies of their times. Churches and cathedrals were erected in honor of Mary, who had assumed many of the aspects of the Goddess.

As time passed, the church began its movement to quash the old beliefs. In Richard Kieckhefer's book *European Witch Trials: Their Foundations in Popular and Learned Culture, 1300-1500*, he makes the point that the lower classes were concerned with magic and sorcery as a way to improve daily life, while some of the more learned individuals sought to punish the so-called devil worship. The clergy was foremost among the educated classes. Clearly, the clergy's role in exterminating nearly 200,000 people accused of witchcraft in Europe during an otherwise brilliant period in the history of civilization warrants scrutiny. Some historians consider the total number of people put to death for heresy closer to nine million. The religious intolerance that gripped the thirteenth to eighteenth centuries spawned sincere fanaticism, and the resulting torturers, Grand Inquistors and witch hunters prove Kieckhefer's thesis only too well.

According to historian Pennethorne Hughes, three waves of persecution can be said to have peaked at periods when the influx of new ideas was challenging the authoritarian framework of the Church and eroding faith among the congregations, thereby threatening its very existence. The first peak came in the thirteenth century after the Crusades had died down. By then, clashes between Norman and Mohammedan forces were limited to skirmishes along Europe's eastern border. Nonetheless, Europe's restricted contact with the knowledge, mysteries and luxuries of the Near East stimulated latent heresies at home, where modernism was already loosening the strictures of asceticism. The Church retaliated in 1233 with the Inquisition. Pope Gregory IX assigned the Dominicans the responsiblity of combatting heresy.

Witchcraft was declared a heretical act which implied an intellectual process of guilty defiance of the Christian God and His vicar on earth. One of the earliest records of trial and punishment for worshipping a non-Christian god dates from 1324 in Ireland. Dame Alice Kyteler of Kilkenny, a woman of high social status and the leader of an Irish coven, was tried by the Bishop of Ossory and found guilty. While her title saved her, her followers were all burned.

The second peak of persecution came in the beginning of the fifteenth century. After the Black Death had decimated at least 25 million people in Europe, and after the Hundred Years' War had ended the struggle for control of France, and after the Great Schism between rival popes who fought for the sole control of the Roman Catholic Church, a sense of nationalism developed that brought with it a renewed interest in witch hunting.

The French heroine Joan of Arc was caught in this wave of witch hunting. Compelled by a clairaudient experience, she led her countrymen against the English in 1428. This peasant girl came to be known as the Maid of Orleans. She was captured in 1430 by the Burgundians, who turned her

Above: **A newsletter about the public burning of three witches at Dernberg, Germany in October 1555.**

Below: **Hanging was another method for executing witches. This drawing of the public hanging of Joan Prentice, Joan Cony and Joan Upney appeared in an English pamphlet in 1589.**

over to the English. After an ecclesiastical trial in 1431—where she refused to say the Paternoster and insisted on the authenticity of her personal revelation—she was burned at the stake as a witch. Ironically, she was later canonized by the very church that had denounced her for heresy.

Even today some authorities maintain that Joan of Arc was a witch. Professor Murray suggests that Joan was really the head of the Dianic cult. She points to Joan's admission that the voices that she heard, she had also heard in the woods of her native Domremy, where the peasants danced around a sacred tree in a fairy wood. In addition, Joan's use of the form 'my Lord' instead of 'Christ' indicated to Professor Murray that Joan could have meant the head of the cult.

In 1484 Pope Innocent VIII wrote a papal bull declaring the misguided actions of '… many persons of both sexes, unmindful of their own salvation and deviating from the Catholic Faith, have abused themselves with devils… .' Further, he declared that the heretical depravities these persons participated in would be examined by professional inquisitors.

Two prominent Dominican professors of theology of the Order of Friar Preachers, Henrich Institor and Jakob Sprenger, were delegated as the inquisitors. They approached the witch problem intellectually and reasonably by writing a book entitled *Malleus Malleficarum*, which translated means 'The Hammer of the Witches.' Its publication in 1486 gave clergy and witch hunters alike a detailed guidebook to undoing curses, and identifying, charging, trying, torturing, convicting and sentencing witches. The authors presented complex historical arguments on the existence of witchcraft, and then systematically refuted the overwhelming evidence that witches were a natural phenomenon. This 250,000-word book proved to be a powerful, and deadly, tool. The novelty of the printing press greatly contributed to the book's fame. Just thirty years after the Gutenberg Bible was printed to the amazement of the civilzed world, the printing press made the *Malleus Malleficarum* available to German, French, Italian and English speakers in over 35 total editions.

By the end of the fifteenth century, the Inquisition was in full swing. First established in Spain by the Catholic monarchs Ferdinand and Isabel in 1478, by 1492, the Grand Inquisitor was forcing the conversion or expulsion of Spanish Jews. In 1499 came the forced conversion of people of Moorish ancestry.

The Inquisition provided the clergy with

a veil of legitimacy for the illegal seizure of property. Powerful citizens could be denounced as heretics if they were perceived as a threat to the town's clergy.

The third violent outburst of persecution against witches came in the sixteenth and seventeenth centuries, when the Italian Renaissance and the Protestant Reformation had significantly altered the fabric of Catholic Europe. The Italian Renaissance lasted from about 1450, when Florence was considered the capital of Renaissance learning and art, to 1527, when the powerful Medici family that had ruled the Florentine Republic was expelled.

In 1509 Henry VIII made himself head of the English Church after being excommunicated by the Pope. Martin Luther started the Reformation in Wittenberg, Germany by posting 95 theses on the abuses of the Catholic Church on a church door. Pope Leo X condemned him of 41 counts of heresy and issued a papal bull of excommunication to him on 3 January 1521. From Spain the Inquisition spread to Portugal in 1531. In 1535 the Reformation came to England. One year later, John Calvin established the Presbyterian form of Protestantism in Switerland. In 1541 John Knox led the Reformation in Scotland and established the Presbyterian Church there. In response to the overwhelming rebellion of the Protestants and dissent within the Church hierarchy, in 1542 Pope Paul III established the Inquisition in Rome.

During this era, new currents in scientific thought were reaching audiences across Europe. In 1543, the Polish scholar Nicolaus Copernicus published his thesis *On the Revolution of Heavenly Bodies* and shook the very foundations of the Church's claim on the divine origin of the laws of the universe. Copernicus proved that the earth was not at the center of the universe as astronomers before him believed, but that the earth and all the planets revolved around the sun.

Giordano Bruno was a Dominican friar who expanded the theory of Copernicus into a form of pantheism and attacked the Christian doctrine of immortality. He was expelled for heresy; however, his views also brought him into conflict with both Calvinists and Lutherans. In 1600 he was burned at the stake.

In 1598 the Protestants were given the right to worship without fear of the auto-da-fé after the signing of the Edict of Nantes. However, less than 100 years later, Louis XIV, the self-proclaimed absolute monarch of France, revoked the Edict, causing thousands of Protestants to flee.

THE WITCH HUNTERS

Inquisitors were quite thorough in their physical examinations of accused witches, which usually began with shaving the entire body and stripping the woman in public. ('Witch' and 'woman' will be used interchangeably here. Some authorities claim that nearly 80 percent of the estimated nine million witches executed were women.) Public humiliation, physical and mental exhaustion, torture, dunking, whipping, solitary confinement and denial of sleep were all used to wrest a confession from the accused. Whether given a 'merciful' death by being choked to death, beaten into unconsciousness before being burned, or simply being burned alive, practicing witchcraft was a crime and death by burning was punishment for the heretic.

Pennethorne Hughes recorded the story of a witch hunter in Newcastle-on-Tyne, who in 1649 confessed to causing the death of 220 women in groups of 20 at a time. Jesuit-trained Peter Binsfeld, Suffragan Bishop of Trier, Germany, is said to have been responsible for the deaths of 6500 women, men and children in the late 16th century. He was ruthless and believed that 'light' torture was equivalent to no torture. While today, legally sanctioned murder is abhorrent to most people, his *Treatise on Confessions by Evil Doers and Witches* was a highly respected source book among his peers. Opposition to witch hunters was usually met with swift and terrible punishment. One Dutch scholar, Cornelius Loos, attempted to voice his outrage at Binsfeld's callous disregard for humanity, but he was condemned and forced to retract his statement publicly.

The Inquisition was not abolished until 1834, by which time most European countries had ceased burning the accused witches at the stake: England had stopped in 1684, France in 1745, Germany in 1775, Spain in 1781, Switzerland in 1782 and Poland in 1793.

Above and below: **The 1971 Warner Bros film, *The Devils*, dealt with witchcraft in seventeenth-century France. In these scenes we see an accused witch about to be burned at the stake.**

WITCHCRAFT IN AMERICA

In the United States there were two main strains of traditional witchcraft. From 1673 to 1708 the scholarly type was practiced in the Pennsylvania German community, especially in the brotherhood established under Johannes Kelpius in Germantown, now part of Philadelphia. To the brothers, witchcraft was a religion of nature and they celebrated the summer solstice according to early German tradition. They blended pagan, Christian and Jewish elements into a religion that held nature as the source of sacred power. By discovering the secrets of that power and learning to control it, a person could change reality for the sake of the greater good.

The second type of witchcraft practiced in the colonies was less cerebral and more practical. These witches were sometimes called 'the cunning folk' and were often asked to heal the sick, find lost items or precious metals, or send fair wind to a sailing ship. They resembled Native American shamans in their relationship to their communities.

There were also witches who were thought to use their powers to the disadvantage of others and could harass their enemies, and induce sickness or even death. Many times these witches were poor, elderly, eccentric or mentally ill women who were outcasts from their communities. The late Dr Margaret Murray, a leading authority on witchcraft, suggests that there are three common theories on witchcraft: that there were women who

possessed supernatural power and the evidence given at their trials was correct; that the women who were tried for witchcraft did not have supernatural powers but either were themselves deluded or were tortured until they admitted to things they did not do; and that there were witches who did what they admitted to, but did not have supernatural powers.

A fourth type of witch was said to be more evil than the others because she was in league with the devil. By making a pact with Satan, the witch would earn her power, paying later for it with her soul. The Christian influence apparent in this description of a witch shows witches in direct opposition to all that is good or godly. Frequently, the supposed evil and Satanic witches were harrassed by the authorities.

The so called 'proof' that incriminated many innocent people was known as the witch mark. It was believed that witches who were in league with the devil bore a mark of their pact somewhere on the body. Alternately, the marks were considered nipples where familiars were nursed. According to legend, familiars were imps or minor demons who assumed the shape of small animals such as dogs, cats, hares, toads and rodents. Once a witch mark was found it was pricked with a pin to see if it would bleed or cause pain to the accused. The usually natural phenomena of scars, birthmarks, corns, hemorrhoids, warts or supernumerary breasts which would not bleed if pricked were enough to convict innnocent people of sorcery. Reputed witch finders regarded the discovery of such a spot as final and irrefutable evidence of guilt.

In the winter of 1692, the small New England village of Salem, in the Massachusetts Bay colony, was the setting for one of the worst epidemics of witchcraft in American history. For the colonists it was a year of political uncertainty as the once cohesive Puritans experienced Protestant dissension.

Although there were 60 trials for witchcraft in the colonies before the Salem episode, events at Salem Village (later Danvers) began in the home of the town minister. There the minister's nine-year-old daughter, Betty Parris, and her 11-year-old cousin, Abigail Williams, spent hours in the company of a West Indian slave named Tituba who taught them something about

Below: **Death by hanging. According to some estimates, 9 million people, mostly women, were executed for witchcraft from the fifteenth to the seventeenth century. Once accused, the individual was considered guilty until proven innocent — which rarely happened.**

the magical traditions she had learned. Tituba could read fortunes in the patterns of egg white in a glass. Eventually, the exotic occult lore she recounted to the girls attracted the attention of others of the neeighborhood's adolescent girls. Compared to the thrift, sobriety, industry and prudence of Puritan life, Tituba's stories and charms brought an element of adventure to the girls' sheltered existence.

Betty and Abigail fell into trances and began screaming, sobbing or racing around on all fours and barking like dogs. The other girls experienced seizures and saw spectral shapes. When 12-year-old Ann Putnam described her struggle with a witch who attacked her with a long knife, neither the doctors nor the ministers could find anything physically wrong with the girls and the diagnosis of witchcraft was speedily pronounced.

The inquest was moved to the local courthouse. Gradually, the testimonies escalated until Betty named Tituba a witch. The other girls added that Sarah Good and Sarah Osborne were also guilty of witchcraft. Sarah Good lived on the fringes of the Salem community, an eccentric, pipe-smoking beggar. Sarah Osborne defied Puritan decency laws by living openly with a man before marriage. It is possible that these two women in particular were accused because they were already seen as outcasts and would not have the support of the community to fight the charges. Tituba confessed that she had atacked Ann Putnam in her spectral shape with a knife. Her confession of guilt saved her life and she was sold by the Parrises. The others, however, were not so fortunate. Before the witch trials were over, 19 women had been hanged, and one man who refused to testify had been pressed to death by heavy stones.

Cotten Mather, the celebrated New England Puritan, was foremost among the Salem witch hunters and published several witch-hunting pamphlets.

According to Catherine L Albanese, author of *America: Religions and Religion*, the clearest statement of the depth of colonial witchcraft beliefs was the admission of spectral evidence at the trials. This meant that claims by the girls that they had been attacked or harassed by a phantom in the shape of the accused individual could be used as evidence. Defense was useless because it was a commonly held belief that the specter of a witch could travel anywhere, leaving the physical body at will.

Below: **The title pages from Cotton Mather's witch-hunting pamphlets. Mather was the driving force behind the Salem witch persecution of 1692. Many of those accused of witchcraft were not practicing witches. Rather, they were the old, the senile, the mentally ill and the handicapped.**

The Wonders of the Invisible World.

OBSERVATIONS

As well *Historical* as *Theological*, upon the NATURE, the NUMBER, and the OPERATIONS of the

DEVILS.

Accompany'd with,

I. Some Accounts of the Grievous Molestations, by DÆMONS and WITCHCRAFTS, which have lately annoy'd the Countrey; and the Trials of some eminent *Malefactors* Executed upon occasion thereof: with several Remarkable *Curiosities* therein occurring.

II. Some Counsils, Directing a due Improvement of the terrible things, lately done, by the Unusual & Amazing Range of EVIL SPIRITS, in Our Neighbourhood: & the methods to prevent the *Wrongs* which those *Evil Angels* may intend against all sorts of people among us - especially in Accusations of the Innocent.

III. Some Conjectures upon the great EVENTS, likely to befall, the WORLD in General, and NEW ENGLAND in Particular; as also upon the Advances of the TIME, when we shall see BETTER DAYES.

IV. A short Narrative of a late Outrage committed by a knot of WITCHES in *Swedeland*, very much Resembling, and so far Explaining, *That* under which our parts of *America* have laboured!

V. THE DEVIL DISCOVERED: In a Brief Discourse upon those TEMPTATIONS, which are the more Ordinary *Devices* of the Wicked One.

By *Cotton Mather*.

Boston Printed by *Benj. Harris* for *Sam. Phillips*. 1693.

The Wonders of the Invisible World:

Being an Account of the

TRYALS

OF

Several Witches,

Lately Excuted in

NEW-ENGLAND:

And of several remarkable Curiosities therein Occurring.

Together with,

I. Observations upon the Nature, the Number, and the Operations of the Devils.

II. A short Narrative of a late outrage committed by a knot of Witches in *Swede-Land*, very much resembling, and so far explaining, that under which *New-England* has laboured.

III. Some Councels directing a due Improvement of the Terrible things lately done, by the unusual and amazing Range of *Evil-Spirits* in *New-England*.

IV. A brief Discourse upon those *Temptations* which are the more ordinary Devices of Satan.

By *COTTON MATHER*.

Published by the Special Command of his EXCELLENCY the Governour of the Province of the *Massachusetts-Bay* in *New-England*.

Printed first, at *Boston* in *New-England*; and Reprinted at *London*, for *John Dunton*, at the *Raven* in the *Poultry*. 1693.

In 1692, there was an outburst of witch persecution in Salem Village, Massachusetts. During an eight-month period, 19 women were hanged and one man pressed to death.

Hollywood examined the events in *Maid of Salem* (*below*), as did Arthur Miller in his excellent play, *The Crucible*.

WITCHCRAFT IN THE TWENTIETH CENTURY

Below: **Margaret Hamilton's portrayal of the Wicked Witch of the West in MGM's 1939 classic,** *The Wizard of Oz,* **has probably done more to influence popular opinion about what a witch is and what she does. As Dorothy herself said, 'Witches are old and ugly.' Little did she know.**

Despite the persecution of witches throughout history, witchcraft survived into the twentieth century. Interestingly enough, the old dichotomy between black and white witchcraft prevails. Two of the more flamboyant examples representing the black side, a decidedly male perspective, are Aleister Crowley and Anton LaVey.

Aleister Crowley began to feed his appetite for the occult arts in twentieth century London. A member of the Hermetic Order of the Golden Dawn, he was expelled when he attempted to take control of the Secret Society.

Called 'The wickedest man in the world,' a magician and a charlatan, Crowley himself preferred the appellation the Great Beast. He practiced a variety of magic he called sexual magic. Orgies, human and animal sacrifice, beastiality and drugs were all part of Crowley's quest for personal power and the manifestation of evil.

As a magician and a showman, Crowley would hold mysterious ceremonies he claimed were the seven rites of Eleusis before a paying audience. It is not certain what his place is in furthering the history of witchcraft, but his colorful presence has left an indelible mark on the footnote of history.

Another footnote to the history of witchcraft is San Francisco's Satanist Anton Szandor LaVey, whose practice of black witchcraft mirrors Crowley's. LaVey founded The Church of Satan, where his followers share his belief that sexual energy produces great occult power.

Though most people tend to associate witchcraft with the Satanism of Crowley and LaVey, 'Satan' is a Christian concept and

witchcraft predates Christianity. Sybil Leek, one of the best known modern day witches, says that witchcraft is 'a return to a nature religion' that 'teaches people their place in the universe.' The white witchcraft that Leek represents is experiencing a rebirth with the renewed interest in ancient beliefs and a rise in the symbolism that legitimizes and celebrates female power.

Z Budapest, a native of Hungary who now lives in Oakland, California, stresses the connection between witchcraft and feminism, referring to the renewed interest in witchcraft as 'the fourth wave of feminism.' (The first wave occurred early in civilization with the old matriarchal religions, the second with the suffragist movement of the late nineteenth and early twentieth centuries, and the third with the feminism of the 1970s.)

Another advocate of white witchcraft is Starhawk, who has founded two covens in California. She is a licensed minister of the Covenant of the Goddess, a legally recognized church. A leader of the goddess movement, she addresses the need to be

political. 'We need to talk about what would happen if we really did value air and water and fire and earth and other humans. What kind of world would we have of we honored these concrete things instead of abstracts like profits or a god "out there"?'

Seen as a new religion, this form of witchcraft appeals to people who reject the Christian doctrine of original sin, the idea that humans have been in a fallen state since Adam and Eve disobeyed God's order and ate from the tree of knowledge. Witches believe that divinity is 'immanent'—inside of the individual and in nature—rather than out there.

Holidays are not associated with messiahs but rather with the change of seasons and humanity's interconnectedness with the earth. Perhaps the most distinctive feature of witchcraft today is that women are seen not as evil Eves or pure Virgin Mary, but as goddesses representing all aspects of life—birth, death and rebirth. In correspondence with the traditional beliefs, witchcraft emphasizes ecology and maintaining all life on earth.

Left: In contrast to Margaret Hamilton's Wicked Witch, Elizabeth Montgomery's Samantha Stephens on television's *Bewitched* was a good witch who struggled to be mortal, but was continually tempted to use her powers, invoked by the twitch of her nose.

Above: Aleister Crowley—aka 'the Beast 666'—was a real life witch, perhaps the best known in the twentieth century. A practitioner of black magic, he bore no resemblance to most of the witches depicted in movies and on television.

GHOSTS & THE SPIRIT WORLD

These pages: **Inspired in part by the successful spectral photographs made at Raynam Hall in England in 1936, Walter Riley Hewett undertook an intensive study of a house in Indianapolis that was alleged to be haunted by the ghost of a woman who had lived and died there in the early part of the twentieth century.**

Hewitt's search lasted for nearly three years and resulted in these remarkable photographs that were taken in November 1954. Hewitt tried for several months to duplicate this remarkable series, but the ghost never again would manifest herself to the photographer.

 eople have believed in ghosts since time immemorial. At the heart of this belief is the assumption that the individual is composed of two distinct elements: mind and body. Most of the world's religions maintain that the body is temporal, existing only for a brief time, but the mind—or spirit—endures after the death of the body and then moves on to a higher realm, be it heaven, nirvana or 'the other side.' In some cases, however, the spirit is trapped in the material world and becomes a ghost.

Popular theory holds that spirits cannot leave the physical world when the death of the individual is marked by violence or tragedy, such as murder or suicide. The spirit remains part of the world, forever haunting the site of its demise. However, this is not always the case, as history is filled with numerous tales of ghosts who did not leave the world under violent circumstances. For example, Nathaniel Hawthorne, the American writer whose stories reflected the influence of unseen forces, frequently saw ghosts and believed that his house was haunted. Hawthorne repeatedly encountered the ghost of the Reverend Dr Harris at the Boston Athenaeum. Although they knew each other only by sight, both men frequented the Athenaeum, and Dr Harris continued to occupy his favorite chair by the fire even after his death. Although there may have been others present in the room, only Hawthorne was aware of the ghostly presence.

In the early part of the twentieth century, scientists and researchers began to seriously study haunted houses and poltergeist activity. Foremost among the 'ghost hunters' of the era was Harry Price, a magician with a penchant for exposing fraudu-lent mediums. Price's tools of the trade included felt overshoes for walking noise-lessly, steel tape measures to check walls for secret passages, a still camera, a remote-control movie camera, fingerprinting equipment and a portable telephone for instant communication with other investi-gators.

In 1929, Price launched an investigation of Borley Rectory in Suffolk, England. The old rectory had a reputation for being haunted, and when Price arrived on the scene, the current tenants, the Reverend G Eric Smith and his wife, were troubled by moving furniture, keys falling out of locks, and the sound of footsteps and a woman's voice. After three days of intensive study, Price declared he could find no natural cause for the disturbances. Moreover, he claimed to have made contact with the ghost of the Reverend Mr Bull, who had built the dwelling in 1863, and to have glimpsed a shadowy figure—supposedly a nun who had been buried alive in a con-vent wall.

Price resumed his investigation a year

later, shortly after new tenants, the Reverend Lionel Algernon Foyster and his wife, Marianne, had moved in. The Foysters were plagued by what seemed to be a poltergeist, or 'noisy ghost.' Windows were broken, doors were locked, household items vanished, furniture was thrown across the room, strange smells filled the air, and peculiar noises echoed through the halls.

Mrs Foyster in particular seemed to be victimized more than the other members of the household. She was thrown from her bed at night, nearly suffocated with her mattress, given a black eye and slapped by an invisible hand. Pleas for help addressed to Marianne appeared on the walls of the rectory.

Price suspected Mrs Foyster of concocting the incidents herself, but he nonetheless remained convinced that the house was haunted, and when the rectory was again in need of a tenant he leased it himself so that he could complete his investigation.

With the assistance of 48 volunteers, he carried out an extensive battery of tests, which culminated in the 1940 publication of a book entitled *The Most Haunted House in England*.

Price spent 40 years investigating psychic phenomena, and while he was not without his detractors, he had a reputation for innovation and integrity. After his death in 1948, his methods were called into question. The Smiths, the first tenants he met during his investigation of Borley Rectory, claimed that they never believed his findings. Later, in 1956, the Society for Psychical Research reviewed Price's methodology in the Borley case and concluded that he had manipulated evidence, and so the question of whether ghosts reside within the walls of Borley Rectory remains unanswered.

Borley Rectory is just one of many ancient manors in England that are supposedly home to spectral visitors. In her research for *The Stately Ghosts of England*, Diane Norman contacted 30 families and 28 responded that ghosts did indeed inhabit their homes. Roger and Alexandra Moreton-Frewen of Brede Place in Sussex provided Norman with one of her most fascinating case studies. Built in 1350, Brede Place had been in the Frewen family since 1708, and ever since the first Frewen had occupied the estate, it had been associated with ghosts.

To assist her in her investigations, Diane Norman called on psychic Tom Corbett. According to Corbett, several ghosts dwelled within the walls of Brede Place, including a man and a woman who could be seen walking through the eastern bedrooms and a priest who occupied the chapel and the room above it on the west side of the mansion. His findings were corroborated by present-day family witnesses, as well as by ancient family records.

At Frampton, another English estate, three-year-old Margaret Sheridan announced at breakfast one morning that she had just seen a small boy dressed in a sailor suit. Her announcement was greeted with silence, as her grandmother tried to distract her with toast. Soon after her encounter with the Sailor Boy, Margaret's family received word that her father had been killed in World War I. Years later Margaret Sheridan learned that the Sailor Boy was an ancestor who had been drowned at sea, and his appearance signalled misfortune for the family.

Though there have been many documented sightings of ghosts, their very existence defies all the laws of the rational

Below: Wisecracking comedian Bob Hope combined comedy with horror and a sheet-draped 'ghost' in *The Ghost Breakers*.

world and no theory can satisfactorily explain them. What we do know is that ghosts transcend our notion of time. Numerous sightings have confirmed that ghosts carry on as they did in their own lifetimes.

As he was repairing pipes in the cellar of a medieval building, Harry Martindale of York, England heard a trumpet blast. He looked up and saw a soldier with a trumpet walk through a wall. The ghostly apparition was followed by troops from the distant past. It was later determined that the soldiers were part of the Roman Legion of the fourth century. As they marched along in a dejected manner, Martindale could not see their feet, and he concluded that they were marching on the surface of a long-ago buried road. The town locals regarded Martindale's vision as the product of an overactive imagination, but seven years later two archaeologists saw the same scene—right down to the minutest detail, including the blast of the trumpet. The soldiers were dressed in the same green kilts and leather helmets, and, as Martindale had reported earlier, they carried round shields and assorted weapons, from short swords to long spears.

Researchers have also concluded that ghosts often appear as a harbinger of death. Referred to as crisis apparitions, these ghosts make their appearance when a person has died or is on the verge of death. For her book *The Probability of the Impossible*, psychologist Thelma Moss studied the files of the British Society for Psychical Research and noted that crisis apparitions are a worldwide phenomenon. Some theorists have hypothesized that crisis apparitions are a form of mental telepathy, while others have suggested that these apparitions are the subconscious mind's response to loneliness and worry.

In 1917, a young Englishwoman living in India felt compelled to turn around as she was dressing her baby. When she turned, she was startled to see her brother, who was serving in the military. Concerned about leaving the baby unattended, she immediately turned her back on her brother, and when she looked again he was gone. So convincing was the apparition that she searched the house for him, assuming he had arrived unexpectedly and was simply hiding from her. He was nowhere to be found, and she later learned that he had been killed in action the day he had appeared to her.

Around the turn of the century, a woman in Chicago reported waking up in a depressed mood. As she went into the kitchen to prepare a cup of tea, she saw an apparition of her brother, Ed, falling forward, his legs caught in a loop of rope. The woman cried out, 'My God! Ed is drowned,' and indeed only six hours earlier her brother, a stoker on a tugboat, had fallen overboard and drowned.

Poet and writer Robert Graves recounted his encounter with a ghost in *Good-Bye to All That*. While stationed with F Company at Wrexham, Wales during World War I, Graves met Private Challoner. On the eve of Challoner's joining the First Battalion, Challoner told Graves, 'I'll meet you in France, sir.' Challoner was killed the following May, but in June, Challoner's ghost passed by Grave's C Company billet in France, looked in the window to where the men were dining, saluted and walked on.

Daniel Defoe's short story 'A True Relation of the Apparition of One Mrs Veal' is very likely based on a newspaper account

Below: **With Death keeping watch, a ghostly figure plays dice aboard a phantom ship doomed to forever sail the Seven Seas.**

of a crisis apparition. In both fact and fiction, Mrs Bargrave is visited by her old friend Mrs Veal. Mrs Bargrave is surprised by the impromptu visit, for she has not seen her friend in over two years and Mrs Veal rarely traveled without her brother. During her two-hour stay, the two women made much of Mrs Veal's dress, which was unusual because it was made of scoured, or heavily washed, silk.

Two days later Mrs Bargrave visited the home of the Watsons, relatives of Mrs Veal. The Watsons had just learned that Mrs Veal had died the week before — 24 hours *before* she had made her mysterious call on Mrs Bargrave. Mrs Bargrave mentioned the dress of scoured silk, and discovered that only Mrs Watson and Mrs Veal knew that it was made of scoured silk.

In addition to ghostly apparitions of people, legend tells of phantom animals and things. One of the best known examples of an apparition of an object is the legend of the *Flying Dutchman*, a spectral ship, doomed to forever sail the seas with its crew of a lone skeleton because its captain defied a warning to turn back at the Cape of Good Hope.

A castle was spotted by writer Barbara Cartland on a walk through the Austrian countryside. After returning to the village where she was staying she learned that the castle had been torn down long before.

Many pet owners have reported seeing their pets after they have died. In one instance a pet appeared along with its deceased owner. In 1910, members of the Tweedale family encountered the ghost of a long dead aunt. With the woman was her dog. Although no one in the Tweedale family had ever seen the dog before, the family knew that the dog had been the aunt's companion.

Another form of ghostly activity is supposedly caused by a poltergeist, or 'noisy spirit.' Unexplainable household noises and disturbances are said to be the work of a poltergeist. Typical poltergeist effects include such things as pots and pans flying across the room, drawers opening and closing, doors slamming and pictures falling off walls. In other words, poltergeists are responsible for any sort of movement by an inanimate object. More bizarre examples of poltergeist activity include water running from walls and stones passing through walls.

One bizarre incident attributed to poltergeist activity took place at a farm in Macomb, Illinois. During a two-week period, 200 fires started for no apparent reason, and eventually the house, two barns, the milk house and the chicken house were burned to the ground.

In another incident, workers in a law office in Rosenheim, Germany reported light bulbs turning in their sockets, file cabinets opening and closing, and telephones repeatedly dialing a certain number.

In the nineteenth century, poltergeist activity was believed to be the work of a malevolent spirit force. In the twentieth century, various psychological theories have been advanced, foremost among them the hypothesis that poltergeist activity is a form of psychokinesis, the mind's ability to move matter. (Please refer to the final chapter for a detailed discussion of psychokinesis.)

Below and below right: **History is filled with tales of ghost ships and their ghostly crews. Perhaps the most famous legend is that of the *Flying Dutchman*, which was condemned to an eternal voyage when its captain attempted to navigate the Cape of Good Hope.**

THE SPIRIT WORLD

Since ancient times, people have been fascinated by the spirit world. Interest in the spirit world crosses all cultural boundaries. Shamans—the seers and medicine men—of tribal people are honored among their people because they have the power to communicate with deities and spirits. To contact the spirit world, the shaman usually goes into a trance. This altered state is induced through meditation, intense concentration on the rhythmic sounds of drums, or through hallucinogenic drugs. Once in touch with the spirit world, the shaman receives a message in the form of a song, prayer or ritual to be performed.

Black Elk, an Oglala Sioux Indian medicine man, first visited the spirit world when he was nine years old. At that time he became deathly ill, and two spirits came down from the sky to take him back to their world. There, in a tepee adorned with a rainbow, he met the six Grandfathers—the powerful spirits of the East, West, North, South, Earth and Sky.

The six Grandfathers taught Black Elk about the spiritual values of life and to respect the beauty and goodness of the earth. After his lesson, Black Elk was returned to his home, his illness cured and with a wisdom far beyond his years.

In the United States, Spiritualism as a movement dates back to 1847 and the publication of *Nature's Divine Revelations* by Andrew Jackson Davis. Davis argued that the human spirit remains alive after the death of the physical body and moves on to another world, or 'sphere,' where it begins another existence. Davis hypothesized that since the spirit still existed it could make contact with the people it had left behind on earth.

That same year, Davis' theories seemed to find support in Margaret and Kate Fox, two teenage girls, who made the claim that they had communicated with the spirit world.

In December 1847, the Fox family moved into a supposedly haunted house in upstate New York. Three months after the Foxes moved in, the two daughters, Margaret and Kate, aged 15 and 11, respectively, were so frightened by strange noises at night that they asked to spend the night in their parents' room. Distressed by a rapping she had heard every night, Kate finally snapped her fingers, calling out 'Mr Splitfoot, do as I do.' She clapped her hands and heard clapping in reply. Her sister Margaret then commanded the strange force to 'do just as I do.' She clapped four times and was answered with four raps. Finally, Mrs Fox asked a series of questions, and through raps and knocks, the family ascertained that the mysterious rapper was the spirit of a man who had been murdered in the house years before. Indeed, an investigation 50 years later led to the discovery of a skeleton under the house, a fact which was

Above: **Tatankaya Iyotake, a Native American shaman. Among tribal peoples, shamans, or medicine men, are revered for their ability to communicate with the spirit world.**

Tatankaya Iyotake, who is better known as Sitting Bull, became chief of his tribe and led the Sioux in their victory against General Custer.

Below: **Ritual hypnotism and dance were integral elements of the shaman's communication with the spirits. Here, we see Big Foot's band of Miniconjou Sioux in costume at a Ghost Dance ritual.**

The Ghost Dance religion of the late 1880s originated with the Paiute shaman Wovoka and quickly spread to other Basin and Plains tribes, proclaiming that a messiah would come and unite all tribes against the whites. The movement died out by the early 1890s, when no messiah had yet appeared.

Above: Sir Arthur Conan Doyle, the creator of Sherlock Holmes, was a noted supporter of spiritualism.

Below right: The Progressive Think- er, published by Mr JR Francis, circa 1900, claimed to be a publication that no spiritualist could be without. (See the caption on page 36.)

Opposite page: Harry Houdini, the great magician, waged a personal war against mediums who resorted to trickery. According to Houdini, Margery, a well-known and respected medium of the 1920s, was nothing but a fake.

Margery was one of the mediums investigated by the ASPR, which was itself divided by its members' views on the enchanting Margery.

construed as coincidence by some and as evidence by others.

Almost overnight, the Fox sisters were famous. In 1849 at Rochester, New York, they gave a demonstration of their ability to communicate with the dead, and soon were conducting séances for the public. Skeptics accused the Fox sisters of being frauds, and the sisters later confessed that the original rappings had been faked, only to recant their confession later on. Whether they had indeed communicated with spirits seemed not to matter, for they launched a movement that persisted for fifty years, into the early years of the twentieth century.

Others were soon to follow the Fox sisters, and all over New York, hundreds of self-proclaimed mediums—those who claimed the ability to contact the spirit world—held séances. A séance would begin with the medium going into a trance. Once in this altered state, the medium's body would become the channel for a spirit. Most mediums communicated through one primary spirit, who acted as a guide through the spirit world.

Mediums belonged to two categories: mental and physical. Mental mediums conveyed only spoken or written messages from the spirit world, whereas the more spectacular physical mediums produced an array of special effects, from moving tables to tooting trumpets. By far the most bizarre special effect was ectoplasm, the diaphanous matter believed to be the essence of a materialized spirit.

The spiritualism movement spread quickly across the country, with a heavy concentration of mediums in Philadelphia and the Midwest, and across the Atlantic Ocean to England and the rest of the Continent.

Among the most impressive mediums of the era was the flamboyant Daniel Dunglas Home. A native of Scotland, Home was educated in the United States, but was best known throughout England and the Continent. His séances were accompanied by such unusual effects as disembodied hands

and an accordion that played under its own power. Home's body also seemed to elongate itself before the eyes of the participants. Try as they might, his detractors were never able to produce evidence that Home had relied on trickery.

Home's most astounding séance took place in 1868. While in a trance, the medium's body was mysteriously transported out one window and back in another. As reported by Lord Lindsay to the Committee of the Dialectical Society in London, 'The distance between the windows was about seven feet, six inches and there was not the slightest foothold between them, nor was there more than a 12-inch projection to each window, which served as a ledge to put flowers on.'

As mediums flourished, scientists began to study the phenomenon. In 1882, a group of distinguished scientists—among them Sir William Crookes, Sir Oliver Lodge, Professor Charles Richet and Alfred Russell Wallace—founded the Society for Psychical Research (SPR) in London to research mediumship, as well as hypnotism, telepathy and clairvoyance. Sir Arthur Conan Doyle, the creator of Sherlock Holmes, was also interested in studying spiritualism. Three years later, under the guidance of Harvard psychologist William James, the American Socitey for Psychical Research (ASPR) was established in Boston. With some of the most brilliant minds of the day, researching spiritualistic phenomena the movement earned credibility in the scientific community.

One of the ASPR's early investigations focused on Mina Crandon, the wife of an eminent Boston surgeon. Dubbed Margery by her psychic investigator at ASPR, she was not only one of the most convincing mediums of the day, but also one of the most controversial. A physical medium, Margery was famous for her displays of ectoplasm, which was more solid than the typical vaporous material of other mediums. During a séance, phantom limbs of ectoplasm would grow from her body. Detractors noted that Margery's ectoplasm was not unlike lung tissue, the implication being that her husband, Dr Le Roi Goodard Crandon, had obtained the tissue, but to say so outright would have been to accuse a respected member of society of perpetrating a fraud.

In 1922, Margery entered a contest conducted by *Scientific American*. The magazine agreed to pay $2500 to any medium who was able to prove that he or she possessed bona fide talents. The panel of judges included J Malcolm Bird, the associate editor of *Scientific American*; Walter F Prince, an ASPR researcher; and the magician Harry Houdini, who was dedicated to exposing fraudulent mediums. Bird became an ardent supporter of Margery and wrote a glowing report of her in his magazine. As other sources picked up the story, Houdini's support was implied, even though he had yet to investigate Margery. Outraged, Houdini rushed back to Boston to conduct his own research. It took only a few séances for Houdini to declare that Margery was a fraud, an opinion that was seconded whole-heartedly by Walter Prince of the ASPR.

The event occasioned a falling out between Prince and Bird, with Prince intimating that Bird had perhaps been swayed by the lady's charms rather than by concrete evidence. When Bird joined the ASPR, Prince left the organization for the Boston Society for Psychic Research. Other researchers at ASPR did the same, creating a rift at the ASPR between the Margery and anti-Margery contingents. As for Margery herself, she seemed to lose interest in spiritualism after the death of her husband.

Both the ASPR and the SPR, as well as Italian and French researchers, investigated an Italian woman named Eusapia Palladino. Researchers were divided on whether Palladino had genuine psychic abilities or was an outrageous fraud. A hot-tempered and superstitious woman, Palladino seemed to be as authentic as she was deceitful. Frederic W H Myers, one of the cofounders of the SPR, witnessed Palladino at work in France and believed that she possessed genuine abilities, yet when he brought her to Cambridge for further study he concluded that she was a highly practiced fraud.

Among Palladino's supporters was Hereward Carrington, and even Carrington admitted that she had resorted to trickery during her séances. Nevertheless, after conducting extensive testing at Columbia University in New York, Carrington concluded that she did have the ability to communicate with the spirit world and that her tricks were simply for the amusement of frustrating her pompous investigators.

As more and more mediums were exposed as frauds, scientific support rapidly evaporated. Even as scientists, as well as the general public, were dismissing spiritualism as nothing more than hocus-pocus and mediums as nothing more than sharks who preyed on the gullibility of others, one woman stood out for her honesty—Eileen Garrett.

HARRY HOUDINI

COPYRIGHT 1911 BY THE STROBRIDGE LITHO CO CINCINNATI & NEW YORK

Yours Truly,
J. R. Francis

Above: **Mr JR Francis, the Chicago, Illinois publisher of** *The Progressive Thinker*, **a magazine designed to keep spiritualists informed. (See the caption on page 34.) Mr Francis also wrote** *The Encyclopedia of Death and Life in the Spirit World, Search After God* **and** *Is the Devil Dead?*

Born Eileen Jeanette Vancho, in County Meath, Ireland, Garrett left her native country for London and France, eventually settling in the United States. Garrett did much to advance psychic research. A willing laboratory subject, she also traveled worldwide giving lectures on the subject. She never took money for conducting séances and held them only privately on request.

Garrett's spirit guide was an entity named Uvani, who functioned as something of a manager, controlling the other spirits wishing to speak through Garrett. Garrett's most famous séance was held in London on 7 October 1930. The participants in the séance were Harry Price, the director of the National Laboratory of Psychic Research; his secretary, Miss Ethel Beenham; and Ian Coster, an Australian newspaperman. Hoping for a story, Coster had contacted Price about obtaining a reputable medium to contact the spirit of Arthur Conan Doyle, the creator of Sherlock Holmes who had died only a few months earlier. Conan Doyle had been an avowed spiritualist, and Coster reasoned that a man of his beliefs would be a prime candidate for making contact with the living.

Arthur Conan Doyle did indeed make contact through Eileen Garrett, but his message was overshadowed by the other events of the evening. The séance began with the voice of Uvani, but he was immediately interrupted by an urgent voice who cried 'The whole bulk of the dirigible was too much for her engine capacity.' The speaker was Flight Lieutenant Carmichael Irwin, who, along with 47 others, had been killed two days before in the tragic crash of the dirigible R-101 as it made its maiden flight. The crash was the worst in British aviation history up to that point, and critics called for an end to the airship program, which had been the topic of heated debate. Irwin's message to Garrett further stimulated the controversy.

From a technical standpoint, Irwin's message was detailed and accurate, but skeptics soon pointed out that the R-101 had been thoroughly discussed in the papers and very little, if any, information had been denied to the public. Garrett's reputation for honesty stopped the skeptics from accusing her of fraud, but it was suggested that she had telepathically received her information from the journalist Coster. As was her style, Garrett offered no explanation.

Though its heyday is long since past, interest in spiritualism persists in some sectors of the population to this day, and interest seems to revive whenever there is an increase in the number of premature deaths. For example, spiritualism experienced a resurgence in France during World War I. Robert Graves, whose encounter with the ghost of Private Challoner is recounted above, noted that there were a number of ghosts in France at that time, an opinion that was shared by medium Gladys Osborne Leonard.

Leonard's séances provided comfort to many grieving families whose sons and fathers were casualties of World War I. Noted physicist Sir Oliver Lodge was one who turned to Leonard, and he was so convinced of her abilities that he later wrote the introduction to her autobiography, asserting that 'to communicate with the spirit world' is 'not out of accord with the doctrines of modern physics.'

Leonard's spirit guide, Feda, possessed knowledge that Leonard herself could not have known. For example, Feda told Mrs Hugh Talbot exactly where she would find a small book that had belonged to her deceased husband. Mrs Talbot had never seen the book before and therefore could not have conveyed the information telepathically to Gladys Leonard. Much to Mrs Talbot's surprise, the contents of the book were as described by Feda.

The 1960s saw a revival in the spiritualism movement in Canada and the United States with the televised séance arranged by James L Pike, the former Episcopal bishop of California, through the mediumship of Arthur Ford. The séance took place in Toronto in September 1967.

Ford was a well-known medium who had previously attracted the public's attention with his claim that he had communicated with the spirit of Harry Houdini. But what etched the televised séance into the public's mind was Pike's conversation with his son Jim, who had committed suicide the year before. Through Arthur Ford, Jim spoke to his father, telling the elder Pike that neither he nor the rest of the family should feel responsible for his suicide.

Throughout the course of the séance, Ford was also the channel for various people known to Pike, including Marvin Halverson; Louis Pitt, dean of the Virginia Theological Seminary; and George Zobrisky, a lawyer.

The birth of the New Age movement in 1980s renewed the pursuit of contacting the spirit world. The New Age movement grew out of a state of religious confusion, and many religious authorities view the movement as a direct outgrowth of the countercultural values of the 1960s. As the once idealistic youths of the 1960s became the affluent consumers of the 1980s, many of them reached a crisis point at midlife and began searching for a meaning to life. The New Age movement guided them in their quest.

According to Carl Raschke, a professor of religious studies at the University of Denver and an authority on new religious movements, 'the New Age movement is a whole panoply of attitudes and beliefs derived from the human potential movement, psychology, occultism and holistic health. It's more of a lifestyle—a quasi-religious lifestyle. There is no New Age orthodoxy. These people are chronic questers.'

For many people the quest concerns contacting the spirit world. A 1990 poll conducted by the University of Chicago National Opinion Research Council reported that 42 percent of Americans believe they have had contact with someone who has died—usually a dead spouse or a sibling. These people turn to channelers, the updated version of the mediums of the spiritualist movement, for help in contacting the spirit world. Channelers claim to be pipelines for deceased humans, as well as for entities that never existed on earth.

Channeling today is big business, complete with agents and organizations designed to find the right channeler for an individual's needs. Detractors of the New Age movement hasten to point out that many channelers reap considerable financial rewards for their efforts, and while sometimes that may be the case, it cannot be overlooked that some channelers provide an integral part in helping people recover from the death of a loved one.

At the height of the spiritualist movement, numerous mediums claimed to be able to communicate with the 'Other Side' (*below*), but as history has shown only a few mediums were truly blessed with this talent.

At that time, however, a number of great minds of the day, such as Sir William Crooke, Sir Oliver Lodge and Sir Arthur Conan Doyle, were ardent believers in spiritualism.

ASTROLOGY

The human race's preoccupation with the stars is seen worldwide. The signs of the zodiac (*opposite page*) adorn a building on the Piazza San Marco in Venice, and in the Republic of San Marino, a series of stamps depict the constellations of the zodiac: (*above, from top to bottom*) Aries, Leo and Taurus.

strology, the science that describes the influence of the stars upon nature and mankind, was practiced by the earliest civilized peoples of the earth, and in every period of philosophic and spiritual enlightenment was accorded a place of honor by those of high birth and great learning. Indeed, there is no corner of the earth where those who are the wisest of their race and time have not read and pondered what James Gaffarel, astrologer to Cardinal Richelieu, so wisely termed 'the handwriting on the wall of heaven.'

Originally, there were two branches of astrology: natural and judicial. Natural dealt with the relationship between the stars and other material things, such as the rhythms of nature, the weather and the human body. Judicial astrology explored the influence of the stars and the planets on human choice and action.

The earliest known Egyptian astrologers were the nobleman Petosiris and the priest Necepso, who lived at approximately the time of Ramses II. Reference is made to these 'astromancers' in the writings of Athenaeus, Aristophanes, Juvenal, Pliny, Galen, Ptolemy and Suidas. From the testimony of these authors, there can be little doubt that both Petosiris and Necepso left extensive writings on astrological subjects, although little has been preserved to this age. According to Albert Pike, the distinguished Masonic scholar, books on astrology were carried with the deepest reverence in the religious processionals of the Egyptians.

In China, astrology set forth the rules by which both the state and the family were to be governed. The Chinese presumed the relationships existing between terrestrial rulers and their subjects to be controlled by the motions and positions of celestial bodies and other sidereal phenomena. It was to discover these relationships that the Chinese astronomers of all ages primarily directed their efforts.

The astrology of the ancient Chinese is established upon the line of imperial descent, for under the old regime the emperor was the Son of Heaven, the direct descendant of the azure God of the Sky. Among the most important ceremonials of the empire was the annual celebration of the happy new year, which took place on the night of the winter solstice, when Yang, the Spirit of Light, began to increase. South of Peking there is an altar of heaven in the midst of an imaginary well made up of the philosophic diagrams of Fohi. The altar is circular in shape and rises in three tiers, each level being surrounded by a carved marble balustrade. Upon the night of the winter solstice the whole area in which the altar stands was lighted by torches. On the upper terrace, or altar proper, there stood a tablet bearing the inscription, 'Imperial Heaven, Supreme Emperor.'

There were also rows of similar tablets

Above: **The Hindu zodiac is one of the oldest systems in the world, dating back to 1500 BC. Scholars believed that the Hindu zodiac developed concurrently with the Greek and Arab systems but was not influenced by them.**

dedicated to emperors of the divine line who had intervened between the first divine emperor and his then worshipping descendent. Upon the second terrace were tablets to the Sun, the Moon, the five planets, the Great Bear, the 28 principal constellations (lunar mansions) and the other important stars of heaven. The princes of the realm, their great Mandarins, and other dignitaries all stood in their appointed places during the ceremony. When everything was in readiness, the emperor ascended into the presence of the tablet of 'High Heaven' and, bowing humbly before the venerable past, knelt and knocked his forehead against the marble pavement, beseeching the Great Emperor above to look with favor upon his earthly son and to protect the empire.

On the Indian subcontinent, an examination of the Vedas, Puranas and other religiohistorical documents of the ancient Aryans suggest that India was indebted to neither the Greeks nor the Moslems for its astrological doctrines, but rather to its own sages who lived in prehistoric times, for its learning and proficiency. It is not impossible — in fact, there is considerable supporting evidence in the literary fragments of the ancients — that the entire structure of Chaldean, Egyptian, Greek and Roman learning, especially the more occult sciences, was originally derived from Asia. It is recorded of both the Egyptian Osiris and the Greek Orpheus that they were 'dark skinned men' from the East, who brought the first knowledge of the sacred sciences from a race or order of sages who passed an almost fabled existence amidst the highlands of northern Hindustan.

One of the earliest known examples of a horoscope belonged to Rama, a man born prior to 3102 BC. The horoscope of Rama is preserved by Valmiki in the eighteenth chapter of the *Bala Kanda*, as follows: 'Rama was born in Kataka with Chundra and Buru there, Sani in Thula, Kuja in Makara, Sukra in Meena, Ravi in Mesha and Buda in Vrishabha.' Translated into English, this means that Cancer was rising, with the Moon in conjunction with Jupiter in the same sign. Saturn was in Libra, Mars in Capricorn, Venus in Pisces, the Sun in Aries and Mercury in Taurus. The Dragon Head is calculated in Sagittarius.

It should be noted that Hindu astrology differs from that of Ptolemy in one very definite particular. The Oriental calculations are based upon what has been termed a natural zodiac, while that of Western people is based upon what is called an intellectual zodiac. Approximately 1400 years

have passed since these two zodiacs coincided, and there is now a discrepancy of some 20 degrees between the two systems. The Oriental zodiac is, therefore, about 20 degrees behind the Ptolemaic, and in applying Hindu keywords to horoscopes set up according to the Western methods, this difference must be taken into consideration.

The astral philosophy of the Greeks was most certainly derived from that of the Far East. The first allusion to astrology in Greek literature is found in a description of Plato. In his *De Nativitatibus*, Julius Firmicus Maternus calculated the horoscope of this remarkable man: 'If the Ascendant shall be Aquarius, Mars, Mercury and Venus therein posited; and if Jupiter then be placed in the seventh, having Leo for his sign, and in the second the Sun in Pisces and the Moon in fifth House, beholding the Ascendant with a trine aspect, and Saturn in the ninth from the Ascendant in Libra. This Geniture renders a Man Interpreter of Divine and heavenly Institutions, who endued with instructive speech, and the power of Divine Wit, and formed in a manner by a celestial Institution, by the true License of disputations shall arrive at all the secrets of Divinity.'

The horoscope as set up by Firmicus is extremely probable. The sign in which the Sun is placed agrees with Plato's physical appearance, as does the ascendant with the qualities of mind. Pisces confers heaviness and breadth, and 'Aristo named him *Plato* (which implieth Latitude) in allusion to the largeness of his person; others say, to the wideness of his shoulders.' Neanthes relates the term to the breadth of his forehead.

Jupiter, the ruler of Pisces, when powerful, gives the 'divine appearance,' and, according to Hesychius, the philosopher was called *Serapis* from the majesty and dignity of his person. Aquarius was termed the sign of the truth-seeker, and of all men it may be said of Plato that he lived for truth alone. The serenity of Plato's mind, the earnestness of his endeavor, the synthesis which marks his classification of facts, the humaneness and rationality of his soul — all these qualities reveal the highly developed Aquarian type.

The story of the influence of astrology upon the Roman Empire is a history of Rome itself. The emperor Numa practiced all forms of magical arts. H P Blavatsky, in *The Secret Doctrine*, relates that 'Marcus Antonius never traveled without an astrologer recommended to him by Cleopatra.'

Augustus Caesar, before his ascent to the

throne, went to the astrologer Theogenes, who fell on his knees before the youth and predicted his rise to power. Augustus was so impressed that he published his horoscope and had a silver coin struck with the sign of Capricorn, under which he was born, upon one of its surfaces.

Sylla, the astrologer and mathematician, read the horoscope of Caligula, revealing to Caesar the time and conditions under which he would die. This same emperor was admonished by the Sortes Antiatinae that 'he should beware of Cassius,' and by the conspiracy and sword of a man of this name he died.

Otho surrounded himself with seers and astrologers, and sought advice from Ptolemy, being assured by the latter that he should outlive Nero and be a ruler of the Romans. Nero himself practiced astrology, and no more dramatic incident is recorded in the history of Rome than the interview between Agrippina, the mother of Nero, and the Chaldean astrologer. This scheming woman sought the advice of the stars as to the outcome of her life's ambition to make her son the emperor of the Romans. The astrologer cast the nativity and rendered the following judgment: 'If he reigns, he shall kill his mother.'

Without a moment's hesitation, Agrippina, with teeth set, hissed back the answer: 'Let him kill me so that he but reigns!'

Needless to say, the stars gave honest judgment.

In later years, Nero surrounded himself with astrologers, and Bamilus was not only his constant adviser but repeatedly warned the emperor that his reckless course was bringing him to an untimely end.

Hadrian, the Roman emperor from 117-138 AD, wrote from the stars a diary of his own life, even predicting the hour of his own death, all this long before the incidents themselves actually occurred. Septimus Severus caused his horoscope to be inscribed upon the roof of his judicial palace with the statement of his foreknowledge that he would not return alive from his expedition to England. He died at York, as he had predicted.

The eclectic spirit prevailing in Rome caused the Eternal City to become a center for the exchange of ideas—religious, philosophic and political. The temples of various gods were clustered together in the Forum. In this cosmopolitan atmosphere astrology gained many converts among the powerful, the wealthy and the wise. Several new titles were bestowed upon the stargazers. They were called *astrologi*, *mathematici* and *genethliaci*.

The origin of the science caused those proficient in it to also be termed *Chaldaei*, or *Babylonii*. In writings of this period, therefore, astrologers of all nationalities were known as *Chaldeans*, and are so described by Hippolytus, who makes grudging reference to their abilities. According to H P Blavatsky in *The Secret Doctrine*, 'Under the wisest emperors,

Above: A medieval woodcut of the 12 signs of the zodiac as they wheel, with the Sun and Moon, around an earthly kingdom.

Below: Julius Caesar was warned by a soothsayer 'to beware the ides of March,' but he failed to heed the warning and attended a meeting of the Roman Senate on that day. There, he met his death at the hand of conspirators who were waiting for him, daggers ready.

Above: **Man's intimate relationship with the stars is symbolized by this widely reproduced European engraving from the Middle Ages.**

Below right: **A Tibetan mandala. The Tibetan astrological system is extremely accurate, but its methods are a closely guarded secret.**

Rome had a School of Astrology, wherein were secretly taught the occult influences of Sun, Moon and Saturn.' Even when the astrologers fell upon evil times, they continued to flourish.

The Arabs possessed an extraordinary capacity for scholarship, and, like the Chinese, established their social and cultural systems upon the solid foundation of knowledge.

During the Middle Ages a theological blight descended upon the greater part of Christendom, as the priests stripped the occidental countries of practically every vestige of classical learning. Arrogant princes and an ambitious clergy conspired together to the common woe. Thus, Europe continued for centuries in an unbelievable state of superstition and ignorance. It was not until the Moorish conquests of Spain in the eighth century that knowledge, culture and progress regained ascendancy over the selfishness of petty nobles and the bigotry of ecclesiastics.

From all parts of Europe men seeking to learn, who long had been denied intellectual stimulation, flocked to the universities of the Moors. Returning in due time to their own countries, these scholars established schools and clinics for the further dissem-ination of art, philosophy and science. It was from the Moorish professors of Toledo that Gerard of Cremona secured the famous *Canon* of Avicenna, which became the premiere astro-medical textbook of Europe.

Astrology, which had conquered Italy a thousand years earlier, had its triumphant re-entry into Europe with the Moors. It permeated their scientific books and was accepted as an essential part of their curriculums. From Spain, astrology spread first to one country, then to another, until the science, with all its Arabic involvements and complications, came to be generally recognized and accorded a high place in many centers of learning.

The celebrated Caliph Al-Raschid, second only to Solomon in glory and wisdom, was given to the occult arts, and the stories of the *The Thousand and One Nights* abound with references to astrology and astromancy. Al-Raschid ordered the astronomical and astrological books of Ptolemy to be translated into Arabic, and it is now generally accepted that the Caliph—a man profoundly versed in literature and science—was a strong proponent of astrology and frequently employed it in administering grave problems of state.

The Arabs perfected the mathematical aspect of astrology, achieving a high degree of accuracy in spherical trigonometry and other advanced mathematical sciences. The Arabs also devised numerous tables for the calculation of nativities and reduced a vast astrological lore to an orderly and systematic procedure. They formulated many of the terms now used in astrological literature, creating a considerable vocabulary to distinguish the nomenclature of this science from that of other forms of learning.

The Arabian astrologers became proficient not only in natal astrology but in predictions relating to cities, races and religions. Predictions were successfully made from eclipses of the Sun and Moon, comets and other celestial phenomena.

Above: An ancient Arab zodiac. The science of astrology had been lost to European scholars for several hundred years, but its teachings survived in Arabic manuscripts. Thus this ancient lore was able to return to prominence at European universities around the tenth century.

Left: The destinies of the peasantry and nobility alike were ruled by the stars. Whether it was a question of when to wage battle or to plant crops, the answer was determined by consulting an astrologer.

Above: **A plate depicting the signs of the Chinese zodiac. Chinese astrologers concentrated on understanding the impact the motions and positions of the celestial bodies had on their earthly rulers.**

Below: **The Aztec zodiac is divided into 20 signs.**

Their technical name for astrology is 'The Science of the Decrees of the Stars.' The astrologer is called Ah-Kami, or Munadjdjim, the latter name *also* signifying an astronomer. Indeed, it was not until the nineteenth century that any precise distinction was made between an astronomer and an astrologer—and each was presumed to possess the knowledge peculiar to the other.

The ancient people of Central America also developed elaborate systems of natal and judicial astrology. Prescott, in his *History of the Conquest of Mexico*, notes that the Aztecs, when a child was born into their nation, instantly summoned an adivino (astrologer) whose duty it was to ascertain the destiny of the newborn babe. 'The sign,' wrote Lucien Biart, 'that marked the day of his birth was noted, and also the one that ruled during the period of the last 13 years. If the child was born at midnight, they compared the preceding day and the day following.'

Like the Greeks, Egyptians and other ancient peoples, the augurs among the Mexicans foretold events from the positions of the planets, the arrangements of sacred numbers, from clouds, storms, eclipses, comets, the flight of birds and the actions of animals. In ancient Mexico, as in

other parts of the civilized world, astrology was cultivated not by the ignorant and superstitious but by the great and learned. Three of the great names in the whole history of the Aztec nation are intimately connected with this science—Quetzalcoatl, Nazahualpilli and Montezuma.

The Aztec's astrological knowledge was derived principally from the doctrines and revelations of Quetzalcoatl, the first and foremost of their philosophers and teachers. Quetzalcoatl was the Son of Heaven. His true parent was the Universal Creator in the dual aspect of father-mother. In the physical world he was born of the Virgin Sochiquetzal, and his coming was annunciated by a heavenly apparition, which declared that it had come as an ambassador from the god of the Milky Way to discover among mortals the blessed Virgin who was to become the mother of the Divine Incarnation.

Nazahualpilli was the king of Tezcuco. Of this king, Torquemada writes in the second book of *The Indian Monarchy*, 'They say that he was a great astrologer and prided himself much on his knowledge of the motions of the celestial bodies; and being attached to this study, that he caused inquiries to be made throughout the entire of his dominions, for all such persons as were at all conversant with it, whom he brought to his court, and imparted to them whatever he knew; and ascending by night on the terraced roof of his palace, he thence considered the stars, and disputed with them on all difficult questions concerned with them.'

Montezuma was the most outstanding organizing genius of the Aztec world. This last king of the Indians was not only a great general, statesman and prince, but also a distinguished patron of the occult arts, especially astrology.

In his *Mexico, A Study of Two Americas*, Stuart Chase relates that, 'In astronomy the American mind reached its climax, and the Mayas were its high priests. Starting with observations of the heavens some 4000 years ago, the Mayan calendar was developed to a point where it was possible to distinguish, without duplication, any given day in 370,000 years! This was far in advance of European astronomy, more accurate than anything so-called Western civilization achieved until very recent times.

The Aztecs borrowed Mayan principles but never achieved such mathematical elegance. Their solar calendar, however, was more accurate than that of the Spaniards. They were found in full knowledge of

the year of Venus, eclipses, solstices, equinoxes and such phenomena… It is not unreasonable to suppose that, during these 150 years (450 to 600 AD), the Mayas were the most civilized people on the planet?'

The astrological systems of the Aztecs and the other nations of Central America and Yucatan are evidently identical in origin with that of the Mayans, differing only in minor details from those of the more northern Indians. Alexander von Humboldt, an authority on these subjects, has pointed out the numerous correspondences which exist between the astrological symbols of the Mexicans and those of the Chaldeans, Greeks and Egyptians. Though present knowledge of Aztec metaphysics is extremely fragmentary, evidence does suggest the vastness and profundity of their theories.

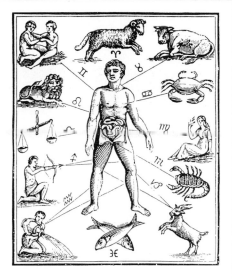

Above: **A phlebotomic figure illustrating the relationship between every part of the body and the signs of the zodiac. During medieval times, physicians used charts like this to determine when a patient must be operated on or have his blood let.**

Below: **Man is the symbolic center of the universe in this zodiac chart from the Renaissance.**

WESTERN TRADITIONS

Western literature and science is filled with many illustrious exponents of astrology, both ancient and modern. In an article on astrology in the writings of Shakespeare, John Cook thus summarizes the results of an extensive research: 'The numerous allusions to the practice of astrology, the striking metaphors and apt illustrations, scattered throughout the plays of Shakespeare, at once attest to his intimate acquaintance with the general principles of the science, and the popularity of astrological faith… He has left us sufficient evidence to show that he was largely influenced by a subject which has left indelible marks in the language and literature of England.'

The bard of Avon puts the following words into the mouth of King Lear: 'It is the stars, the stars above us govern our conditions.'

Even more striking is Shakespeare's flair for astrologic humor. He makes a disgruntled player to complain: 'It is impossible that anything should be as I would have it; for I was born, Sir, when the Crab was ascending; and all my affairs go backwards.'

Dante's astrology is written in majestic measure. We follow him into the vastness of space in his *Paradiso* (Canto XXII):

'… I saw
The sign that follows Taurus, and was
  in it.
Oh glorious stars! Oh light impregnated
With mighty virtues, from which
  I acknowledge
All of my genius whatsoe'er it be,
With you was born, and hid himself
  with you.
He who is father of all mortal life,
When first I tasted of the Tuscan air;
And then when grace was freely given
  to me
To enter the high wheel which turns
  you round
Your region was alloted unto me.'

'For Dante, astrology was the noblest of the sciences,' writes H Flanders Dunbar in *Symbolism in Medieval Thought.* 'For Dante, the principle of individualization is the influence of planets and stars, or, more accurately, of the intelligences by which they are moved. The ego, created directly by God, in its connection with the body comes under stellar influence, and at birth is stamped like wax by a seal. All impressions from the stars are good, since there is no lovableness that does not reflect the lovableness of God. It is the harmonizing and proportioning of these good qualities in their true relationships that make this or that person more or less perfect. It is likely that the modern reader, with his oversimple conception of astrology, will lose much

Above: Galileo Galilei (1564-1642) was the first astronomer to use a telescope. What he saw through his telescope convinced him of the truth of Copernicus' view that the earth rotates on its axis and revolves around the sun. In Galileo's day, astronomy and astrology were not seen as separate and distinct disciplines as they are today.

Right: This 'map of the heavens,' with its pictorial representation of the constellations, was commissioned by Pope Gregory XIII in the sixteenth century.

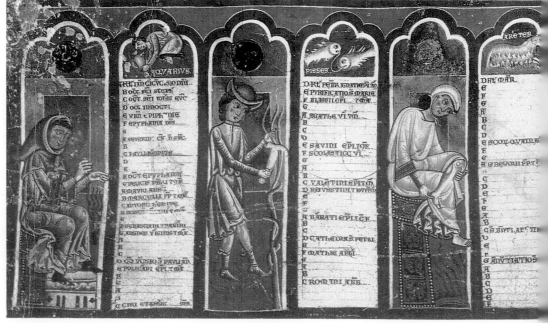

Above: A fresco by Giovanni Maria Falconetto depicting the astrological sign of Cancer.

At bottom: An Italian calendar depicting the first six signs of the zodiac.

Above: Nicolaus Copernicus (1473-1543), the father of modern astronomy and one of the most distinguished astrologer-scientists in the Western world.

Below: The horoscope of Agostino Chigi. This fresco shows the position of the planets and the constellations at the time of Chigi's birth on 30 November 1466.

of the meaning of Dante… Astrology was both more complicated and more scientific in method than the familiar birth-month pamphlets suggest.'

Goethe commits himself in no uncertain terms to both the theory and practice of astrology. He begins his autobiography thus: 'On the 28th of August 1749, at midday, as the clock struck twelve, I came into the world, at Frankfurt-on-Main. The aspect of the stars was propitious: the Sun stood in the sign of the Virgin, and had culminated for the day; Jupiter and Venus looked on with a friendly eye, and Mercury not adversely; the attitude of Saturn and Mars was neutral; the Moon alone, just full, exerted all the more as her power of opposition had just reached her planetary hour. She, therefore, resisted my birth, which could not be accomplished until this hour was passed. These auspicious aspects which the astrologers subsequently interpreted very favorably for me may have been the causes of my preservation.'

Nor is science represented by less impressive names. According to Thorndike in his *History of Magic and Experimental Science*, 'A trio of great names, Pliny, Galen and Ptolemy, stand out above all others in the history of science in the Roman Empire.' Needless to say, all these distinguished thinkers not only admitted the influence of the planets upon human life but wrote at some length on the science of astrology.

The names of other astrologer-scientists are certainly no less renowned: Hippocrates, the father of medicine; Vitruvius, the master of architecture; Placidus, the mathematician; Giordan Bruno, the martyr; Jerome Cardan, the mathematician; and Copernicus. In *Galileo*, Emile Namer wrote that 'Galileo himself, father of modern science, read his children's horoscopes at their births.'

'In the traditions of astrology,' wrote Sir Francis Bacon, 'the natures and dispositions of men are not without truth distinguished from the predominances of the planets.'

At this point it is appropriate to insert three well authenticated accounts of astrological prediction. The Archbishop of St Andrews, having a disease which baffled the physicians of England, sent to the Continent in 1552, begging assistance of the mathematician-astrologer Jerome Cardan. After erecting the horoscope of the prelate by which the disease was discovered and cured, Cardan took his leave in these words: 'I have been able to cure you of your sickness, but cannot change your destiny, nor prevent you from being hung.' Eighteen years later this churchman was hung by order of the commissioners appointed by Mary, Queen of Scots. As he was passing through the city of London on his return home, Cardan was also engaged to calculate the nativity of King Edward VI.

The second example relates to a celebrated prophecy by the noted astronomer Tycho Brahe. From a study of the great comet of 1577, Brahe was led to declare that, 'In the north, in Finland, there should be born a prince who should lay waste Germany and vanish in 1632.' Time proved the accuracy of the comet's warning. The prince, Gustavus Adolphus, was born in Finland, ravaged Germany during the Thirty Years' War, and died as the astronomer had predicted, in 1632. The *Encyclopedia Britannica* comments thus upon the circumstance: 'The fulfillment of the details of this prophecy suggests that Tycho Brahe had some basis of reason for his prediction.'

The third account is taken from Lord Bacon's *Essay on Prophecy*. He writes: 'When I was in France, I heard from one Doctor Pena, that the Queen Mother, who

was given to curious arts, caused the king, her husband's, nativity to be calculated under a false name; and the astrologer gave a judgment that he would be killed in a duel; at which the Queen laughed, thinking her husband to be above challenges and duels; but was slain, upon a course at tilt, the splinters of the staffe of Montgomery going in at his bever.'

The Holy See can boast of several astrologer-popes, including Sylvester, John XX, John XXI, Sixtus IV, Julius II, Alexander IV, Leo X, Paul III, Clement VII and Calixtus III. According to Temple Hungad, Maresilio Ficino, the astrologer to the household of Lorenzo the Magnificent, casting the horoscopes of the children of that illustrious de Medici, predicted that little Giovanni was destined to become a pope. When, later, this occurred and he ascended to the holy chair as Pope Leo X, he became a distinguished patron of astrology and a great believer in the ancient science. Pope Julius II had the day of his coronation set by astrology, while Sixtus IV arranged his audiences according to planetary hours. It is said of Paul III that he never held a consistory except when the heavenly bodies were propitious.

The four greatest conquerors of historic times—Alexander the Great, Julius Caesar, Genghis Khan and Napoleon I—devoutly

Above: Tycho Brahe (1546-1601), the great Danish astronomer-astrologer. At an address to the University of Copenhagen, he declared, 'We cannot deny the influence of the stars without disbelieving in the wisdom of God.'

Left: A birth chart is constructed from the following information: the date and place of birth; the longitude and latitude of the place of birth; the birth time in hours, minutes and seconds; and the birth time in Greenwich Mean Time.

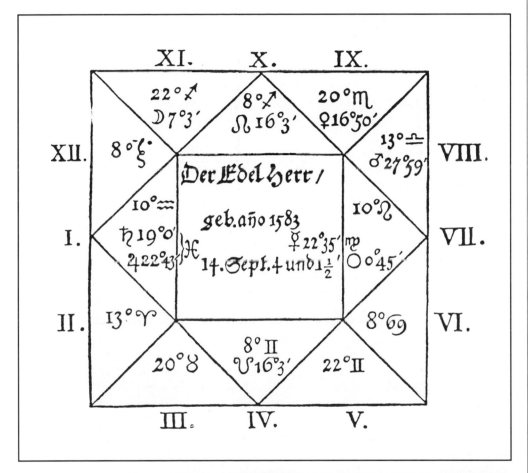

Above: **Michel de Nostredame, better known as Nostradamus, is history's most famous seer. Though the bitterly pessimistic visionary died in 1566, he claimed that his prophecies would remain valid until 3797.**

Events in this century that he predicted include the abdication of Edward VIII in 1936, the rise and fall of the Third Reich, the assassination of President John F Kennedy and the rise of Saddam Hussein.

Below: **Centuries after the fall of the Roman empire, the Eternal City's once great buildings stand in ruins, noble reminders of this once great civilization. Like the Roman Forum, their astrology is also preserved for posterity in the *Astronomicon*, a work from the first century AD.**

Opposite page: **A sixteenth-century woodcut of the celestial sphere, according to the Ptolemaic view of the universe. Ptolemy wrote one of the earliest known textbooks on astrology, circa 150 AD.**

believed in the 'heavenly' government of the world.

The Brahman sages revealed to Alexander not only the time of his death but the manner thereof—that he should perish from a cup. When Alexander reached the walls of Babylon the astrologers warned him away, saying 'Flee from this town where thy fatal star reigns.' Alexander was deeply impressed by this warning and for a time turned aside from Babylon. Later he entered the city where he came by his death.

According to Lucian, Caesar noted the revolutions of the stars in the midst of his preparations for battle. The mathematician Spurina warned the immortal Julius that his Mars threatened violence during the Ides of March, and the outcome of this latter admonition is, as they say, history.

Genghis Khan appointed astrologers to positions of honor in his suite, and one of them, Ye Liu Chutsai, was his constant advisor during Khan's victorious march across half the world.

Napoleon pointed out his guiding star to Cardinal Fesch, his uncle, but that worthy churchman had not the vision to perceive it. The first emperor of the French put such faith in the 'testimony of the suns' that he frequently sought the advice of the cele-

brated French seeress Mademoiselle Lenormand. In justice to the ability of this remarkable woman, it should be remembered that she warned him repeatedly *against* a Russian campaign.

Catherine de Medici was profoundly versed in the heavenly lore and was the patroness of Nostradamus, the most famous of the French astrologers and physician to King Henry II and Charles IX. The prophecies of Nostradamus, 'set forth in a pamphlet, were read all over the world. Although he died in 1566, his forebodings were believed in as late as the eighteenth century, for at its beginning a Papal Edict forbade the sale of the booklet, as it proclaimed the downfall of the Papacy.' He also prophesied the great fire of London in 1666, the French Revolution and the advent of Napoleon centuries before these circumstances took place, and in the case of Napoleon gave a very accurate description of his person and temperament. Nostradamus' prediction of the London fire is as follows:

> 'The blood o' th' just requires,
> Which out of London reeks,
> That it be raz'd with fires,
> in year threescore and six.'

Nostradamus also predicted the rise and fall of the Third Reich (1933-1945) and the

Above: A nineteenth-century German map of the northern sky, showing the constellations of the zodiac (counterclockwise, from the top)— Jungfrau (Virgo), Grosser Lowe (Leo), Krebs (Cancer), Zwillinge (Gemini), Stier (Taurus) and Widder (Aries).

Above: This is the southern sky counterpart to the map on the opposite page. Moving counterclockwise from the top is, once again, Jungfrau (Virgo), then Waage (Libra), Skorpion (Scorpio), Schutze (Sagittarius), Steinbock (Capricorn), Wasserman (Aquarius) and Fische (Pisces).

Above: **A plate bearing the likenesses of the gods and goddesses of ancient Greece, (clockwise from the top): Ares, Eros, Aphrodite, Zeus, Pallas Athena, Apollo, Demeter, Poseidon, Hephaestos, Selena, Hermes, Hera and Artemis. They, too, were subject to the power of the stars.**

Below right: **A nineteenth-century woodcut by the famous French popularizer of astrology, Camille Flammarion.**

assassinations of the Kennedy brothers (1963 and 1968) and possibly the Gulf War of 1991.

Benjamin Franklin, the great American scientist, philosopher, diplomat, and the founder of the *Saturday Evening Post*, published a series of almanacs under the pseudonym of Richard Saunders, or Poor Richard. He borrowed this name from a distinguished astrologer-physician of the preceding century, whose great textbook on medical astrology, published in 1677, contained an introduction by the most celebrated of the English astrologers, William Lilly.

An outstanding exponent of astrology in early twentieth century America was Evageline Adams, a descendant of John Quincy Adams, sixth president of the United States. Ms Adams successfully defended astrology before the courts in 1932, and at the end of the case the judge said, 'The defendant raises astrology to the dignity of an exact science.

Every fortuneteller is a violator of the law, but every astrologer is not a fortuneteller.'

The humble and the great flocked to Ms Adams' studios in Carnegie Hall in New York City. King Edward VII, Enrico Caruso, John Burroughs, Geraldine Farrar and Mary Pickford were among her clients. To quote the *New York World* of 11 November 1932, 'Businessmen came too; even J Pierpont Morgan (Sr) and two former presidents of the New York Stock Exchange, Seymour

Cromwell and Jacob Stout. "I read Mr Morgan's horoscope many times," Ms Adams said. "He was skeptical at first. But I convinced him. During the last years of his life I furnished him a regular service. It explained the general effects of the planets on politics, business and the stock market."'

Adolf Hitler, born under the sign of Aries on 20 April 1889, was a believer in astrology, as were many other persons of high position within the German Reich between 1933 and 1945. The British Foreign Secretary Lord Halifax was also a believer, and in 1940 he hired Hitler's former astrologer Ludwig von Wohl as a consultant on Hitler's horoscope.

According to von Wohl, Adolf Hitler had first consulted the astrologer Baron Rudolf Freihern von Sebottendorf in 1923. The Baron, whose real name was Adam Glandeck, advised Hitler *not* to undertake anything of importance during November of that year, but Hitler ignored him. When the famous 'Beer Hall Putsch' of 8 November 1923 failed and Hitler found himself in jail, he became a believer.

During the first years of World War II, one of the major astrologers in the service of the Third Reich was Karl Ernst Krafft, who was a psychological consultant to Heinrich Himmler's Office for State Security. One of Krafft's predictions is credited with saving the Fuhrer from an assassination attempt in November 1939. However, this did not spare him from arrest in June

1941 on the orders of Rudolf Hess as part of a general, official campaign against astrology. Nonetheless, many astrologers, including Krafft and the mysterious Dr Wulff of Hamburg, continued to serve the aims of Germany's war effort.

During April 1945, when the Nazi empire was on the verge of collapse, Hitler had two horoscopes done—his own and that of the Reich itself. They suggested victory would be snatched from the jaws of defeat in the same way as it had been for Frederick the Great at the end of the Seven Years' War. The death of President Franklin D Roosevelt a few days later was seen as auspicious, but Hitler was nonetheless doomed. It seems that his astrologers had given him false data in order to save their own lives.

Many, indeed most, great world leaders have been followers of the stars. In May 1988, for example, it was revealed that former US President Ronald Reagan and his wife Nancy were firm believers. Through the well known San Francisco astrologer Joan Quigley, Mr and Mrs Reagan used the stars to guide their highly successful eight-year tenure in the White House. Ms Quigley predicted that late March 1981 would be dangerous for the president. Thus, after the 30 March assassination attempt during which Mr Reagan was severely wounded, presidential appearances were no longer scheduled without first consulting Ms Quigley.

In 1987 Ms Quigley was consulted to pick the precise hour for the signing of the historic treaty with the Soviet Union which limited the number of intermediate nuclear weapons in Europe. She accomplished this by casting the horoscopes of both President Reagan (Aquarius) and Soviet Premier Mikhail Gorbachev (Pisces).

Tortured as a sorcerer in one era, ridiculed as a charlatan in another and raised to highest honors in more generous times, the astrologer has survived the numerous 'physical changes in the moral and intellectual world.'

Like the fabled phoenix, astrology has risen again and again victoriously from its own ashes. Vilified and traduced by the sophists of every age, but vindicated and evidenced by Nature herself, astrology still gathers luster from its own stars, and now in the twentieth century it may truthfully be said that the whole civilized world is astrology conscious.

Above: The Roman gods Mercury, Jupiter, Cupid and Minerva, surrounded by the signs of the zodiac.

Below: In this depiction of apocalyptic despair by Peter Breughel, we see the role the zodiac plays in the calamitous events that befall mankind.

TEMPVS OMNIA ET SINGVLA CONSVMENS.

Solis equus, Lunæque, inuectum quattuor Horis,
Signa per extenti duodena volubilis Anni,

Proripiunt Tempus: curru quod præpete secum
Cuncta rapit: comiti Morti non rapta relinquens.

Pone subit, cunctis rebus Fama vna superstes,
Gætulo boue vecta, implens clangoribus orbem.

THE ESSENCE OF ASTROLOGY

Above: **A zodiac showing the 12 signs and their corresponding symbols.**

Below: **The square, dark panels in this ceiling fresco represent the 12 signs of the zodiac.**

A horoscope is a map or diagram of the heavens cast for a particular moment of time and read according to well-established rules. The horoscope is calculated by a mathematical process—free from the elements of chance or divination. Predictions are deduced from the horoscope in a demonstrable and strict mathematical way, to quote Rapahel's *A Manual of Astrology*, 'according to a certain chain of causes which for ages past have been found uniformly to produce a correspondent train of effects.'

The annual revolution of the Earth around the Sun is divided into 360 degrees of a circle, a division that mathematically and astronomically is universally accepted. The subdivisions of the circle into 12 equal arcs, distinguished by names, are known as the signs of the zodiac. They no longer bear any but the most rudimentary relationship to the constellations of the same names.

Persons born 'on the line' between two signs of the zodiac partake of qualities found in both those signs, or more strictly speaking, have a blend of traits that may compose an individual nature. Due to variations in astrological calendars, this may become apparent during the last few days of a departing sign, but the 'cusp,' as it is termed, pertains chiefly to the first week of the incoming sign. While the new sign is gaining its ascendancy, the influence of the old persists, but gradually loses its hold day by day, until by the seventh day, the new sign is in full control.

To give fuller interpretation to the signs of the zodiac, they have been divided into periods of approximately 10 days, called the 'decans' or 'decantes,' which cover modifications of individual traits. These are attributed to minor planetary influences,

which temper or blend with the ruling influence of the period. A study of these is therefore helpful in forming the individual horoscope, but they are always to be regarded as subordinate to the ruling planet.

From the earliest days of astrology, special note was given to the planets, or 'wanderers,' which followed their own special paths among the fixed stars of constellations that form the signs of the zodiac. These planets—seven in number—were simply the members of the solar system that were continually visible from Earth, namely: the Sun, the Moon, Mercury, Venus, Mars, Jupiter and Saturn. (According to astronomers and those who believe in a *heliocentric* universe, the Sun and Moon are not technically planets.)

Each sign of the zodiac was regarded as under the control of one special planet. The Sun became the governing influence of Leo, while the Moon held sway over Cancer. The other planets were each given two signs: Mercury controls Gemini and Virgo, with Venus influencing Taurus and Libra, Mars dominating Aries and Scorpio, Jupiter ruling Sagittarius and Pisces, and Saturn governing Capricorn and Aquarius. In recent centuries, however, some astrologers have seen fit to reassign Aquarius to Uranus and Pisces to Neptune. No astrological affiliation is usually attributed to Pluto.

Although the signs of the zodiac make up only a fraction of what the science of astrology entails, the characteristics of individuals born under each sign have achieved a place of prominence in modern popular culture.

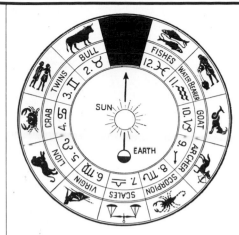

Above: **The zodiac for Aries and** (*below*) **its symbol, the Ram.**

ARIES: The Ram

The first sign of the zodiac is represensted by the head and horns of the ram. It is a symbol of offensive power—a weapon of the gods, hence an implement of the will. The Babylonians sacrificed rams during the period when the Sun occupied this sign, which occurs annually from 21 March to 20 April.

Aries, a fire sign, is ruled by Mars and exalted by the Sun. Though quick to anger, Aries people often calm easily. They are naturally humorous and quick of wit, and enjoy music and entertainment. They say the right thing at the right time, and as students, they are often keen and have the ability of applying whatever they learn to the best advantage.

In business, Aries people are specially suited to being good salespeople, and their drive is valuable in real estate and financial fields. Professionally, they are fine actors, capable lawyers and statesmen. They are also qualified for literary and artistic work.

In love and marriage, Aries persons frequently find harmony and understanding with those born in Leo, Sagittarius or under their own sign. Marriages with Gemini or Libra are regarded as specially suited to the Aries temperament.

TAURUS: The Bull

The second sign of the zodiac is represented by the head and horns of a bull. The Sun is in Taurus annually from 21 April to 20 May. Ironically for so masculine an image as a bull, this earth sign is ruled by Venus and exalted by the Moon.

Strength is the predominating feature of this sign. With it, however, there is a stubborn, firm-set nature that is difficult to change. The governing planet, Venus, emotional and fraught with primitive urges, fur-

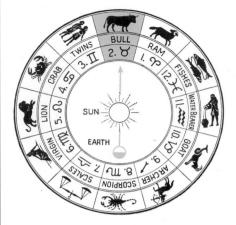

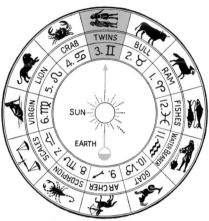

Above: **The zodiac for Taurus and (*right*) its symbol the Bull.** *Below:* **The zodiac for Gemini and (*at bottom*) its symbol, the Twins.**

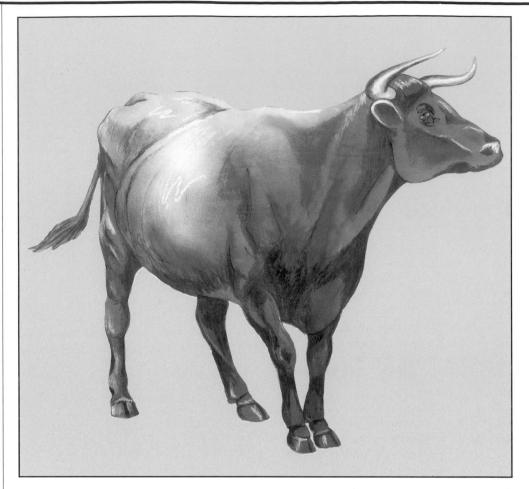

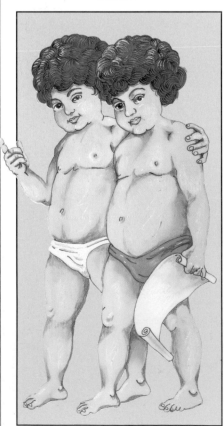

thers these Taurian trends rather than repressing them.

In business, the practical mind of Taurus is suited to constructive fields. They can succeed in all mechanical lines, as engineers, builders and contractors. Often mathematical-minded, they are capable cashiers and accountants. Here, their trustworthy nature, once recognized, may raise them to high position in financial circles. They are good teachers, due to their natural sympathy. Their artistic ability is often on the practical side, producing photographers and landscape architects.

In love and marriage, Taurus and Scorpio often prove ideal, each being strong or forceful, while supplying qualities that the other needs. Taurus and Virgo are well suited because of the latter's analytical abil-ity. Taurus may do well with Libra, who adds good judgment to the union, but there is often an element of uncertainty here. Taurus and Capricorn are a very fine marital combination.

GEMINI: The Twins

The third sign of the zodiac is represented by two pieces of wood bound together, symbolic of the unremitting conflict of contradictory mental processes. The Sun is in Gemini annually from 21 May to 20 June. Ruled by Mercury, Gemini is an air sign.

A duality of nature is a concomitant of the Twin sign, and while cases of split personality are comparatively rare, the Gemini mind runs to contradictions. Gemini people have a way of going from hot to cold, like the swing of a pendulum. Their friendly attitude may shift to mistrust when they encounter problems. They are often unconventional as well as skeptical, and their keen foresight may suffer through overenthusiasm, causing them to let real opportunities languish while they go after something else. Above all, Geminis should never waste what they have gained, for though they picture each success as building to something bigger, they may overlook the obstacles that can ruin such hopes.

In business, Gemini people fit almost anywhere.

They are good salespeople, promoters and often successful speculators. They do well in advertising, publishing, television, transportation and other fields where they must keep up with trends.

In love and marriage, Gemini and Libra

are well suited, as are Gemini and Aquarius. But some restraining force is needed, due to the wavering natures in both cases. Gemini gains drive from an Aries marriage and exuberance from a mate born under Leo. Gemini and Sagittarius form an unusually good marital combination

CANCER: The Crab

The fourth sign of the zodiac is symbolized by what is presumably the folded claws of a crab and is thought by Nicholas DeVore to symbolize the joining together of a male and female essence.

The Sun is in Cancer annually from 21 June to 22 July. A water sign, Cancer is ruled by the Moon and, in fact, Cancerians are occasionally referred to in literature as 'Moon children.'

Cancerians cling to tradition, yet their moods—and even their purposes—may become as changeable as the Moon itself. This self-contradiction is understandable, when recognized as part of the individual's innate nature. These people are home centered, and are fond of family life and domestic tranquillity, but they also enjoy travel and adventure. Cancerians have strong determination and great perseverance; otherwise they would not go to the extremes that they do. So, despite some seemingly contradictory characteristics, Cancer can be developed into one of the best of signs by persons who subordinate the morbid side and refuse to dwell in the past.

In business, people of this sign succeed along established lines. They do well as manufacturers and merchants, for with them, quality is important and they take pride in what they produce. However, they must learn to be aggressive. Otherwise,

they can vacillate and find themselves left far behind.

Professionally, they are good teachers, librarians, historians and scientists. They are capable lawyers and politicians. Many Cancerians rise to a high rank in art, literature and music.

In love and marriage, the home-loving nature of Cancer is a highly important factor, but it must be remembered that Cancer mates can suffer through neglect. As in business, Cancer and Capricorn are usually admirably suited to matrimony. Cancer and Pisces are a good combination; while Scorpio and Libra also mate well with Cancer.

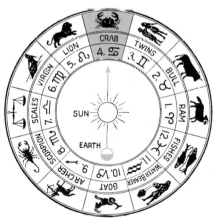

At top: **The zodiac for Cancer, and (*above*) its symbol, the Crab.** *Below:* **The zodiac for Leo.**

LEO: The Lion

The symbol for the fifth sign of the zodiac is possibly an emblem representing the phallus, used in ancient Dionysian mysteries. It is also an emblem of the Sun's fire, heat or creative energy. The Sun is in Leo annually from 23 July to 22 August. A fire element, Leo is ruled, of course, by the Sun itself.

Both ambition and idealism are present under Leo, for the brilliance of this sign reflects the grandeur of its governing

planet, the Sun. But Leo, as well as being high-minded, can be high-handed. When people of this type fall victim to their own shortcomings, the result can prove disastrous.

Leos love the spotlight, perhaps because to them it is the Sun in miniature. They insist upon charting their own course and do so with an inherent vigor. They override their own faults so naturally that they often are not even aware of them.

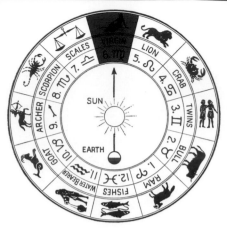

Above: **The zodiac for Virgo, and** (*below*) **its symbol, the Virgin.** *Below right:* **The Lion, the symbol for Leo.**

Leo people enjoy everything that is active, including outdoor life, for they crave the warmth of the Sun that is so predominant in their sign. Indolence is the greatest of drawbacks to the Leo temperament. Leos will revel in ease and luxury until they are forced to action, either through necessity or their own self-imposed demands.

In business, Leo offers unlimited prospects. Along strictly commercial lines, Leo people star in special fields. Anything requiring promotion or enthusiastic development falls in the Leo's domain. Thus, Leos make capable hotel managers, restauranteurs, real estate developers, pub-

lishers and executives, for their spirit is contagious.

Leos also succeed in many professions because they have a flair for showmanship, which can sway clients just as effectively as audiences. Many noted actors were born under this sign, and, in the literary field, they have had a strong trend toward the dramatic—all part of the Leo makeup.

In love and marriage, the Leo exuberance is also generally helpful, though not always harmonious. Leos are perhaps best suited to Aries, Sagittarius or Aquarius, but they also have excellent marital prospects with Cancer and Virgo, as well as those of their own sign.

VIRGO: The Virgin

The sixth sign of the zodiac, Virgo's symbol, is probably a reference to the immaculate conception of a messiah. Virgo is usually depicted as a virgin holding in her hand a green branch, an ear of corn or a spike of grain.

The Sun is in Virgo annually from 23 August to 22 September. Ruled by swift, sure Mercury, Virgo is an earth sign.

Virgo people have inquiring minds that will not rest until they have learned all they want to know about a subject. They are skilled at drawing information from people, then filling in from other sources or ratio-

nalizing facts into a complete and remarkably accurate picture.

Order and harmony are essential to the Virgo mind. Therefore, Virgo people should simplify their lives and purposes, or they will bog down under a mass of detail that their exacting minds cannot ignore. The less little things bother them, the greater their capacity for higher aims. Virgo people are usually tolerant, but once blind to their own faults, they may become even more opinionated than those whom they criticize.

Imagination rules the Virgo mind, mak-

ing them fearful of accidents, illness and financial problems. They are sensitive to pain and any kind of suffering, which makes them superficially sympathetic to those who experience misfortune.

In business, Virgo people are suited to special lines, where their quick minds see new opportunities or productive deals. They are good at evaluating business conditions and market trends. They become good writers, editors, lawyers and professors because they size up things quickly and apply their conclusions ingeniously. Many become architects or designers. However, as actors, lecturers and showmen they must overcome their self-conscious-

ness to succeed, and the same often applies in sales.

Love and marriage present problems for Virgos because of the exacting, fault-finding and sometimes demanding nature evidenced by this sign. One of the best marital combinations for Virgo is with another of the same sign, as each may understand the other's critical moods. Virgos may find happiness with those born under the sign of Pisces, while Aries, Taurus and Capricorn would also prove compatible. Virgo and Libra could be helpful to each other, but their strong minds might too often come in conflict, making this a dubious union.

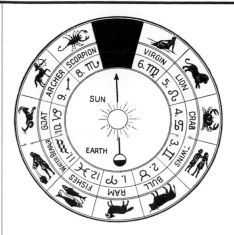

Above: **The zodiac for Libra, and (*below*) its symbol, the Scales.**

LIBRA: The Scales

The seventh sign of the zodiac, Libra's symbol, represents the balancing scales, and, as such, is emblematic of equilibrium and justice. The Sun is in Libra annually from 23 September to 23 October. An air sign, Libra is ruled by Venus and exalted by Saturn.

Everything in Libra has to do with balance; hence the susceptibility of the Libra individual is counterbalanced by a strong-mindedness that can become firm and unflinching in purpose. Libra is the sign of justice, and indicative of persons who balance everything to a nicety, always trying to promote good will and friendship, even if they must go to extremes to do so. This is actuated by their inherent love of harmony and beauty, as reflected by the beneficial gleam of Venus.

Intuition is a guiding force with Librans and often enables them to ferret out deceit and insincerity, no matter how much it is glossed over. However, if they prejudge a matter, or listen to persons in whom they trust or sympathize, Librans can be carried far astray. They are so vulnerable to the influence of those who impress them that they will imitate the manners of such persons and actually pick up their traits.

Compassion and understanding are paramount with Librans. They are never deaf to an appeal from family or friends and they will often champion the underdog, if they seem to represent a deserving cause, even against their sounder judgment. Such is their need to equalize matters and produce harmony.

In business, Libra people often rise to high positions, as their judgment, when properly exercised, is of the executive type. Similarly, their understanding toward subordinates can prove a powerful asset.

Their intuitive ability makes them excellent merchants and their hunches aid them in speculative fields. However, they should curb their gambling instinct or it may run away with them. Yet, at the same time, such an instinct can serve as an asset in certain fields.

Libra people often become inventors, researchers or historians. Their talent to play a part makes them fine actors, and they are excellent musicians and singers as well. They are also mathematically minded and

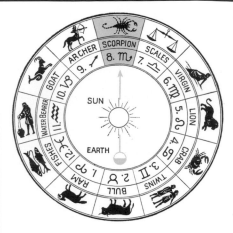

Above: **The zodiac for Scorpio, and** (*below*) **its symbol, the Scorpion.**

are suited to many arts and crafts. Since Librans rely on their own judgment, they should be wary of business partnerships.

In love and marriage, Libra does well with Aries because of the latter's drive. Libra gains animation from marriage with Leo. Perhaps the susceptible Libra and jovial Sagittarius are the best mating of all, but Libra also harmonizes with Aquarius and can benefit from a pairing with Gemini or Scorpio. There is a natural attraction between Libra and Virgo, but conflicts of interests may result, and Libra and Pisces are seldom a suitable combination.

SCORPIO: The Scorpion

The symbol for the eighth sign of the zodiac resembles that of Virgo, but with an arrow on the tail—doubtless to represent the sting. It is symbolized by the asp or serpent, harking back to the serpent of the Garden of Eden, and indicating that the will governs, or is governed by, the reproductive urge. It is sometimes symbolized by the dragon, and is frequently linked with the constellation Aquilla, the Eagle.

The Sun is in Scorpio annually from the second thirty-degree arc after the Sun's passing of the Fall Equinox, occupying a position along the ecliptic from 210 degrees to 240 degrees. Scorpio, a water sign, is ruled by Mars and exalted by Uranus.

That noted Scorpio, Theodore Roosevelt, was fond of the slogan, 'Speak softly and carry a big stick,' a phrase which aptly sums up the characteristics of this sign. Scorpio people are quiet, even secretive, in manner, yet highly observant. Once roused to action, they are determined, aggressive and dominant, always ready to champion a cause. When they work for the good of others, they rise to great heights and are much respected. But Scorpio people, always well-satisfied with themselves, can easily become domineering and condescending.

Scorpios are blunt, argumentative and natural fighters, and their coolness under fire deceives the opposition and adds to their strength. Always, in the showdown, Scorpio is apt to have the upper hand. Thus, they should control their tempers, as well as their actions.

In business, a powerful Scorpio personality can succeed in practically any line. They range from managers of branch offices to the heads of large companies. They have the greatest of opportunities in the expanding world of today, for as heads of bureaus, committees and other investigative groups, no other sign can begin to equal them. Professionally, those born under the sign of Scorpio frequently become great physicians.

In love and marriage, Scorpio finds three strong choices: Taurus, Cancer and Pisces. Scorpio's crusading spirit is admirably seconded by Taurus. The Scorpio boldness carries along the wavering Cancer disposition and brings the strong point of Pisces to the fore. Scorpio may also find a harmonious marriage with Virgo, while Scorpio's power and Leo's exuberance may prove a satisfactory marital combination.

SAGITTARIUS: The Archer

The ninth sign of the zodiac, Sagittarius was, in Hindu astrology, known as Dhanus. His symbol represents an arrow and a section of bow, typifying aspiration. He is usually pictured as the Centaur, half horse and half man, representing the conflict between the philosophical mind and the carnal instinct of conquest, and also the aspiration supported by the effort that aims at the stars. Sagittarius is said to have been named for the Babylonian god of war.

The Sun is in Sagittarius annually from 23 November to 21 December. Ruled by Jupiter, king of all planets, Sagittarius is a fire sign.

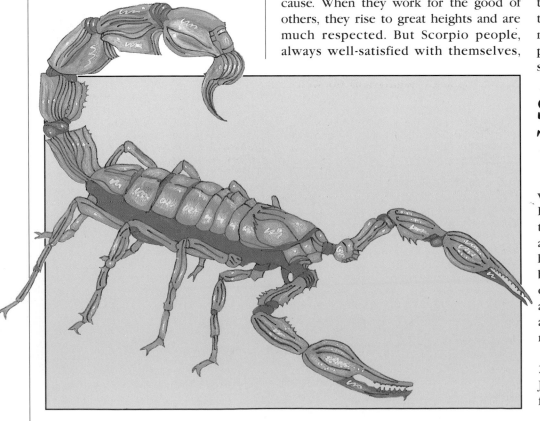

Being workers, not seekers, Sagittarians often accomplish twice as much as others and will apply themselves to charitable or helpful causes with the same energy that they devote to their own aims. When their time is thus divided, they are often happiest, because by doubling their effort—as they like to do—they can still handle their own affairs along with someone else's. When confronted by adversity or failure, these people can usually stage a remarkable 'comeback' by merely stepping up their activity or their output.

Sagittarians are naturally intuitive, with keen foresight, so when they feel sure that something 'can't go wrong' they yield to impulse. However, in their excitement and enthusiasm, they may overlook new problems that might arise. This impetuosity causes Sagittarians great trouble through middle age, when they become irritable and develop unruly tempers, which can be soothed or restrained only by persons whom they trust. Sometimes they literally wear themselves down until their recklessness is merely spasmodic. With their stamina depleted, they then fuss from one minor project to another, getting nowhere.

At their best and strongest, Sagittarius people insist on seeing things through, and their impulsive actions are contagious, bringing them great popularity and a host of followers. Those who achieve success under this sign are usually neat, methodical and orderly.

In business, Sagittarians succeed in anything that provides a multitude of outlets for their active, versatile minds. They like to travel and do well as prospectors, mining engineers, pilots and sea captains. Imports and exports are good avenues for their progressive, systematic minds. They also do well as bankers and financiers, but in all well-established endeavors they should avoid too many side interests, remembering that time is money.

Inventors, writers and large farm operators are all found under Sagittarius. They are very strong in scientific and mechanical fields, and in a partnership with Aries or

Gemini they can achieve great results. The spontaneity of Sagittarius and the exuberance of Leo is also an effective combination, though it may prove less sustained.

In love and marriage, Sagittarius is aptly called 'the bachelor sign' because these freedom-seeking folk can get along quite well on their own. However, they are cheerful, considerate and willing to share burdens, so potentially they might prove to be fine spouses. Sagittarians do well to marry someone born under their own sign or a person born in Gemini, due to the mutual urge toward varied interests. Sagittarius also may marry well with Aries or Leo, which are themselves impetuous to a degree. Sagittarius and Libra are often a good marital team, due to their mutual recognition of intuitive qualities.

At top: **The zodiac for Sagittarius, and (*above*) its symbol, the Archer.**

CAPRICORN: The Goat

The tenth sign of the zodiac, Capricorn was considered by the ancients to be the most important of all the signs, and is known in Hindu astrology as Makarar. Its symbol represents the figure by which the sign is often pictured—that of the forepart of a goat, with the tail of a fish—vaguely suggesting the mermaid. Sometimes Capri-

corn is depicted as a dolphin, or 'sea goat.'

The Sun is in Capricorn annually from 22 December to 20 January. This earth element is ruled by Saturn. Capricornians need encouragement early in life so they may gain confidence and strengthen their genial and witty qualities. The more gregarious they become, the more diver-

Above: **The zodiac for Capricorn, and (*at bottom*) its symbol, the Goat.** *Below:* **The zodiac for Aquarius.**

sified and realistic their interests, the better they can elude the ever-haunting specters of pessimism and despair.

Self-interest is strong in Capricorn, for these people are used to finding their own way. However, those who are fully matured are by no means selfish. Fear of the future often makes them economical, but they share their possessions with others, sometimes too generously. Once a dark mood has passed, a Capricorn person often manages to forget it. Their desire for success is usually so determined that it rouses petty jealousy on the part of others. If Capricornians do not fall victim to despair, they can outlast their problems and overcome

all limitations, and thus become true optimists.

In business, people of this sign are good managers, superintendents, bookkeepers and accountants. Their pragmatic foresight makes them good financiers. They succeed in many professions, as lecturers, teachers and lawyers, to name a few. They also usually evidence strong literary qualifications.

In love and marriage, Capricorn probably does best with Virgo, though Capricorn and Taurus may prove an equally fine union. Capricorn and Aries also promise good marital prospects. All three of those signs have qualities which are helpful to Capricorn's fluctuating moods.

AQUARIUS: The Water Carrier

The symbol for the eleventh sign of the zodiac represents a stream of water, symbolizing the servant of humanity who pours out the water of knowledge to quench the thirst of the world. Aquarius is thought to represent Ganymede, son of Callirrhoe, the most beautiful of mortals, who was carried to heaven by an eagle to act as cup bearer to Jupiter.

The Sun is in Aquarius annually from 21 January to 20 February. Before the discovery of the planet Uranus in 1781, Aquarius, an air sign, was identified with the planet Saturn. Since the existence of Uranus has become known, astrologers have been inclined to identify it as the ruler of

Aquarius. Still others point to Neptune—discovered in 1846—because the persona of its namesake (Neptune, king of the sea) is so starkly similar to that of Aquarius.

More famous persons have been born under Aquarius than any other sign, and in the great majority of cases they have risen from obscurity or have made up for early failure, sometimes succeeding despite seemingly insurmountable odds. Invariably, they have done this on their own, through the full application of all that they have learned. Self-reliance, confidence and the belief that they are right are the qualities that lay the foundation of the Aquarians' success.

Aquarians who develop the honesty and kindly sentiments of this sign are sure to attain great heights. They have mild dispositions and can curb their tempers. They are both active and volatile, and once their ambitions are sparked, they can scale unprecedented heights. The Aquarian's greatest fault is indolence, for if they delay or treat life lazily, they will never get anywhere. They must also maintain their natural, quiet dignity, for without it, they may become boastful and surly, losing the fame that otherwise may carry them far.

In business, Aquarians are good bargainers, keen buyers, capable auctioneers and make excellent promoters, as they know how to stimulate interest. They do especially well in law and politics. Their mechanical skills are well developed, and many noted scientists, as well as famous inventors, have been born under this sign.

In love and marriage, Aquarius does well with most signs, for the Aquarian has an understanding nature. Gemini, Leo and Libra are especially good, as they respond strongly to the sympathies of Aquarius.

PISCES: The Fishes

The symbol of the twelfth and final sign of the traditional zodiac represents a pair of great seahorses or sea lions, yoked together, who dwell in the innermost regions of the sea. It is also symbolic of life after death, and of bondage—the inhibiting of self-expression, except through others—as well as of the struggle of the soul within the body.

The Sun is in Pisces annually from 21 February to 20 March. Traditionally thought to have been ruled by Jupiter, Pisces, a water sign, is more properly affiliated with Neptune, a planet that was unknown to all but a select few until 1846.

Because of their unselfish disposition, Pisceans sometimes fail to fully realize their own possibilities. The greater their honesty, the more doubtful they become as to their own ability. This in turn produces fear of the future, which then increases their immediate worries. Subsequently, Pisces people are perhaps the most cautious of all the signs where their own affairs are concerned. In contrast, however, Pisceans often rely upon the promises of other people and thus are easily and frequently duped. Though they themselves are sincere and trustworthy, they are often blamed for the mistakes of others, who have shunted the burden onto the kindly

Pisces person. Often, a Pisces individual becomes the victim of a subtle, cunning plot, which is never suspected.

There are two saving factors to this sign. One is the optimistic trend inspired by Jupiter. Most other planets would be deadly if they held chief sway over Pisces, but thanks to their jovial dispositions, Pisceans can make their way through deep troubles almost as if they were trifles. The other factor in their behalf is that their true worth is always sincerely appreciated by real friends and good people, who help them to accentuate their strong points and even serve as buffers against unscrupulous persons.

In business, Pisceans tend to gravitate to large organizations, where their honesty and executive capacity can be appreciated. They do well in government jobs and scientific pursuits. Many of them also succeed as engineers. They are interested in historical subjects and all forms of nature.

While a marriage between two persons born under Pisces is harmonious, it is difficult for one to bring out the other's more forceful qualities. Pisces would do better in a pairing with Cancer, Virgo or Scorpio, but other signs often prove helpful, with the exception of Libra, which is too prone to weigh the Pisces shortcomings.

Above: **The zodiac for Pisces, and (***below left***) its symbol, the Fishes.** *Below:* **The Water Carrier, the symbol for Aquarius.**

PALMISTRY & PHRENOLOGY

Above: **The ancient Greeks probably developed their system of palmistry before recorded history.**

Opposite page: **An illustration from a seventeenth-century book on palmistry. Note that a sign of the zodiac has been ascribed to each phalange of the fingers.**

almistry, the study of the human hand as a method for understanding an individual, is an ancient art. Though there is no conclusive evidence, it seems very likely that the origins of palmistry date back to the ancient Egyptians. The first documented records of palmistry are found in the Indian literature of the Vedic period (circa 2000 BC). In Western cultures, the works of Aristotle (384 to 322 BC) contain the earliest references to palmistry, but both of these cultures suggest an earlier, oral tradition of palmistry. Indeed, palm prints are found in Stone Age cave paintings, suggesting that since the dawn of time, people have been fascinated by the message contained in their own hands.

The name palmistry is somewhat misleading, for the entire hand—not just the palm—is used to interpret the individual. In fact, palmistry relies on both hands. The left hand is said to indicate the characteristics that one is born with, while the right hand indicates one's nature at the present time. If an individual is left-handed, then the situation is reversed. The shape and feel of the entire hand, the individual fingers, and the lines and mounts of the palm are all taken into consideration. Once the pieces are put together, palmistry deals with tendencies and probabilities rather than certainties. A palmist will never predict that someone will achieve sudden wealth; instead the emphasis is on the pattern that one's life may follow.

THE SHAPE OF THE HAND

Palm readers have traditionally divided hand shapes into seven categories:

The **elementary** hand is thick and broad, with short fingers. The hand is stiff and awkward and indicates a person of low intelligence who relies on brute force. This type of hand is rare.

The **square** hand indicates a practical nature. The hand is actually more rectangular in shape, with squared-off fingertips. The person with this type of hand is orderly and conventional.

The **spatulate** hand is spade-shaped and straight-fingered. The entire hand suggests a spatula and may take two forms. In one version, the palm is wider at the wrist than at the base of the fingers, while in the second kind, the palm is wider at the top than at the wrist. This is the hand of the active, energetic individual. The person with the spatulate hand can be found in all fields, but whatever the occupation there is always the urge to be active, to excel and to be original.

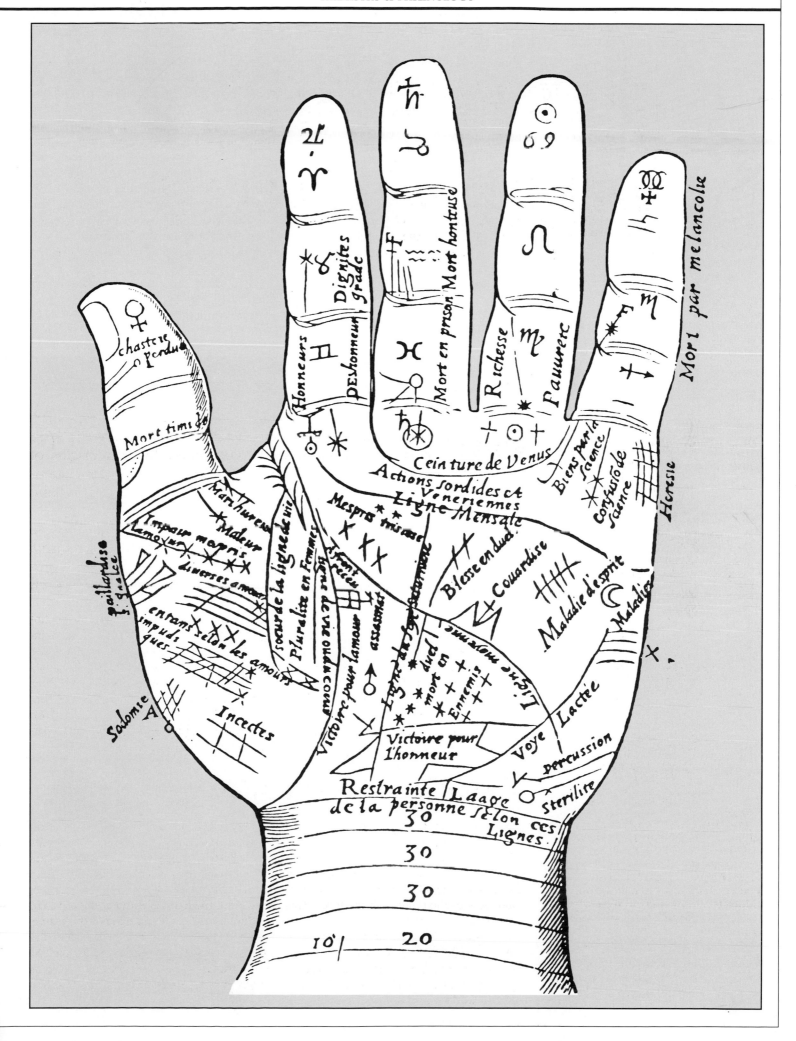

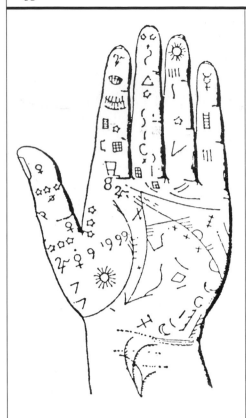

Above: **A chart of Napoleon's hand. Both he and his wife, Josephine, were fervent believers in the science of palmistry.**

Right: **Some palmists like to do a reading from a handprint rather than from the hand itself.**

Opposite page: **Types of hands: (1) elemental, (2) square, (3) spatulate, (4) philosophical, (5) artistic, (6) idealistic, (7) mixed, (8) practical, (9) intuitive, (10) sensitive and (11) intellectual. Numbers 8 through 11 are the modern classifications.**

The **philosophical** hand has a broad palm and heavy joints on the fingers and thumbs. The fingers can vary in shape, either square or conical. This long and lean hand denotes the thinker, a person with a logical, cautious nature. People with this type of hand tend to be introverted and analytical. Often teachers, they are the people who seek knowledge.

The **conical** hand is long and flexible, with tapering fingers. This hand is indicative of an artistic nature. People with a conical hand are creative, sensitive and impulsive rather than methodical. They enjoy companionship and are social minded.

The **pointed** hand (also known as the psychic hand) is even longer and more slender than the conical hand. The pointed hand reveals an idealistic nature and an intuitive mind. People with this sort of hand tend to be dreamers, often with an unrealistic view of the world. They can become martyrs to their own ideas or hold extremist philosophical or religious beliefs.

The **mixed** hand is a very common type because few people fit neatly into one category. The fingers on a spatulate hand, for example, may belong to two or three different categories. Thus, the palmist must analyze all the fingers, combining the results. The thumb tends to function as a modifier. For instance, a square thumb will temper the idealistic nature of a pointed first finger.

A modern classification divides hands into only four types: practical, intuitive, sensitive and intellectual. These four modern types are linked to the past through

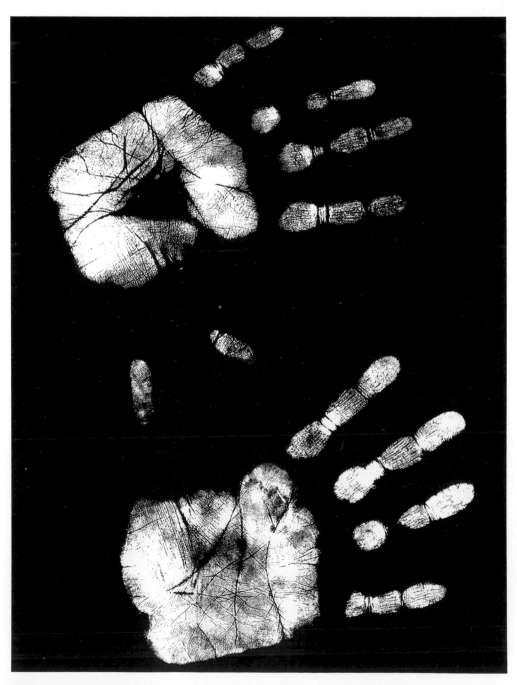

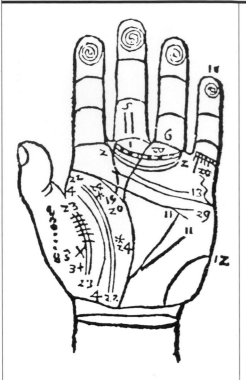

Above: An illustration from the book on palmistry published in the seventeenth century that is believed to be the first reference to the patterns found on fingerprints.

Below right: Types of thumbs, from left to right: stiff-smooth, clubbed, supple-jointed, waisted, knotty-jointed and thick.

their association with the four elements of the ancient world: earth, fire, water and air.

The **practical** hand has a square palm with short fingers.

This honest, hard-working, sensible person is connected with the element of the earth.

The **intuitive** hand has a long palm and short fingers. The person with this sort of hand is energetic and restless, with an individualistic nature. This person is associated with the element of fire.

The **sensitive** hand has a long palm with long fingers. Linked with the element of water, this person is imaginative and emotional, often moody.

The **intellectual** hand has a square palm with long fingers. This person is clever, rational and orderly and is connected with the element of air.

FLEXIBILITY OF HANDS

Highly flexible hands have fingers that bend backward, almost at right angles to the palm. A high degree of flexibility indicates an extremist nature. People of this sort prefer an unconventional lifestyle and are often talented individuals.

Hands with medium flexibility have fingers that bend back slightly. People of this sort are reasonable and willing to compromise.

Stiff fingers do not bend, nor does the individual. These people are unyielding and set in their ways, but will always honor their word, once they give it.

TEXTURE OF HANDS

Flabby hands are loose-skinned and have a swollen feeling. Persons with this type of hand are variable; sometimes pleasant, sometimes irritable. Flabby hands are often found among those who are lazy.

A soft hand feels limp, but its owner must not be underestimated. Successful and famous people often have soft hands.

A firm hand is indicative of a determined person. People with firm hands are rational, accepting the good with the bad. Firm hands belong to the hard worker.

Persons with hard hands are hard to convince. They are generally stubborn, but the individual with a well-shaped thumb will be willing to listen to reason.

THE THUMB

The **thumb** is one of the most important indicators of a person's temperament. Many palmists give the thumb as much significance as all the other fingers combined, and some Hindu practitioners base their entire reading on the thumb alone.

The thumb is divided into three parts, or phalanges. The first phlange, which runs from the tip to the joint, represents will power. The second phalange, the area from the joint to the palm, is associated with

reason. If the first phalange is longer than the second, will power is stronger. A short second phalange indicates a tactless person with a lack of reasoning power. The third phalange of the thumb is actually part of the palm known as the mount area of Venus. This area embodies love, affection and sympathy.

An average thumb reaches to the middle of the bottom phalange of first finger. A long thumb is considered more forceful

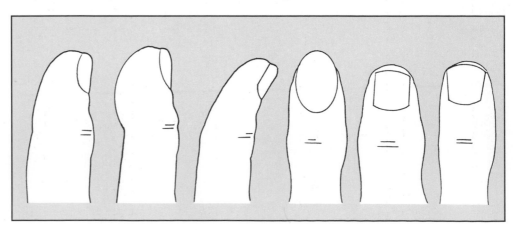

and can strengthen weak lines on the palm. This person is clear-minded and makes a good leader. A very long thumb, however, indicates a tyrant. A short thumb is impressionable and indecisive, often ruled by emotion rather than logic.

A thumb is usually broader than it is thick. A thumb that is as thick as it is broad indicates an unbalanced, perhaps violent nature, while a slender thumb signifies patience. A 'waisted' thumb—when the second phalange is narrower than first—points to an understanding of both people and animals. A knotty joint on the thumb suggests an analytical mind, whereas a smooth joint betokens an impulsive nature.

THE FINGERS

Each finger is considered an extension of the mount directly below it and modifies the quality of the mount, with short fingers decreasing the value and long fingers increasing the value. Very long fingers may exaggerate. The overall appearance of the finger is also significant.

The **first finger**—the index or forefinger—is the most important. The finger of Jupiter, it represents ambition. If the top of the first finger is level with the bottom of the nail on the second finger, the person has the ability to be a leader. If the finger is the same length or longer than the second finger, the person is self-centered and a dictator determined to make people obey. If the top of the finger is below the bottom of the nail on the second finger, the person has a tendency to be timid and avoid responsibility.

An index finger that curves toward the second finger indicates acquisitiveness, which can range from simply collecting things to hoarding possessions in a miserly fashion. If only the top phalange curves toward the second finger, the person has a tendency to be stubborn and persistent.

If the first finger is a normal length and shorter than the third finger, the person is a good organizer and is capable of taking charge, but prefers to work with a partner. If the finger is the same length as the third finger, the person is well balanced, but if it is longer, the person is proud and desirous of power.

A long and smooth first finger signifies good prospects professionally and socially. A short finger indicates a lack of confidence and stamina, while an extremely short finger indicates a person afraid of the outside world.

A thick first finger suggests a dogged and determined individual. A thin finger indicates an imaginative but unrealistic individual. A crooked finger signifies a crooked person. Finally, if the phalanges are marked with deep, straight vertical lines, the person is overworked and fatigued.

The **second, or middle, finger** repre-

Below: **Types of fingers, from left to right: long, short, large, square, spatulate, tapered, slender, and thick and short.**

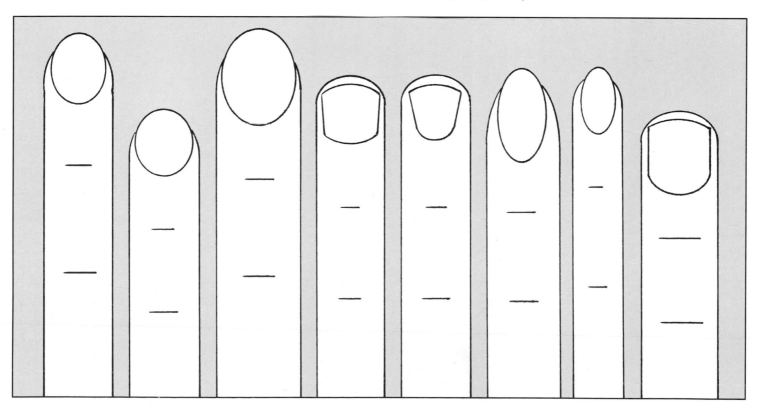

Above: For a fee, Jean the psychic will tell your fortune by reading your palm or the tarot cards.

Below: When doing a reading, a palmist considers the entire hand. For example, the long, narrow fingers of the hand on the left reveal very different characteristics from the short, thick fingers of the hand on the right.

Opposite page: The handprint of William Ewart Gladstone, British statesman and orator. Gladstone (*inset*) served as Prime Minister of Great Britain in the late nineteenth century.

The line of Mars (the curved line closest to the thumb) added strength to Gladstone's life line. The long length of the line points to Gladstone's active life as a member of parliament for 60 years.

sents Saturn, and if it is strong denotes a melancholy and serious temperament. A straight middle finger, in good proportion to the rest of the fingers, denotes a sensible individual, able to concentrate and plan ahead. A long, strong and heavy middle finger suggests a serious and thoughtful person and one who is likely to have a hard life.

If the finger is the same length as the first and third fingers, the person is irresponsible. A finger that is slightly longer than the first and third fingers indicates an irresponsible person, while a very long finger reveals a morbid and melancholy person. A short middle finger belongs to an intuitive individual. If the middle phalange is the longest, the person loves the country and is said to be 'green-fingered.'

If the middle finger curves, it takes on the qualities of the finger toward which it is curved. A crooked middle finger signifies a person full of self pity.

The **third, or ring, finger** represents Apollo and the individual's inner concerns. A strong and smooth ring finger indicates an emotionally balanced person, while a smooth finger with smooth joints suggests creativity.

A long third finger indicates a longing for fame. These people do well in show business and advertising. A very long finger, however, reveals an introverted individual. A short finger signifies a person lacking in emotional control. If the third phalange is the longest, the individual craves money and luxury.

A third finger that bends toward the second finger indicates a person who is apt to be anxiety-ridden and always on the defensive. If the third and second fingers bend toward each other, the person is secretive. A third finger that droops toward the palm when hand is relaxed suggests a person who has difficulty dealing with the intuitive aspects of his personality. A crooked or otherwise distorted finger reveals emotional difficulties.

The **fourth, or little, finger** represents Mercury and human relationships. If the fourth finger reaches above the top crease on the third finger, the person is highly intelligent and articulate, but if the finger reaches the nail on the third finger, the individual is untrustworthy. A short fourth finger discloses that the individual has difficulty in making the best of himself.

A long first phalange reveals a knowledgeable person, with an interest in education. However, a first phalange that is considerably longer than the others means the person has a tendency to exaggerate or embellish the truth. A short or almost nonexistent third phalange signals a depraved person.

If the fourth finger bends toward the third finger, the person is shrewd and clever in business. If the finger bends toward the palm when the hand is relaxed, the person has sexual difficulties.

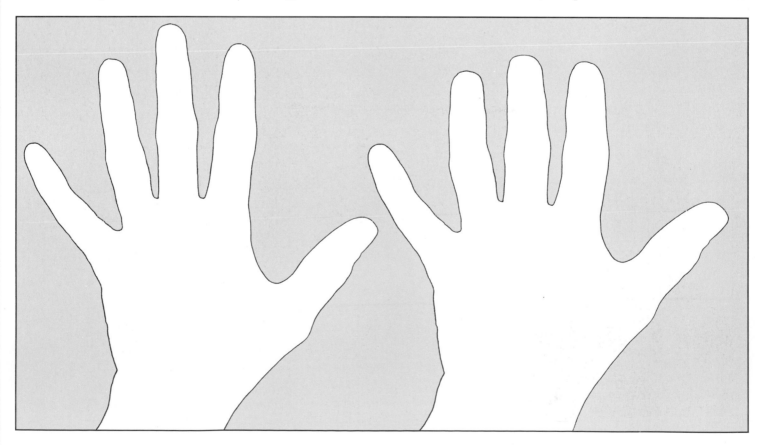

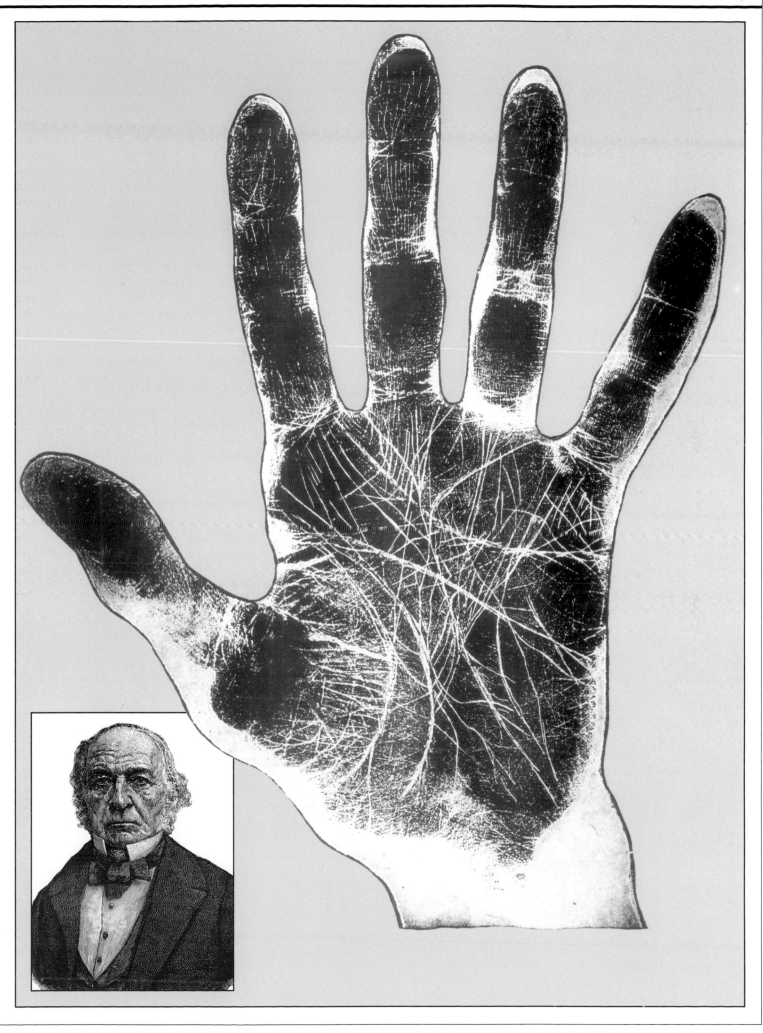

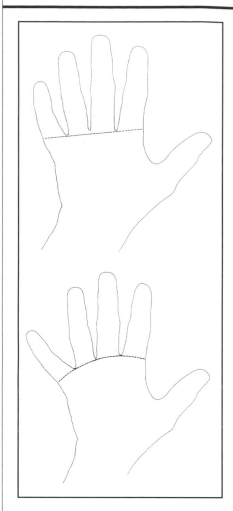

Above: **The set of the fingers adds to the interpretation. An individual with fingers set straight across (*at top*) tends to be practical and have a positive outlook. An uneven set (*above*) is the most common and indicates that the person must endure life's ups and downs.**

A twisted or crooked little finger denotes a liar, someone not to be trusted.

Palmists also look at the set of the hand—how the fingers join the hand. For a square hand, the normal set is a straight line across the palm. For all other types of hands, the normal set is a gentle curve, with the first finger set a little lower than the second and third fingers and the fourth finger set slightly lower. A finger that is set noticeably low detracts from the value of the mount.

An additional consideration is the span of the hand, or the distance between the fingers. If the fingers are held together stiffly, the person is likely to be cautious, suspicious and unsociable. If the fingers are evenly spaced, the person has a well-balanced mind and is capable of succeeding in any field. Well-separated fingers indicate an independent and freedom-loving nature. A wide gap between all fingers reveals an open and trusting, almost child-like, disposition.

If the widest space is between the thumb and the first finger, the person has a tendency to be outgoing and generous. If the widest space is between the first and second fingers, the person is not easily influenced by others. If the widest space is between the second and third fingers, the person is light-hearted and anxiety-free. If the widest space is between the third and fourth fingers, the person is an independent and original thinker. If the fourth finger is set far apart from the other fingers, the person is apt to have difficulties in personal relationships and feel isolated and alienated.

The joints add to the meaning of the fingers. Smooth joints reveal an impulsive nature, while knotty joints suggest a deep-thinker. Large joints typify a methodical, rational individual.

A pointed fingertip adds idealism; a square tip, practicality; and a spatulate tip, action.

The palmist bases the reading on the total picture. Thus, a square finger with smooth joints is influenced by the practicality indicated by the square shape and the impulsiveness betokened by the smooth joints.

THE NAILS

The shape and color of the nails offer clues into a person's character.

Short nails reveal a curious and energetic personality; very short and broad nails, an irritable one. Broad, long nails indicate a person of sound judgement. Long, almond-shaped nails point to an artistic personality. Large, square nails tend to belong to cold, selfish individuals. Wedge-shaped nails are a sign of an overly sensitive person.

White nails reveal a selfish nature, while pink nails imply a warm, outgoing personality. Red is indicative of a violent temper and blue is the color of poor health.

THE MOUNTS OF THE PALM

The palm is divided into sections called mounts. Beginning with the area below the first finger the mounts are as follows: Jupiter; Saturn, under the second finger; Apollo, under the third finger; Mercury, under the fourth finger; Upper Mars, below Mercury; Luna (also called the mount of the Moon), beneath Upper Mars; Venus, at the base of the thumb (this area is technically the third phalange of the thumb); and Lower Mars, above Venus. The area at the center of the palm is called the Plain of Mars.

The mounts are the keys to an individual's traits and abilities. The higher the mount or the more space it takes, the greater the significance of the area.

The **mount of Jupiter** symbolizes ambition and social prestige. If the mount is more developed near the side of the palm, family pride drives the individual, but if the development is closer to the head line, the desire to lead is the primary motivator, but the individual should guard against arrogance. If the mount is more developed closer to Saturn, the individual is driven by the pursuit of knowledge.

The **mount of Saturn** is seldom highly developed and is usually influenced by either Jupiter or Apollo or both. Saturn's characteristics are caution and reserve. If the mount is developed closer to the heart line, those characteristics are intensified. If the mount is developed toward Jupiter, the person tends to have a serious outlook on life, but if development is toward Apollo, interest in the arts exerts a strong influence.

The **mount of Apollo** is connected with the arts and signifies brilliance in any field of endeavor. If the mount is developed toward Saturn, a seriousness is added, while development toward Mercury adds a practical, business mind to the artistic talents. An overdeveloped mount suggests a tendency to overrate one's abilities.

The **mount of Mercury** represents hope and typically combines cheerfulness with practicality. The influence of Mercury is seen in a wide range of people, from top level business executives to housewives, for the qualities of Mercury are needed to succeed. If the mount is developed toward Apollo, the person possesses a love of all things beautiful and artistic, and if developed toward the percussion (the side of the palm), a sense of humor is evident. If the mount is developed toward Upper Mars, the person will vigorously support a cause. People of this sort are utterly reliable. An overdeveloped mount can work both positively and negatively, supplying the initiative for inventive minds and successful sales people but also for criminals and swindlers.

The **mount of Luna** represents imagination, intuition, creative ability and motivation. This is a large area and can vary in form, from bulging all over or in just a few places to thin and almost flat. When the mount is developed toward Upper Mars, the person has the ability to turn dreams into reality. If the percussion bulges, there is the need for physical activity combined with creativity. If development is near the wrist, the person is sensual or imaginative, and if near Venus, romantic and emotional. Development near the Plain of Mars indicates an aggressive nature.

These characteristics are intensified if the mount has a reddish color. A bluish cast reflects a melancholy nature. A pale color tends to lessen the effects listed above.

The **mount of Venus** represents love, sympathy, passion and vitality. All of these characteristics come into play if the area is evenly padded and centered. If the mount is developed toward Lower Mars, the person is antagonistic, but if it is developed near the base of the thumb the person is likely to be highly emotional. Development near the wrist indicates an affectionate, sensual nature, while development near Luna reveals self-indulgence.

A low, flat mount indicates a cool, dispassionate nature, while a highly cushioned one reveals a person dynamic in love and friendship. If the area is hard and muscular, the person is resentful.

The **mount of Lower Mars** represents the will to fight for a cause, be it for family, country or self. The action can be either mental or physical. An overdeveloped mount indicates an abusive temperament, while an underdeveloped area reveals a fearful, reticent individual.

The **mount of Upper Mars** represents endurance, bravery and fortitude. These characteristics signify moral courage rather than physical courage, and complement the action that is the hallmark of Lower Mars. If development of the mount is high or stronger near Mercury, there is no stopping this person, but if the development is near the Plain of Mars, the tendency is to become overly aggressive. Development toward Luna reveals the potential to inspire others, while development toward the percussion suggests a physically reserved individual. An overdeveloped mount means cruelty, while underdeveloped signifies a morbid person.

The **Plain of Mars**, the area in the center of the palm, is influenced by the mounts of Lower and Upper Mars. A high plain indicates good control of one's emotions especially in arguments, while a flat plain reveals a restrained individual who holds a negative attitude about the world in general.

Above: **Types of nails, from the top, left to right: short and broad; broad and long; long; large and square; wedge; and short.**

THE MAJOR LINES

The three major lines—the head, heart and life—are found on almost every palm.

The **life line** represents a person's life energy and vitality. The line begins halfway between the thumb and forefinger and curves around the thumb, ending at or near the wrist. According to the old wives' tale, the life line indicates the length of one's life, and while some palm readers today reject this notion, there are others who believe it is as valid. If the line begins high, near the forefinger, the person is ambitious and not easily deterred. If it starts at the head line, it reveals someone who exhibits an average degree of organization and control, albeit with a measure of caution.

A slight degree of separation between the life and head lines indicates an energetic person capable of succeeding in any walk of life, while a large separation symbolizes an impulsive, uncontrolled person. The gap between the life and head lines also is a good indicator of independence. The wider the gap and the earlier it starts, the greater the tendency to be independent.

Lines that branch upward and end under the first finger show a desire for wealth and power. Lines that drop down toward the thumb indicate a strong need for love and affection.

When the life line ends in the mount of Luna rather than near the thumb, the person requires change, such as travel, new surroundings or a variety of occupations.

A branch line extending to the mount of Jupiter, under the first finger, portends great success, either in business or marriage.

A line to Saturn, under the second finger, signifies a deeply religious person, often with a strong need for solitude.

A line to Apollo, under the third finger, reveals wealth or fame. If the line is straight, wealth is achieved with the help of family or friends. If wavy or broken, the path to fame and fortune will be filled with obstacles.

A strong, connecting line to Mercury denotes prosperity in business, usually with the assistance of loved ones.

A line to Upper Mars suggests unusual bravery or physical strength, often in the service of one's country.

Small lines that intersect the life line are interpreted as situations that hinder business or cause unhappiness in one's personal life. Those lines that radiate from the thumb and go through the life line show a tendency to be easily influenced by family and friends.

The **head line** is associated with mental attitudes—the level of intelligence, breadth of understanding and use of one's intellectual potential. The longer the line, the greater the importance of intellectual concerns.

This line starts near or at the same place as the life line, about midway between the thumb and forefinger, and crosses the palm toward the outside of the hand.

If the head line is joined to the life line, it reveals a cautious nature. The longer the two lines are joined, the greater the caution. Being joined a long time also shows being close to or dependent on one's family for a long time.

A separation between the two lines shows a desire to forge ahead, but if the separation is great, this becomes a restless, headlong quality.

A line that goes across the palm, gently sloping to the area between Upper Mars and Luna is considered the average head line and indicates a good intellect and a practical nature. The line typically extends to Apollo or Mercury but not to the edge of the hand.

A long and straight line reveals a shrewd individual with a good memory.

A line that slopes toward the mount of Luna belongs to a person who is sensitive and imaginative. If the line slopes even further and ends at the top part of Luna, the person has a talent for self-expression, but if it ends at the lower part of Luna, the imagination is over-active. A line that ends at the lower part of Luna can even indicate madness.

If the line runs toward the center of the wrist, the individual is out of touch with reality.

A line that curves upward to the heart line reveals an aptitude for business and the ability to make money, but a line that runs close to the heart line suggests a narrow

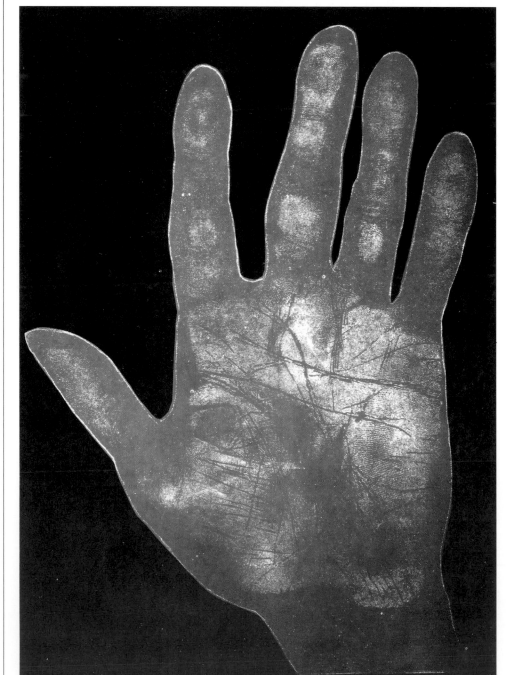

Below: **The handprint of Mark Twain. His fate line curved toward the mount of Jupiter—an indication of success through effort.**

outlook on life.

A clear, firm line denotes common sense, while a thin, light line signifies indecision. A red line reveals an aggressive nature. A short line means that the person will need assistance to achieve success, while a very short line indicates insufficient ambition or energy to complete one's goals.

A head line that ends under Saturn portends low intelligence, insanity or premature death if there are other indicators of poor health.

If the line ends under Apollo, the individual is light-hearted and cheerful and often succeeds in the arts. Persons of this sort generally desire the easy path to wealth.

If the line ends under Mercury, the person will make an excellent manager in any field.

A forked ending pointing to Luna shows imagination that is restrained by common sense, but a fork that ends on the heart line reveals a person willing to sacrifice all for the sake of all.

A strong branch line stemming from the head line to Jupiter indicates high ambitions that lead to success.

A heavy branch line to Saturn expresses religious fervor.

A branch to Apollo signals the ability to attain success through one's talents.

A branch to Mercury is a sign of success in business.

A branch line to the Luna area is closely associated with the imagination, but the final analysis is dependent on the reading of the total hand.

The **heart line** represents the emotional and physical traits associated with the heart. The first horizontal line on the palm, the heart line usually starts in the mount of Jupiter and runs across the palm at the base of the mounts to the opposite edge.

A heart line that starts high, almost at the base of the forefinger, signals a jealous person, while a line that starts low and runs in a straight line indicates affection for family but with little show of emotion.

A line that starts between the first and second fingers reveals sensual love, a tolerant nature and a generous attitude.

A line that starts between the second and third fingers belongs to a person with a negative attitude toward love. This person will need to be loved by an understanding individual.

If the heart line drops down and joins the head line, the head is said to rule the heart.

If the heart, head and life lines all start at the same point, the person is an extremist unwilling to use good judgement.

If the heart line starts in a fork on the mount of Jupiter, the individual is lovable and makes a good marriage partner. However, if one prong of the fork lies on Jupiter and the other on Saturn, the person is apt to be moody and difficult to live with.

A double heart line indicates an increased capacity for love and affection, whereas a missing line means a selfish person.

A branch line that runs to the head line indicates an attachment formed at work or a married couple that works together.

A branch line to the life line expresses sorrow over the loss of a loved one.

A branch line to Mercury indicates the collapse of a business due to family or a loved one.

A line to Saturn reveals unrequited love.

A line to Apollo indicates that career may interfere with home life.

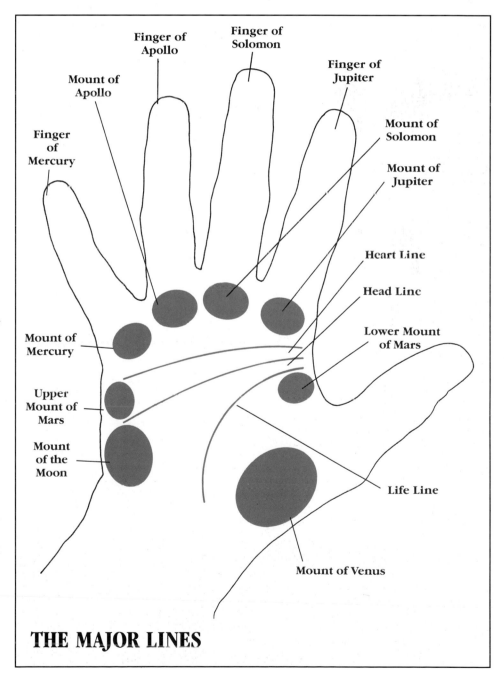

THE MAJOR LINES

Above: **The title page from a seventeenth-century book on palmistry.**

THE MINOR LINES

The secondary lines may or may not be present on every hand, and, in fact, a line such as Saturn, or fate, is more likely to appear later in life.

The **line of Saturn** starts at the base of the palm, near the wrist, between the life line and the edge of the mount of Luna. It moves straight up the palm to the mount of Saturn under the second finger. A line like this is the sign of a successful, untroubled life.

If the line starts at the life line, success will be achieved through one's own resources with possible assistance from friends or family at some time. If it starts inside the life line on the mount of Venus, assistance will come from the family at the onset. This can take the form of an inheritance or financial support for education or for a business endeavor. At the very least, parental guidance is involved.

A line that begins at the rascette, the wrist lines, indicates that numerous difficulties must be overcome before success is achieved.

If the line begins from the mount of Luna, success will be achieved without help from the family. The imaginative forces from Luna help propel the individual to an unusual and prosperous career. Travel may be involved.

If the line begins at the middle of the palm, or from the heart line or head line, success will come later in life or a career will be relatively brief.

If the line of Saturn ends on the mount of Saturn, responsibilities may begin early in life. If the end is near the head line, life is marked by changes in career or surroundings. If it ends near or on the heart line, the person will make sacrifices in the name of love or duty. A line that ends in a fork, with one prong on Jupiter and the other on Apollo, augurs well, for Jupiter provides ambition, Apollo, brilliance and Saturn the caution needed to make it all work.

The **line of Apollo** is also known as the line of the sun, the fortune line and the line of brilliance—the names of which suggest the importance of this line. The line of Apollo increases the value of the line of Saturn, and if Saturn is absent, Apollo replaces it.

The line of Apollo normally begins near the rascette on the wrist and moves straight up to the mount of Apollo under the third finger. Such a line signifies a quick wit, as well as popularity and perhaps even fame. The clearer the line, the greater the chance of financial gain.

If the line begins and is joined to the life line, talent is cultivated or financially sponsored by the family.

If the line begins at the head line, the person is well-organized and ingenious and success comes readily.

If the line starts at the heart line, success will probably arrive late in life.

If the line originates in Luna, creativity and imagination plays a role in choosing a career. Writers, poets, artists, composers and musicians often have a line like this. In some cases, these people will be extremely attractive to the opposite sex and will be idolized by the masses.

A line that ends in Apollo but leans toward Mercury adds business acumen to artistic ability. However, if the line leans toward Saturn, the person weighs every decision carefully.

A line with a triple forked ending—in Apollo, Saturn and Mercury—is unusual but indicates a remarkable ability to attain fame and fortune.

The **line of Mercury** is also known as the line of health or the hepatica line. The line normally begins at the wrist and moves up to the mount of Mercury. A solid line is a positive sign, signaling good health and a successful career. According to Gypsy legend, absence of this line is also interpreted as a sign of good health.

A broken, short line, however, signifies poor health and a wavy line indicates uncertainty and irritability.

If the line of Mercury forms a triangle with the line of Saturn and the head line, the person is said to possess psychic abilities.

THE LESSER LINES

The **rascettes** (bracelets) are the lines that appear on the wrist. If the lines are parallel and clearly marked, the person should enjoy a healthy and prosperous life.

A chain-like top bracelet denotes eventual happiness after a hard and difficult life.

On a woman, the top bracelet arching into the palm is a sign of possible reproductive difficulties.

The **girdle of Venus** is an arc-shaped line that starts between the first and second finger, curves down to the heart line, and finally ends between the third and fourth fingers. This line complements the heart line. Broken or fragmentary lines indicate disappointments in love, while double lines signify nervousness and a triple formation reveals a person prone to hysteria.

The **ring of Solomon** is a line under the first finger. A small line, it should not be confused with the crease where the finger joins the palm. A solid, curved line shows an aptitude for psychic powers; a straight line indicates an interest, rather than an aptitude, in the occult. Short, overlapping lines reveal one who is sympathetic of other's emotional and mental problems.

The **ring of Saturn** is a semicircle under the second finger. A solid line indicates a depressed individual, while a broken line shows a tendency for suicide.

The **line of Mars** runs parallel to and inside the life line and reinforces the qualities of that line. A short line of Mars adds bravery and strength in a time of need. A very long line indicates an extremely active life, often one that will end far from one's place of birth. If the line appears only in the left hand, the person is said to have psychic abilities.

The **line of intuition** is a curved line near the percussion of the palm, running from the lowest part of Luna to Mercury. This line is an indicator of psychic powers.

The **lines of affection** are also called the lines of union. One, two or three lines, they are located on the side of the palm in the mount of Mercury. These lines represent love affairs, marriages and marital problems. Usually one line is stronger than the others and symbolizes the most significant relationship. A long, straight line betokens a long and happy marriage.

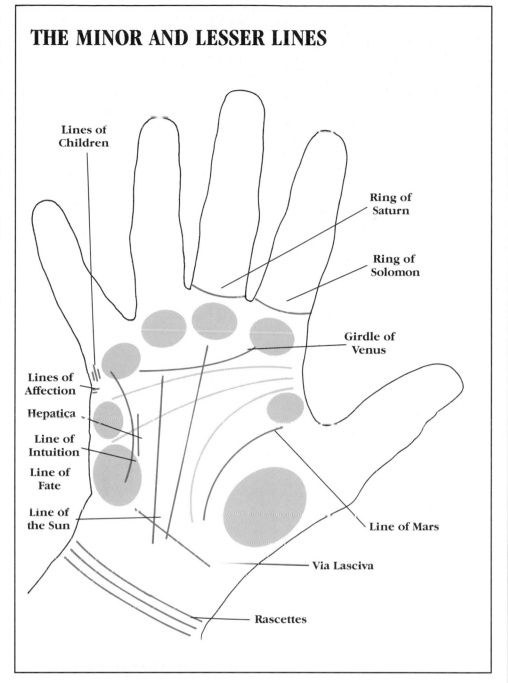

THE MINOR AND LESSER LINES

Lines of Children

Ring of Saturn

Ring of Solomon

Girdle of Venus

Lines of Affection

Hepatica

Line of Intuition

Line of Fate

Line of the Sun

Line of Mars

Via Lasciva

Rascettes

SIGNS AND SMALL MARKINGS

The many small markings seen on the palm provide additional clues for the palmist. Usually the markings are imperfectly formed. A triangle, for example, may have only two sides. The meaning of the sign varies somewhat depending on its location. While a square denotes protection, its specific meaning is interpreted according to location. On the mount of Mercury, a square protects against mental stress, while on the heart line it provides protection from unhappiness in love.

A chained line represents weakness or instability in some form.

A forked line indicates divided ability.

A double line adds strength and reinforcement.

An island (similar to an eye in shape) signals a loss, weakness or illness.

A triangle means good fortune.

A circle on Apollo is the sign of great success. This is very rare.

A square signifies protection from danger.

A star indicates a surprising event, either good or bad.

A bar means an obstacle.

A cross is a bad sign, indicating a shock, upheaval or obstacle.

A spot represents a shock or temporary illness.

A grill denotes instability.

PHRENOLOGY

Phrenology, the study of the 'bumps' on the head, was once the most popular of the psychic sciences. In 1796, after extensive research, Franz Joseph Gall, an Austrian physician, proposed his theory of phrenology. Gall reasoned that the way one thinks affects the shape of the brain, and consequently the shape of the skull. The skull could thus be examined and the 'bumps' read in much the same way as the lines and mounts of the palm.

Gall classified 26 bumps, which he referred to as faculties or organs. His followers isolated more faculties, increasing the total to 42 by the middle of the nineteenth century, when interest in phrenology was at its height.

A phrenologist first studies the overall shape of the head. A round head indicates a strong, confident personality, while a square head reveals a reliable, thoughtful and purposeful individual. A wider head is a sign of an energetic nature, a narrower head, an introspective person. An ovoid, or egg-shaped, head belongs to the intellectual.

Next, the phrenologists moves his fingertips over the head, gently but firmly, to determine the contours of the skull. He studies each faculty, determining its size in relation to the other parts of the head. A faculty that is underdeveloped indicates that particular quality is lacking, while one that is well developed indicates the quality is a major part of the individual's personality.

Below: **A phrenological chart from the nineteenth century, illustrating the 'Natural Language of the Faculties.'**

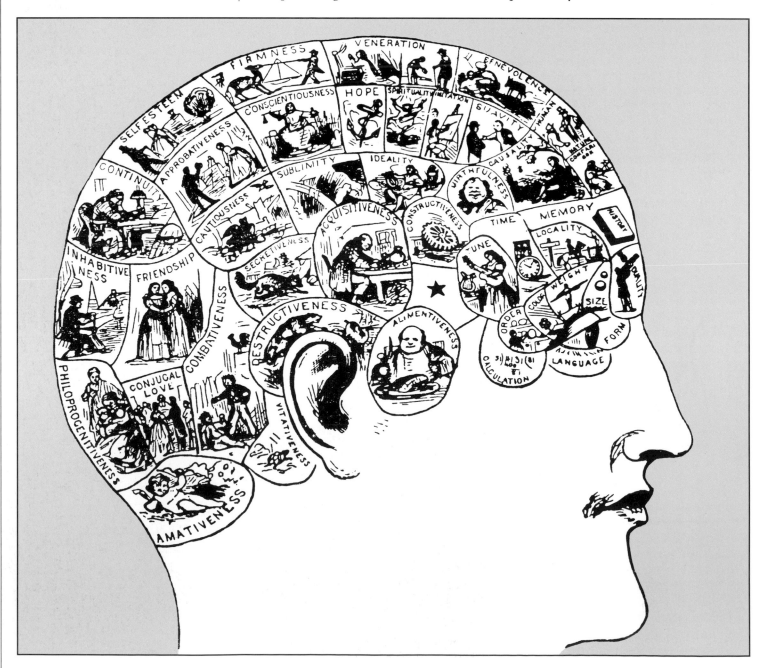

The Faculties

The numbers correspond to the numbered areas on the drawing on the facing page.

1. **Amativeness:** When this area is developed, the person is strongly interested in the opposite sex. When overly developed, the person overindulges in all desires. Lack of development indicates indifference.

2. **Conjugality:** Normal development in this area means the person is capable of constant, faithful love. Overdevelopment indicates a demanding love, while underdevelopment suggests a fickle nature unwilling to make a commitment.

3. **Philoprogenitiveness (parental love):** Developed, this area shows a love of children, pets and anyone in need of attention. Overdevelopment indicates the tendency to overindulge one's children, while underdevelopment shows disregard for children and dependents.

4. **Adhesiveness (friendship):** Normal development of this area shows a person who enjoys the company of others. Excessive development shows a tendency to become involved with unsuitable people or to become easily infatuated. Lack of development represents the inability to make friends.

5. **Inhabitiveness:** When this area is developed, the individual is attached to home and country. Overdevelopment indicates homesickness, while underdevelopment indicates the need for constant change and travel.

6. **Continuity:** Developed, this area relates to the ability to concentrate and to reason. When overdeveloped, the person tends to focus too much on unnecessary details. Underdevelopment is a sign of too many interests and the inability to concentrate.

7. **Vitativeness:** Normal development is a sign of vitality and the ability to stay healthy. Overdevelopment indicates hypochondria, while lack of development denotes ill health.

8. **Combativeness:** When this faculty is reasonably developed, the individual is courageous and energetic. Overdevelopment leads to an antagonistic nature; lack of development makes one fearful.

9. **Execution:** Development of this area indicates an efficient and ruthless individual, but overdevelopment leads to a vindictive nature. Lack of development reveals an inability to make decisions or give orders.

10. **Alimentiveness:** This faculty rules the appetite. When developed, the individual is a good eater, with a love of food and drink. Overdevelopment, however, is a sign of gluttony and alcoholism, while under-

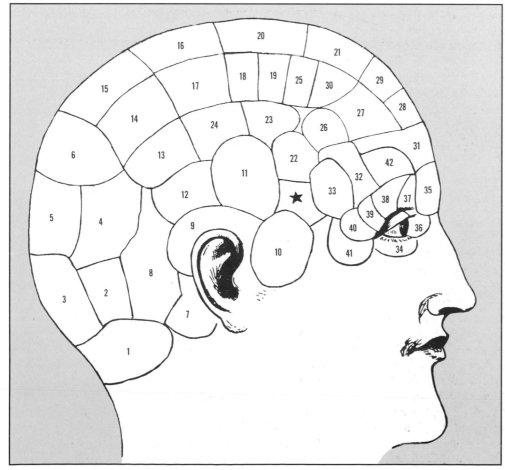

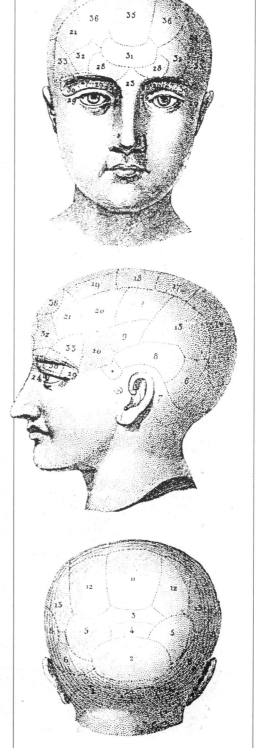

Below: **Three views of an early phrenological chart. As the science of phrenology developed, physicians pinpointed more areas, or faculties, as evidenced by the chart on the *left*.**

Below: **In contrast to most phrenological charts, this one is based on a drawing of a skull to better accentuate the 'bumps' on the head.**

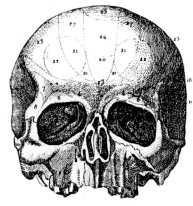

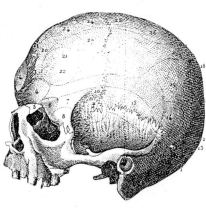

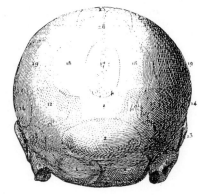

development suggests a finicky eater and perhaps a teetotaller.

11. **Acquisitiveness:** Normal development of this faculty shows a thrifty person, capable of attaining great wealth. Excessive development indicates a miser, while lack of development points to a spendthrift.

12. **Secretiveness:** Properly developed, this faculty is a sign of a tactful, discreet person. Overdevelopment denotes deceit and doubledealing, and underdevelopment typifies the individual who cannot keep a secret.

13. **Cautiousness:** Development in this area tends to make one careful and unwilling to take risks. When overly developed, the person tends to be unwilling to attempt anything and tends to postpone everything. If the faculty is underdeveloped, the person rushes headlong into any situation.

14. **Approbativeness:** When this area is developed, the person enjoys being popular, but with excessive development, the individual becomes a publicity seeker. A lack of development represents an unconventional nature unconcerned with popular opinion.

15. **Self-esteem:** Development in this area is indicative of an authoritative, self-confident individual. When the faculty shows a high degree of development, the person is arrogant and domineering. A deficiency in this area signals an individual lacking in confidence and consequently often incompetent.

16. **Firmness:** Development in this faculty is the mark of endurance and stability. Overdevelopment indicates a stubborn, willful individual, while underdevelopment reveals instability.

17. **Conscientiousness:** Individuals with normal development of this faculty exhibit a high degree of integrity. Those with excessive development are overly critical of others, while a deficiency of this faculty makes one unprincipled.

18. **Hope:** When this area is developed the individual has an optimistic outlook on life. Overdevelopment reveals an unrealistic dreamer, and underdevelopment, a pessimist.

19. **Spirituality:** Development of this faculty is a sign of devotion, intuition and psychic abilities. Excessive development suggests a superstitious nature, while lack of development reveals the skeptic.

20. **Veneration:** Developed, this faculty denotes a respect for customs and tradition. Overdevelopment betokens an obsession with high ideals or hero worship. Lack of development is the sign of a disrespectful, cynical individual.

21. **Benevolence:** Development in this area is the mark of a humanitarian, but excessive development is the sign of an overly sympathetic individual. Deficiency indicates a selfish individual, indifferent to the sufferings of others.

22. **Constructiveness:** When developed, this area represents mechanical ability, often highly inventive or skilled in design. When overdeveloped, there is a tendency to be unfocused and get caught up in the *act* of designing an object. Underdevelopment points to a lack of mechanical ability.

23. **Ideality:** Development of this area indicates a love of beauty and perfection. Overdevelopment reveals a person so moved by the aesthetic that they have a total disregard for all things practical. Undevelopment typifies the vulgar individual.

24. **Sublimity:** When this faculty is developed, the individual possesses a love of art, both manmade and natural. Overdevelopment is the sign of a person given to exaggeration, while underdevelopment suggests indifference to the world's finer things.

25. **Imitation:** Development of this area reveals a flair for the dramatic. With excessive development, the person tends to lose his sense of individuality to the imitation. A deficiency in this area reveals an inept individual.

26. **Mirthfulness:** This faculty deals with wit. When developed, it indicates a cheerful disposition and a sense of humor. Overdevelopment points to a practical joker, while underdevelopment reveals a serious nature, a person unable to have fun.

27. **Causality:** Development in this area symbolizes the thinker, someone with good reasoning skills. Overdevelopment means the individual cannot translate theory to action, while underdevelopment is indicative of poor reasoning power.

28. **Comparison:** When this faculty is developed, the person possesses strong analytical skills and is able to use examples and analogies to support an argument. Overdevelopment indicates a constant nitpicker; underdevelopment, a person incapable of drawing a logical conclusion.

29. **Humanity:** Development in this faculty is the sign of a good judge of character. Overdevelopment denotes an overly critical nature, while underdevelopment means a lack of discrimination in choosing friends and associates.

30. **Agreeableness:** An individual showing development of this faculty is persuasive and charming. Excessive development is an indication of insincerity in speech and

action. A deficiency in this faculty results in an unpleasant disposition.

31. **Eventuality:** Development in this area denotes an excellent memory for facts, events and experiences. Excessive development leads to a proclivity for retelling stories in long, boring detail. A lack of development suggests a poor memory.

32. **Time:** Developed, this faculty denotes a sense of timing and a good memory for dates. When overdeveloped, the person becomes a fanatic for punctuality, but a lack of development makes for a total disregard for time.

33. **Tune:** When this faculty is developed, the person has an ear for music. Overdevelopment denotes the non-stop desire to sing and play, while underdevelopment means the person is tone deaf.

34. **Language:** Development in this area points to an eloquent speaker and writer, perhaps with the ability to learn foreign languages. Excessive development indicates an overly talkative individual, while a deficiency in this area represents an inarticulate person.

35. **Individuality:** Developed, this faculty represents the ability to particularize. Overdevelopment indicates a meddlesome personality, while underdevelopment is evidence of poor powers of observation.

36. **Form:** Development of this faculty is said to be a sign of 'a good eye.' When overdeveloped, the individual is apt to be easily annoyed by anything that is not pleasing to the eye. Deficiency in this area indicates a lack of artistic ability.

37. **Size:** When this area is developed, the individual has the ability to judge proportions, sizes and measurements. Excessive development signals the need to make unnecessary comparisons, while a lack of development means the person cannot judge distances or proportions.

38. **Weight:** Development in this area indicates good balance and judgement of weights. Overdevelopment is linked to a love of high altitudes. A deficiency indicates a lack of balance or poise.

39. **Color:** Developed, this area represents a love of color and a skill in blending them. When overdeveloped, the person is sensitive to colors that clash. Lack of development shows no interest in color.

40. **Order:** When developed, this faculty provides the ability to be organized, systematic and tidy. Overdevelopment promotes fussiness, and underdevelopment indicates an untidy individual.

41. **Calculation:** Individuals showing development of this faculty possess mathematical ability. Overdevelopment of the area indicates an obsession with numbers, while underdevelopment reveals an inability to perform even the simplest mathematical functions.

42. **Locality:** When this faculty is developed, the individual adapts easily to new surroundings and enjoys travel, but with excessive development, the love of travel becomes a constant need to explore. Lack of development signifies a poor memory for places and little interest in new places.

Although phrenology had it origins in medical science, the field soon attracted a large number of quacks and eventually lost the support of the scientific community. Medical science has since shown that the brain simply does not work in the manner described by Gall, but even so, some people today continue to find value in Gall's theory.

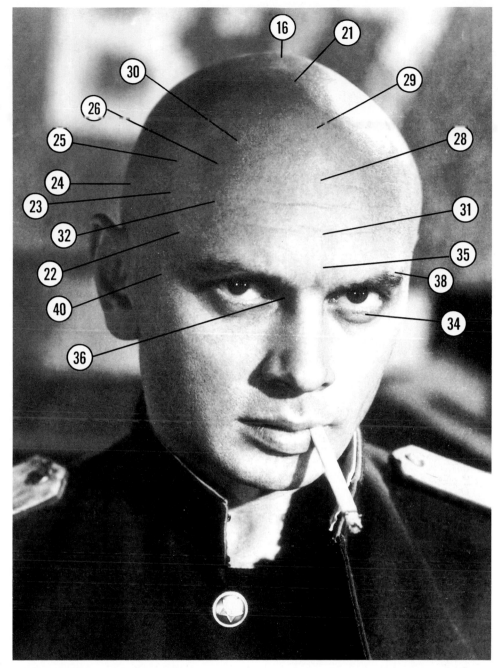

Above: **Yul Brynner, the actor, shaved his head for his role of the king of Siam in *The King and I.***

Brynner's shaved head made him famous, but for students of phrenology, it illustrates the relationship between the bumps on Brynner's head and his personality.

Development in area 21 is the sign of a humanitarian. Late in life, Brynner was active in the cause of gypsy rights. Area 38 shows a good sense of balance: he was a trapeze artist as a teenager. His fluency in languages is indicated by area 34.

NUMEROLOGY

Above: **The ancient Egyptians were the first to develop a system of numerology, making it one of the oldest of the occult arts.**

Opposite page: **A numerological analysis of Madonna's birth and name numbers reveals much about her character.**

umerology is based on the belief that numbers, especially the primary numbers from 1 to 9, influence people's lives and personalities. Every person has numbers associated with his birth and name.

One of the oldest forms of occult lore, numerology dates back to the Babylonians and ancient Egyptians. Up through the Middle Ages, numbers were especially important to the Cabalists. The Cabala is the secret mystical lore of the Jews that is based on the *gematria*, the magico-philosophical science of numbers that revolves around the 22 letters of the Hebrew alphabet.

Numerology has attracted many followers in recent years, although the various systems used today differ somewhat from the ones used by the Ancients. Most of the present day systems are based on the theories of Pythagoras, the Greek mathematician and philosopher. Pythagoras believed that the universe was ordered mathematically, and therefore numbers were the key to the universe. In the past, numerology was considered a form of divination, the art of foretelling the future, but today the adherents of numerology regard it primarily as a method for analyzing personalities and potential.

The primary numbers from 1 to 9 form the basis of all numerological systems. All numbers are then reduced to a primary number. The simplest and most popular system for reducing any number to a primary number is to add the figures of the number. If that number totals 10 or more, that number is reduced again. Thus, 25 becomes 2 + 5 = 7, and 87 becomes 8 + 7 = 15.

The same process is used to reduce dates. A number-letter equivalent is used to determine the number for names.

BIRTH NUMBERS

An individual's most important number is the birth number, which is arrived at by adding up the numbers in one's date of birth. The month is assigned a numerical value. January is 1, February is 2, March is 3 and so on. October, November and December—the tenth, eleventh and twelfth months—are reduced to primary numbers:

October (10) becomes 1 + 0 = 1
November (11) becomes 1 + 1 = 2
December (12) becomes 1 + 2 = 3

If a person's date of birth is 12 July 1956, the equation is as follows: 1 + 2 + 7 (for the seventh month) + 1 + 9 + 5 + 6 = 31, which is reduced to 3 + 1 = 4.

A person's birth number is obviously

Above: **Movie star John Wayne typifies the strength and confidence that characterize individuals with a name number 7.**

unchanging and therefore influences a person's character. The influence of the birth number, however, is tempered by various other numerological factors and should be viewed as a guiding factor rather than as a ruling force.

NAME NUMBERS

Every name has a number, obtained by translating the letters of the name into numbers as indicated in the chart below, and then adding their totals and reducing them to primary numbers.

1	2	3	4	5	6	7	8	9
A	B	C	D	E	F	G	H	I
J	K	L	M	N	O	P	Q	R
S	T	U	V	W	X	Y	Z	

This is simply a listing of the letters in numerical order: A = 1, B = 2, C = 3 and so on. From the letter J—the tenth letter—the letters are reduced to primary numbers. Thus, Z, the twenty-sixth letter, becomes 2 + 6 = 8.

A person's name number is determined by the name usually used. Thus, Kathleen Shoultz, who goes by Kate, would use Kate rather than Kathleen.

K A T E   S H O U L T Z
$2+1+2+5 \ + \ 1+8+6+3+3+2+8=41=4+1=5$

In the case of a person who is known by a single name, or moniker, such as Cher or Madonna, the one name can stand as the mark of the individual.

A person's name number reveals acquired traits, and unlike the birth number can, of course, be changed. Numerologists believe that a change in the name, even just adding or dropping a middle initial, can influence one's life.

WHAT THE NUMBERS MEAN

The **number 1** stands for the Sun. People with 1 as a birth number are strong-willed and driven. Ambitious and active, number 1 people are born leaders. With their dominant personalities, they are born leaders, winners and innovators. These people are forceful and untiring and can achieve great things if their goals are well-directed. However, if misguided, people with 1 as a birth number can be self-centered, ruthless and tyrannical.

As a name number, 1 indicates vigor and a desire for action, but that action is best directed toward immediate goals rather than long-term ones. Determination is the hallmark of the name number 1. These people are successful, but they are apt to spend money freely once they have earned it.

The **number 2** represents a search for balance. People with 2 as their birth number have the ability to see both sides of a situation. This sense of fair play can work against them, as their desire for balance can cause them to waver indecisively. The sense of judgement that allows them to give good advice to their friends can prevent them from making up their own minds regarding their own affairs.

Those with 2 as their birth number should learn to deal with situations as they are rather than try to change them to suit their own desires. They should avoid situations that are marked by extremes or that call for decisions.

These people are gentle, kind and tactful. Number 2s are artistic, but as they are given more to thought than to action, they often lack the force they need to carry out their plans. Although they are charming and intuitive, 2s sometimes suffer from a lack of self-confidence. Their greatest fault is overgenerosity, and they should give the same consideration to themselves as they do to others.

As a name number, 2 denotes a person with a keen sense of judgement. But 2s are planners, not doers, and need associates to carry out their plans. In choosing their associates, 2s should rely on their sense of judgement rather than on emotion, as they may be wont to do.

The quest for balance can create an instability in people with 2 as their name number. Though generally happy, their emotional dispositions can make them restless and gloomy; 2s therefore should avoid situations that promote worry. They should make the most of their friendly natures and avoid arguments. These people get along well with their opposites—number 1s.

The **number 3** signals a talented individual. People with the birth number of three are quick learners. They are typically successful in their chosen fields as they are conscientious and independent. They excel at arts, sciences, sports—anything that demands quick-thinking and intuition.

People with this birth number like to be entertained. They attach a great deal of importance to pleasant surroundings and interesting people. Because they have a tendency to think only of the present, 3s should guard against neglecting their plans, thereby allowing others to profit from their ideas.

As a name number, 3 signifies competence and confidence. People with this name number can achieve great success, but 3s tend to be impatient and the promise of instant gratification may lure them away from a career path that offers more in the long run.

The **number 4** represents a steady and practical nature. People with 4 as their birth number have the ability to grasp new ideas quickly, but their temperament is such that they prefer to study a new idea completely.

Honesty, reliability, patience and perseverance are the characteristics of a person with 4 as their birth number. Professionally, 4s do well at any exacting task, such as research or scientific or technical fields.

As a name number, 4 stands for stability. Other people like 4s because they are dependable and trustworthy. Number 4s are even-tempered and good in an emergency. Though some may describe 4s as plodding, their endurance makes up for any lack of brilliance. Persons with 4 as their birth number should never underestimate themselves, for their traits will always be in demand.

The **number 5** indicates an adventurous, enthusiastic personality. Persons with 5 as a birth number enjoy traveling, feel at home anywhere, and are adept at learning foreign languages. Versatile and vivacious, 5s are open to new ideas and often act on impulse. They love the new and unusual and deplore routine. A drawback to their need for change is that 5s may overlook solid opportunities because they are always focused on what lies ahead rather than on the here and now.

As a name number, 5 signifies independence, both in thought and action. Persons with 5 as a name number prefer to learn through their own experiences rather than taking the advice of others. People of this type can be quite successful, providing they can control their restless natures. Ideally, those with 5 as a name number do best in situations where their flair for the dramatic and need for the unexpected are put to use.

The **number 6** represents sincerity. People with 6 as a birth number are dependable and honest. Other attributes include a cheerful disposition, a tolerant nature and an optimistic outlook. People of this sort are peacemakers, fostering harmony among their friends. They enjoy the finer things in life and do not hesitate to share with others.

As a birth number, 6 betokens success, for this sort of person inspires confidence. Whether their goals are political or commercial, people with this name number attract followers and customers. They need not be radical in what they offer as long as they provide what they have promised. 'Honesty is its own reward' is the creed of the 6. Their kind, caring personalities earn them many friends.

The **number 7** symbolizes knowledge. People with 7 as their birth number have scholarly, often poetic, natures and are often inclined to the fanciful. They are imaginative and intuitive and, oddly enough, analytical. Their preoccupation with things mysterious has a tendency to make them moody and depressed.

Number 7 people are inspired by solitude, and are drawn to artistic and philosophical endeavors. However, they become despondent if the rest of the world ignores them, which causes them to withdraw completely. To be happy, number 7 people need to overcome this tendency to withdraw and need to instead become an active part of the world.

As a name number, 7 holds the promise of great things. These people often become composers, musicians, philosophers or writers. To be successful in their chosen field, however, they must overcome their natural tendency to be dreamers, relying instead on careful planning. Financial independence or commercial success will be achieved only with the help of others, for practicality is not part of 7's character. People with 7 as a name number can become great leaders or teachers, as they understand others well and have the ability to inspire.

The **number 8** denotes material success. People with 8 as their birth number are effective planners, capable of carrying their plans to completion. Once their goals have been achieved, they go on to something better and bigger.

Number 8 people have strong, forceful personalities. They are demanding and expect—and get—perfection from their

Above: **Abraham Lincoln exhibited the sincerity and honesty that is the hallmark of those with the name number 6.**

Above: **The pop star Madonna radiates with the assurance and confidence of number 11, her birth number.**

associates. Opposition does not deter them, and may, in fact, spur them on. These people often make great military or political leaders.

People with 8 as a birth number are driven by the need for wealth and power, and though they can be quite ruthless, those around them enjoy the benefits of number 8's success. Wealth and success are also the standards by which number 8 judges other people. The value of an object, too, is measured in monetary terms.

As a name number, 8 seeks prosperity. These people have a constant need to be active and see things happening around them. Momentum is important, for if 8 slows down, progress will be hindered considerably. On occasion, however, a neglected or forgotten project can be turned into a profitable enterprise. Persons with this name number should avoid wasting time and energy. Their motto should be 'Think big and act big!'

The **number 9** is a powerful number, combining influence with intellect. Like 8, the number 9 promises success, but whereas number 8 people find their fortunes in the business world, 9s achieve success through more creative channels.

Persons with 9 as a birth number possess wonderful, magnetic personalities. If they are able to carry out their brilliant ideas in a practical manner, their success will know no bounds. They must understand their capabilities and desires, and set their goals accordingly.

As a name number, 9 betokens a person of influence. If they use their natural talents, these people are capable of accomplishing great things for mankind. Because they have the ability to influence people, 9s should be guided by high ideals. If they behave out of character, their strength is lost. People with 9 as a name number should avoid dull, boring situations, which tend to stifle their creativity.

THE SECONDARY NUMBERS

Some numerologists study the meaning of the numbers beyond the primary numbers of 1 to 9. There are various theories and beliefs about how these secondary numbers are interpreted. The most mystical of numerologists see significance in many numbers, while others hold that only the secondary numbers up to 22 (for the 22 letters in the Hebrew alphabet) are relevant. Most authorities, however, ascribe meaning to only a handful of secondary numbers: 11, 12, 13, 22 and 40. Of these, 11 and 22 are generally considered the most significant.

The **number 11** provides initiative that is lacking in 2, the number to which it is reduced. The number 11 is strong enough to end the indecisiveness of 2.

As a name number, 11 contributes an assurance and boldness to the number 2's sense of judgement.

The **number 12** signifies completeness. It is the number of the signs of the zodiac, the months, the tribes of Israel and the apostles, to name a few examples.

The **number 13** is typically identified with bad luck and the black arts, but in some instances it can be a positive force.

The **number 22** adds a dash of mysticism to the steady nature of the number 4 to which it is reduced. People of this sort tend to focus on the inner self, often to the point of ignoring the world around them.

As a name number, 22 straddles the line between eccentricity and genius. In some cases, 22 takes the exacting, mechanical skills found in 4 and develops them in new and unique ways.

Like 12, the **number 40** is another power number that denotes completeness.

NUMEROLOGICAL ANALYSIS

There are various methods for analyzing individual traits through numerology, but one of the most commonly used follows the procedure listed below.

The first step is to consider the person's birth number, as this is indicative of the person's natural characteristics. The birth number is called the *number of personality.*

Next, the name number is analyzed. Called the *number of development*, the name number reveals developed traits. If a person's name remains unchanged, the power of the name number increases in terms of the person's career. If the person adopts a new name or takes a stage name, then the analysis is based on this new number, the *number of attainment.*

A person's name also reveals additional information. A vowel vibration is arrived at by adding the numerical values of all the vowels in the name and then reducing the figure to a primary number. This is called the *number of underlying influence*.

When a number occurs frequently in a name that number enters into the analysis. This number is referred to as the *number of added influence*.

Some authorities contend that if the birth number is higher than the name number, a person is prone to adhere to the attributes described by birth number rather than those described by the name number. This may create internal conflicts as the individual struggles to develop the qualities of the name number. On the other hand, if the name number is the higher number, then those attributes will predominate, which means that natural characteristics of the individual are directed toward situations of his own choice. In other words, the person is likely to control situations rather than be governed by them.

An individual with the same birth and name number is apt to have a balanced, harmonious disposition. This type of individual is well-adjusted and able to take all things in stride, but it should be noted that few of the world's movers and shakers have such a balance.

The following examples of numerological analyses of well-known personalities illustrate the principles of this ancient lore.

Pop star **Madonna** is an excellent subject for analysis, for her vibratory numbers reveal many basic concepts of numerology.

Madonna was born on 16 August 1958, giving her a birth number of 2, as illustrated below:

$1+6+8+1+9+5+8 = 38+3+8$
$= 11+1+1 = 2.$

In the case of Madonna, however, the higher vibration of 11 has clearly exerted its power, adding force and determination to the number 2.

For her name number, Madonna has both a number of development and a number of attainment. These numbers illustrate how a change in a name impacts a person's life and career. When she moved from her hometown of Bay City, Michigan to New York to seek fame and fortune, Madonna Ciccone made the conscious decision to use only her given name as her stage name. Today, she is known the world over by only her first name:

M A D O N N A
   1   6   1 = 8 (VOWELS)
$4+1+4+6+5+5+1 = 26$
$= 2+6 = 8$

As befits the 'Material Girl,' the number 8 signifies material success. As to be expected of someone with 8 as a name number, Madonna is driven to achieve wealth and success. In a very short time, she has accomplished both. In addition to being a talented performer, she has a reputation as a hard-working business woman. The vowel vibration also works out to 8, strengthening the force of this already powerful number.

An analysis of Madonna's full name is equally illuminating:

M A D O N N A   C I C C O N E
$4+1+4+6+5+5+1 \; + \; 3+9+3+3+6+5+5$
$= 60 = 6+0 = 6$

The number 6 is the symbol of dependability. People with 6 as a name number are often found in positions of trust. As the oldest girl in a family of eight children, Madonna helped care for her younger siblings. She also maintained a straight-A average all through school. She was well-liked by the nuns at her high school and was even a hall monitor.

Elvis Presley was born on 8 January 1935, giving him a birth number of 9:
$8+1+1+9+3+5 = 27 = 2+7 = 9$

The number 9 is the symbol of universal achievement. In the world of music, there is no better example of influence and achievement than Elvis Presley—the King of Rock & Roll. Persons with 9 as a birth number are characterized by their powerful, magnetic personalities, and Elvis is no exception. More than a dozen years after his death, Elvis' fans are still devoted to the King, many with an almost religious fervor.

Elvis' vivacious personality is also reflected in his name number.

E L V I S   P R E S L E Y
$5+3+4+9+1 \; + \; 7+9+5+1+3+5+7$
$= 59 = 5+9 = 14 = 1+4 = 5$

Although the birth number of 9 predominates, the name number 5 offers insights into Elvis' independent and impulsive nature. The King was known for his spur-of-the-moment, midnight forays to the local movie theatre for his own private screening of the latest film.

Since Elvis Presley is known to much of the world simply as 'Elvis,' an analysis of his given name alone is warranted.

E L V I S
$5+3+4+9+1 = 22 = 2+2 = 4$

Most people never advance beyond the plodding nature of 4. Elvis, however, showed the genius of the higher vibration of 22. Persons with 22 as a name number have the ability to create something new and unique, as Elvis did with his music.

Above: Elvis Presley exemplifies the dynamic, successful personality of the birth number 9.

Above: **The negative aspects of Adolf Hitler's name number 2 made him a fanatic who sought to establish a master race.**

Marion Morrison, better known to the world as **John Wayne**, was born on 26 May 1907, giving him a birth number of 3:
$$2+6+5+1+9+0+7=30=3+0=3$$

The birth number 3 expresses John Wayne's talent as both an athlete and an actor. While attending the University of Southern California on a football scholarship, John Wayne was discovered by Hollywood director John Ford. Leaving football for film, John Wayne went on to became one of the biggest box office attractions the silver screen has ever known.

Marion Morrison, Wayne's given name, reflects the initiative that is often missing from the number 2.

M A R I O N   M O R R I S O N
$$4+1+9+9+6+5 \quad + \quad 4+6+9+9+9+1+6+5$$
$$=83=8+3=11=1+1=2$$

Marion Morrison had to work hard to win a football scholarship, but he was able to attain greater things by changing his name to John Wayne.

J O H N   W A Y N E
$$1+6+8+5 \quad + \quad 5+1+7+5+5$$
$$=43=4+3=7$$
$$\quad 6 \qquad\qquad 1\ 7 \quad 5 \qquad \text{(VOWELS)}$$
$$=19=1+9=10=1+0=1$$

As a name number, 7 denotes John Wayne's success as a film star. The characters he portrayed on screen represented the very essence of strength and confidence. Off screen, he projected an equally heroic, almost mythical, image. Wayne's ability to inspire is embodied by his name number. He survived three major operations and became an inspiration for cancer patients around the world. The vowel vibration 1 points to his vigorous personality, and the frequency number 5 points to the underlying influence of adventure in Wayne's life.

Abraham Lincoln was born on 12 February 1809, giving him a birth number of 5:
$$1+2+2+1+8+0+9=23=2+3=5$$

The birth number 5 shows Lincoln's enthusiastic nature. As a young boy, he was eager to learn, though he rarely had the opportunity to attend school. A true self-taught man, Lincoln spent his spare time studying and reading.

With the characteristic zeal of 5, Lincoln tried a variety of endeavors as a young man. He worked on a Mississippi River flatboat, opened his own store, managed the village post office, and did surveying, before running for the state legislature at the age of 25. After he was elected, he studied law.

Lincoln's success at such a wide variety of responsibilities is no surprise, considering that his name number is 6.

A B R A H A M   L I N C O L N
$$1+2+9+1+8+1+4 \quad + \quad 3+9+5+3+6+3+5$$
$$=60=6$$
$$1 \qquad\qquad 1 \quad 1 \qquad\qquad 9 \qquad\qquad 6\,(\text{VOWELS})$$
$$=18=1+8=9$$

The name number 6 gives dependability to the birth number 5's tendency to be unpredictable and impulsive. The name number 6 expresses the sincerity and reliability for which Honest Abe is so well known. In typical 6 fashion, Lincoln gained the confidence of the people of the United States and was elected to the highest office in the land. The vowel vibration 9 is indicative of Lincoln's power and influence.

Adolf Hitler was born on 20 April 1889, giving him a birth number of 5.
$$2+0+4+1+8+8+9=32=3+2=5$$

The birth number 5 shows Hitler's restless nature. As was the case with Abraham Lincoln (see above), Hitler's youth was marked by a number of jobs: carpenter, architect's draftsman and water-colorist. With Hitler, however, the birth number 5 reveals aimless drifting rather than a desire to succeed. In Lincoln's case, the unpredictability of the birth number 5 benefitted from the dependability of his name number 6, whereas Hitler was influenced by the gloomy aspects of his name number 2.

A D O L F   H I T L E R
$$1+4+6+3+6 \quad + \quad 8+9+2+3+5+9=56$$
$$=5+6=11=1+1=2$$

Hitler is a classic example of the negative side of the number 2. The quest for balance can drive a number 2 to extremes, even outright fanaticism, as illustrated by Hitler's plan to establish the German people as the 'master race' in Europe. Emotional and prone to depression as 2s are wont to be, Hitler spent hours, even days brooding, unable to take action in the face of Germany's impending defeat. Eventually, he avoided action completely by taking his own life.

Winston Churchill was born on 30 November 1874, giving him a birth number of 7:
$$3+0+1+1+1+8+7+4=25=2+5=7$$

The 7 reveals Churchill's intuitive side. Several times in his lifetime, Churchill exhibited great powers of intuition. On one occasion, the prime minister was entertaining at No 10 Downing Street. The guests were called to dinner just as a nightly air raid began. The air raids had become so much a part of daily life that no one considered interrupting the party—no one, that is, except Winston Churchill. Leaving his guests for a moment, he ordered his staff to bring all the food into the dining room and then to go down to the bomb shelter.

Churchill then returned to his guests and continued with the meal. A few moments later a bomb hit the rear of the house, completely destroying the kitchen where the staff had been preparing the meal. Thanks to Churchill's premonition, everyone escaped unscathed.

Churchill's name number expresses the traits that made him a great leader.

```
W I N S T O N   C H U R C H I L L
5+9+5+1+2+6+5  +  3+8+3+9+3+8+9+3+3
=82 =8+2=10 =1
   9        6          3        9
=27 =2=7=9                   (VOWELS)
```

The number 1 symbolizes action and aggression, which is what Churchill brought to his role as Prime Minister during England's fight against Hitler in World War II. Courage, self-reliance and purpose are the hallmarks of number 1. The vowel vibration 9 strengthened Churchill's ability to guide the people of England. The frequency number 3, which occurs 5 times out of 16 numbers, points to Churchill's natural talent and versatility.

Above: **As his birth number 7 suggests, Winston Churchill displayed powers of clairvoyance, several times throughout his life.**

NUMEROLOGY IN DAILY LIFE

Numerology can play a part in an individual's daily life by explaining how a given day harmonizes with his birth and name numbers. The day is assigned a number, using the same method that is used to obtain a birth number. This number is then added to the individual's birth and name number and the total is reduced to a primary number. By following this formula, a person can determine which days are better suited for a specific activity.

For example, Ivan Semancik wants to analyze the influence that 2 November 1991 ($2 + 1 + 1 + 1 + 9 + 9 + 1 = 24 = 2 + 4 = 6$) will have on his life. His name number is 4 and birth number is 2.

Birth number + 2
Name number + 4
Date number + 6
Total $= 12 + 1 + 2 = 3$

According to the summary below, this is a good day for Ivan to attend successfully to numerous tasks.

One. This is a day for action. Problems of a business, legal or practical nature can be solved on this day. However, as it represents a day of *single* purposefulness, all plans must be kept simple and be carried out immediately. It is a day of opportunity.

Two. This is a day of contrasts, one that fluctuates between the good and bad. It is a day for planning and weighing matters. If a decision is made, action is best delayed. The influence of 2 makes this a day fraught with indecision.

Three. This is also a day of action. In contrast to a day influenced by the number 1, this day is suited to handling a variety of tasks. Much can be accomplished on this day. Troublesome tasks can be completed with ease and problems can be solved. It is a good day for business as well as pleasure.

Four. This is a day suited to handling mundane and practical tasks. It is not a time for fun and relaxation, as people often find themselves preoccupied with nagging thoughts about the various chores they should be doing. This is not a day for important events or for gambling.

Five. This is a day to expect the unexpected. It is a day of adventure, filled with vitality and the urge to travel and try new things. It is easy to get swept away with the moment, and one should exercise some caution so that the wild schemes dreamed up on this day don't backfire. If an idea has merit, however, this is the day to take risks.

Six. This is a day of contentment and understanding. It is a day for communication with business associates, friends and family, as long as conflict is not involved. It is not a day to embark on new projects, to solve a problem, or to take on a challenge. This is a day to finish projects that have long since been planned and carefully thought out.

Seven. This is a spiritual day, well suited to reflection on the deeper things in life. It is a good day to study, conduct research, or work on artistic projects. This is also the time to contemplate, to consult with others and to finalize plans. The most mystical of days, strange things are likely to happen.

Eight. This is the day to think big. Smaller projects should be avoided unless they lead the way to something grander. Effort and action will bring results, and complicated issues can be settled on this day. It is the day to handle money matters—the bigger, the better—for this is the day that fortunes can be made.

Nine. This day holds the potential for accomplishing great things. It is the time to make important announcements, to make contacts, or to propose ideas. Long-held goals and personal triumphs of an artistic or competitive nature can be realized on this day. This is the day to win!

DIVINATION

Above: **The art of divination, or fore-telling the future, is practiced all over the world. The future can be seen in tarot cards, dice or in the palm of one's own hand, and those who possess the ability to see the future can be found in cities, towns and villages throughout the world.**

Right and opposite page: **A serious young dowser practices this ancient craft.**

 ivination, the art of predicting the future, has intrigued the human race since the dawn of time, and records of many and varied forms of divination can be found in all cultures. The leaders of ancient Greece, for example, turned to oracles before waging war. In other times and places, people have used objects, ranging from live chickens and animal entrails to tea leaves and crystal balls, to unlock the mysteries of the present and the future. In this chapter, we look at only three forms of divination: the *I Ching*, tarot and dowsing.

DOWSING

The age-old practice of using a forked hazel twig to find underground water is seldom explained, but has apparently met with considerable success. The dowser attempts to locate water or a missing object by concentrating and walking slowly over the ground to be surveyed and even saying out loud the name of the object to be found. The sensation is said to resemble a trembling or magnetic pull toward the ground when water is nearby. This practice has also been used to search for minerals, lost objects and even missing persons, under the assumption that all things give off a unique radiation signal that the trained individual is able to detect. Some individuals do not use a rod or tool and instead experience twitching in their hands, arms or legs or perceive painful shocks in their feet when they are near the hidden object.

Map dowsers who are absent from the surveying site claim that by suspending a pendulum or plumb line over a map of the area, they can retrieve the lost item or dis-cover an unknown mineral deposit. This can only be explained in terms of extra-sensory perception.

There are enough serious dowsers in the United States for there to exist The American Society of Dowsers. The clients of professional dowsers might range from land owners who want to dig a well on their property to companies in the petroleum industry who seek new wells.

I CHING

The *I Ching* or *Book of Changes* is an ancient and complex system of divination that originated in China during the third millennium BC. However, the *I Ching* is much more than a means of prediction. It is a book of wisdom that offers advise on how to deal with the fortune. The central feature of the *I Ching* is the hexagram, a pattern of six lines read from the bottom upward. The hexagram is formed, or cast, by tossing yarrow stalks, coins or wands. Once the hexagram is formed, the *Book of Changes* is consulted for interpretation and advice.

Fu Hsi, who according to legend was the first emperor of China, is said to be one of the earliest developers of the *I Ching*. Under the Hsia Dynasty (2205-1766 BC) and the Shang Dynasty (1176-1150 BC) two early books of changes were used for divination. Around 1100 BC, King Wên Wang (died c 1150 BC) developed the 64 hexagrams that comprise today's sets. He also began compiling an explanatory text that his son, the Duke of Chou, continued. Divination throughout the Chou Dynasty (1150-249 BC) followed the oracles in that form. In the fifth century BC, the great writer and sage Confucius is believed to have studied and used the *I Ching*, adding a written commentary of his own. He is credited with saying that it has 'as many layers as the earth itself.'

Under the Ch'in (221-206 BC) and Han (206-220 AD) Dynasties the *I Ching* was used solely as a means of divining the future and lost the Confucian context that held that its higher purpose was one of guiding ethical statecraft.

Wang Pi (226-249 AD) argued that the oracles compiled by China's great leaders were not intended for casual magic and sport, but were a source of wisdom. Present texts are in fact used for determining statecraft as much as for predicting the future of horse races and lovesick individuals.

The Swiss psychologist and philosopher Carl Gustav Jung took a keen interest in the ancient *Book of Changes*. He was hoping to find a connection between 'this oracle technique, or method of exploring the unconscious' and his synchronicity concept. Jung's fascination with coincidence led him to develop the concept of synchronicity, or the 'simultaneous occurrence of a certain psychic state with one or more external events which appear as meaningful parallels to the momentary subjective state.'

Traditionally, the *I Ching* has been used to encourage deep thought and self-examination. At first, the linear signs were meant to represent the answers yes and no. 'Yes' was indicated by an unbroken line (———) and has become affiliated with Yang, the positive, masculine and active side of nature. 'No' was indicated by a broken line (— —) and is today known as Yin, symbolizing the negative, feminine and passive side of nature. It soon became evident that many questions required more than a simple yes or no answer, and the lines were paired:

———   — —   ———   — —
———   — —   — —   ———

Then a third line was added to each of these pairs, thus forming the eight trigrams which are the fundamental tools for forecasting the future.

The eight trigrams represent all that takes place in heaven and on earth. They symbolize the transitional nature of processes in the physical world instead of representing an entity in a fixed state. This relates to the widely-held belief that what occurs in the visible world is merely the

---

These eight symbols were then combined with each other in every possible configuration, and the resulting 64 hexagrams today make up the entire Book of Changes as expounded by King Wên.

	Name	Image	Attribute	Family Relationship
☰	Ch'ien, The Creative	Heaven	strong	father
☷	K'un, The Receptive	Earth	devoted, yielding	mother
☳	Chen, The Arousing	Thunder	inciting movement	first son
☵	K'an, The Abysmal	Water	dangerous	second son
☶	K'en, Keeping Still	Mountain	resting	third son
☴	Sun, The Gentle	Wind	penetrating	first daughter
☲	Li, The Clinging	Fire	light-giving	second daughter
☱	Tui, The Joyous	Lake	joyful	third daughter

effect of an 'image' or idea in the unseen world. Change is not without meaning and the *Book of Changes* is a record of all the complex, interconnected changes, such as night and day.

The trigrams also represent a family unit consisting of a father, mother, three sons and three daughters. Generally, the sons are associated with movement—beginning of movement, danger in movement, rest and completion of movement—while the daughters are associated with devotion—gentle penetration, clarity and adaptability, and joyous tranquility. However, some authors find other themes in the trigrams, such as animals, body parts, time of day and points of a compass.

Each trigram is assigned an attribute—a word or so that describes the potential action in a given combination of lines—and an image of heaven, earth or a feature of one of the two. The image gives added meaning to the interpretation of the trigram.

Above: **A Chinese soothsayer casts yarrow stalks, the first step in the complicated process of consulting the oracle of the I Ching.**

Forming and Reading the Hexagram

There are two ways to consult the oracle. The first is very ancient and complicated. It requires sorting and separating 50 yarrow stalks. These divination tools were used for at least two reasons: as vegetable matter, they were respected as sources of life; and special properties were attributed to them as they were derived from the sacred yarrow plant.

One yarrow stalk is separated from the pile and has no further role. The remaining 49 are divided into two random heaps. One stalk is drawn from the right-hand pile and placed between the ring finger and the little finger of the left hand. The left-hand heap is placed in the left hand and stalks are drawn from it with the right hand four at a time until there are four or fewer stalks remaining. The remainder is placed between the ring finger and the middle finger of the left hand. The right-hand pile is divided by the same method and the remainder is placed between the middle finger and the forefinger of the left hand. Now is the time to count the stalks between the fingers of the left hand. The sum will be either nine or five. Disregard the first stalk held between the little finger and the ring finger. The new total, if it was nine will now be eight, or if it was five will

Below are the names of the 64 hexagrams in the order that they appear in the *I Ching.*

1.	Ch'ien	The Creative
2.	K'un	The Receptive
3.	Chun	Difficulty at the Beginning
4.	Meng	Youthful Folly
5.	Hsu	Waiting (Nourishment)
6.	Sung	Conflict
7.	Shih	The Army
8.	Pi	Holding Together
9.	Hsiao Ch'u	The Taming Power of the Small
10.	Lu	Treading
11.	T'ai	Peace
12.	P'i	Standstill
13.	T'ung Jen	Fellowship with Men
14.	Ta Yu	Possession in Great Measure
15.	Ch'ien	Modesty
16.	Yu	Enthusiasm
17.	Sui	Following
18.	Ku	Work on What Has Been Spoiled
19.	Lin	Approach
20.	Kuan	Contemplation (View)
21.	Shih Ho	Biting Through
22.	Pi	Grace
23.	Po	Splitting Apart

24.	Fu	Return (The Turning Point)
25.	Wu Wang	Innocence (The Unexpected)
26.	Ta Ch'u	The Taming Power of the Great
27.	I	The Corners of the Mouth (Providing Nourishment)
28.	Ta Kuo	Preponderance of the Great
29.	K'an	The Abysmal (Water)
30.	Li	The Clinging, Fire
31.	Hsien	Influence (Wooing)
32.	Heng	Duration
33.	Tun	Retreat
34.	Ta Chuang	The Power of the Great
35.	Chin	Progress
36.	Ming I	Darkening of the Light
37.	Chia Jen	The Family
38.	K'uei	Opposition
39.	Chien	Obstruction
40.	Hsieh	Deliverance
41.	Sun	Decrease
42.	I	Increase
43.	Kuai	Break-through (Resoluteness)

44.	Kou	Coming to Meet
45.	Ts'ui	Gathering Together
46.	Sheng	Pushing Upward
47.	K'un	Oppression (Exhaustion)
48.	Ching	The Well
49.	Ko	Revolution (Molting)
50.	Ting	The Cauldron
51.	Chen	The Arousing (Shock, Thunder)
52.	Ken	Keeping Still
53.	Chien	Development (Gradual Progress)
54.	Kuei Mei	The Marrying Maiden
55.	Feng	Abundance
56.	Lu	The Wanderer
57.	Sun	The Gentle (The Penetrating, Wind)
58.	Tui	The Joyous, Lake
59.	Huan	Dispersion
60.	Chieh	Limitation
61.	Chung Fu	Inner Truth
62.	Hsiao Kuo	Preponderance of the Small
63.	Chi Chi	After Completion
64.	Wei Chi	Before Completion

Above: An eighteenth-century Chinese illustration showing the eight trigrams that make up the 64 hexagrams of the I Ching.

now be four. Four is considered a complete numerical unit and is assigned the value of three. It follows that eight is regarded as a double unit. It is assigned a value of two. If at first, the left-over stalks that were held in the left hand numbered nine, their assigned value would be two. If at first they numbered five, their assigned value would be three. The remaining stalks are gathered again and divided as before. This time the remainders will be eight or four, which bear the assigned values of two or three. This procedure is carried out a third time. Again the remainders will be eight or four with assigned values of two or three.

The sum of the numerical values of the remainders will determine the character of the line. If it is nine, it is an old Yang. If it is seven, it is a young Yang. If it is eight, it is an old Yin. If it is six, it is a young Yin. Yang lines are considered positive, while the Yin are negative. The old Yang and old Yin are moving lines and designated by the symbol o. The young Yang and young Yin are at rest and designated by the symbol X. This entire process is repeated six times. Each time adds a line and the hexagram gradually takes shape. Once the hexagram is established, the interpretation can be looked up in the *I Ching.*

The coin oracle is a much simpler method requiring three coins. Old Chinese bronze coins with an inscription on one side and a square hole in the middle are the preferred type, but any two-sided coin will work. The three coins are tossed together six times. If they land with inscribed side up, that counts as Yin with a value of two. The reverse side up counts as Yang with a value of three. Each toss determines the character of one line in the hexagram. If all three coins are Yang, then the line is a nine. If all three are Yin, then the line is a six. Two Yin and one Yang give the line a value of seven, and two Yang and one Yin yield an eight. By consulting the *I Ching*, and reading the commentaries on the hexagrams, the answer will become evident.

In both methods, the function of 'strong' or 'moving' lines comes into play. A strong Yang line has a circle over the center, while a strong Yin line has a cross in the gap. When strong line(s) appear, the hexagram is first interpreted according to the commentary in the *I Ching*. Then, is read again with the strong lines turned into their opposites—strong Yin becomes Yang, while strong Yang becomes Yin. Thus, a new hexagram is formed, and it too is interpreted according to the *Book of Changes.*

The hexagrams can be read in a variety of ways, each revealing various themes and interpretations. First, the hexagram is read from bottom to top. The bottom line being one and the top six (*below*). The odd-numbered lines are superior in value while the even-numbered lines are inferior. If the hexagram is divided into three pairs (*below*), (a) represents the earth, (b) man, and (c) heaven. Another way of reading the hexagram is by looking at the bottom three and top three lines. They are referred to as the lower (d) and upper (e) primary trigrams. Finally, the nuclear trigrams are those two trigrams (*below*) which are interlocked within the hexagram and bounded by lines one and six. They are the lower (f) and upper (g) nuclear trigrams.

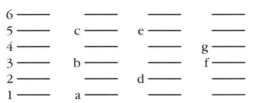

The character of the Yang and Yin lines are by nature positive or negative, 'the firm' and 'the yielding,' but their influence varies according to their relative positions. Reading the hexagrams requires a clear mind and concentration because the judgments of King Wên and the commentaries can be very confusing. The text of the *I Ching* is complex and cryptic, and is best interpreted by an experienced reader.

The text may have up to five sections, depending on the editor. The **judgement**, the essence of the hexagram, is a brief poem of sorts composed by King Wên. The **commentary on the judgement** is self-explanatory and originated with Confucius or during a later period. The **image** (or symbol) is also attributed to King Wên. The image makes the judgement easier to understand by associating King Wên's cryptic words with imagery from the physical world. The **lines** are interpretation of the moving lines by King Wên's son, the Duke of Chou. This section of the text offers more direct advice than the other sections do. Some editors include **other commentaries** that add clarifying remarks to the older parts of the text. These remarks may well show the influence of a particular point of view, such as Jungian psychology.

Below are the eight double trigrams and a brief explanation of their meanings.

1. **Ch'ien, The Creative**
    —— upper Ch'ien, The Creative, Heaven
    —— lower Ch'ien, The Creative, Heaven

The Judgment The Creative works sublime success, furthering through perseverance.

This hexagram is the symbol of the fourth month in the Chinese calendar. Associated with this hexagram are the four attributes of sublimity, potentiality of success, power to further, and perseverance. Whoever draws this oracle will gain success from the primal forces of the universe, and only by persevering in what is right will happiness come to them and others.

The double image of heaven represented by the trigram Ch'ien in the upper and lower position symbolizes the unending course of time. The aspect of time is inherent in the power of the first hexagram. The sign of heaven is the circle and the color is midnight blue.

The Duke of Chou's interpretation of the lines focuses on the dragon. The dragon symbolizes a dynamic, creative force that is electrically charged and manifests itself in the thunderstorm. The early summer is the time when this arousing force is active, and the light-giving power activates the earth's creative forces. During the winter the energy withdraws into the earth.

2. K'un, The Receptive

— — upper K'un, The Receptive,
— —　　　Earth
— — lower K'un, The Receptive,
— —　　　Earth

The Judgment The Receptive brings about sublime success, furthering through the perseverance of a mare. If the superior man undertakes something and tries to lead, he goes astray; but if he follows, he finds guidance. It is favorable to find friends in the west and south, to forego friends in the east and north. Quiet perseverance brings good fortune.

The broken lines of K'un represent the dark, yielding, receptive primal power of Yin. The attribute of the Receptive is devotion and the image is the earth. It is the perfect complement to the Creative, and shares the four fundamental aspects of 'sublime success furthering through perseverance,' but the Creative is associated with the mare rather than the dragon. While the two hexagrams are opposite in structure, they are not opposite in meaning. Both share the aspect of time because their structure is that of doubled trigrams. However, time for the Receptive is a doubling of the earth, and this means the earth carries and preserves all things on it, good or evil.

The sign of the Receptive is the square, a solid, primary form and the symbol of the earth. Yellow is the color of the earth.

51. Chen, The Arousing

— — upper Chen, The Arousing,
———　　　Thunder
— — lower Chen, The Arousing,
———　　　Thunder

The Judgment Shock brings success. Shock comes—oh, oh! Laughing words—ha, ha! The shock terrifies for a hundred miles, and he does not let fall the sacrificial spoon and chalice.

This symbol reflects the first son who seizes the throne with energy and power. The shock comes from the violent movement of the Yang line as it presses upward against the two Yin lines. As thunder bursts over the earth it causes fear and trembling.

It is the spirit of inner seriousness and reverence for God that protects the great ruler from fear. In many cases, the fear caused by this highly charged sign is followed by joy and merriment.

There are three kinds of shock—the shock of heaven (thunder), the shock of fate, and the shock of the heart.

29. K'an, The Abysmal

— — upper K'an, The Abysmal,
— —　　　Water
— — lower K'an, The Abysmal,
— —　　　Water

The Judgment The Abysmal repeated. If you are sincere, you have success in your heart, and whatever you do succeeds.

K'an means a plunging in, and it is illustrated in the hexagram by a Yang line that has plunged in between two Yin lines. The Yang line is bounded by the two Yin lines just like water in a ravine. This hexagram symbolizes the middle son in the family relationships of the eight double trigrams, and as such shares characteristics with the Creative and the Receptive. From the Creative above comes the life-giving property of water, and as it flows on the Receptive earth it brings new life.

'The Abysmal repeated' refers to danger, which if repeatedly encountered can teach a person to rely on inner strength and virtue. On the contrary, by growing used to that which is dangerous, a person can let evil become a part of him, and misfortune will be the result.

52. Ken, Keeping Still

——— upper Ken, Keeping Still,
— —　　　Mountain
——— lower Ken, Keeping Still,
— —　　　Mountain

The Judgment Keeping Still. Keeping his back still so that he no longer feels his body. He goes into his courtyard and does not see his people. No blame.

Above: Each hexagram is associated with an image from the physical world. For example, the image for the hexagram of Ken, Keeping Still is a mountain. In the words of King Wên, 'Mountains standing close together/ The image of keeping still/Thus the superior man/Does not permit his thoughts/To go beyond his situation.'

This can be interpreted as the difficulty of achieving a quiet heart.

This hexagram signifies the end and beginning of all movement, the moment of resting. Whoever acts from this deep level of inner harmony and harmony with the universe makes no mistakes. For example, a heart at rest leads to the complete elimination of egotistic drives and leaves a person free to concern himself with loftier pursuits.

57. Sun, The Gentle

――― upper Sun, The Gentle, Wind
― ―
――― lower Sun, The Gentle, Wind
― ―

The Judgment The Gentle. Success through what is small. It furthers one to have somewhere to go. It furthers one to see the great man.

This is the symbol of the eldest daughter whose image is wind or wood. Its attribute is 'penetrating,' and if this oracle is drawn it signifies the power of light penetrating darkness, of wind clearing the sky of clouds, of penetrating clarity of judgment that foils all hidden motives. It can also portend the influence of a powerful personality who will uncover and dissolve conspiracies in a community.

Change, inherent in each hexagram, is no exception in Sun. However, it should be effected through gentle influence that never lapses rather than through violent means. The oracle of this hexagram encourages deliberation before action, but cautions against repeated questioning or 'penetration,' which will surely bring humiliation on a leader for showing indecision.

30. Li, The Clinging

――― upper Li, The Clinging, Fire
― ―
――― lower Li, The Clinging, Fire
― ―

The Judgment The Clinging. Perseverance furthers. It brings success. Care of the cow brings good fortune.

As a dark Yin line clings to two light Yang lines, the empty space makes the strong lines appear bright. Each of the two trigrams represent the sun. Doubled they represent the repeated movement of the sun and the function of light with respect to time. The ceaseless passage of time reflected in this hexagram reminds human beings that their lives are transitory and conditional.

The cow exemplifies extreme docility. In relation to finding one's place in the world, Li urges cultivating an attitude of compliance in order to develop clarity without sharpness. In the theme of the family, Li is the second daughter.

58. Tui, The Joyous

― ― upper Tui, The Joyous, Lake
―――
― ― lower Tui, The Joyous, Lake
―――

The Judgment The Joyous. Success. Perseverance is favorable.

This double trigram denotes the youngest daughter and is symbolized by the smiling lake. Its attribute is joyousness, indicated by the two strong lines within expressing themselves through the gentleness of the Yin line above. True joy comes from within and must be based on steadfastness, outwardly gentle and inwardly firm.

Tui is the image of a lake which rejoices and refreshes all living things.

Below: The hexagram of K'un, The Receptive is associated with the earth. In its application to human beings, the message is that individuals achieve the height of wisdom when they act as nature does—with tolerance toward all creatures and without artifice.

THE TAROT

The reading of tarot cards is an ancient practice of unknown origins. It is almost certain that their purpose was one of fore-telling the future, and tarot reading today continues to be a popular form of divination.

Noted Swiss psychologist Carl Gustav Jung was interested in all aspects of para-psychology. He was especially intrigued by the repeated occurrence of certain symbols that appeared in dreams of people cross-culturally. He believed that there

Below: **The 22 cards that make up the greater arcana form the heart of the tarot. The most decorated of the cards, they are also the most important and meaningful of the 78 cards. These cards are a French reproduction of an Egyptian set of cards made in 1870.**

    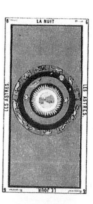

exists a collective unconscious, a reservoir of universal symbols, that the unconscious mind is able to tap. It followed that all instances of psychic experience could be explained, whether coincidence or divination systems such as the tarot.

Some authorities claim that the tarot cards were adapted from the legendary 'Book of Thoth' used by ancient Egyptians. By the fourteenth century AD the decks had surfaced in Europe, where they were called *tarots* and consisted of 78 cards. Of these, 56 were suit cards similar to those of modern decks, except that the suits were swords, rods, cups and coins instead of spades, diamonds, hearts and clubs, respectively. Each suit had four court cards, king, queen, knight, and knave (jack), as well as the number cards from 10 to ace. These suit cards are known as the 'lesser arcana' (from 'arcane' — secret). The 'greater arcana' is comprised of the additional 22

trump cards on which are pictured powerful, archetypal images. A typical list of these images follows: 1) The Juggler, 2) The High Priestess, 3) The Empress, 4) The Emperor, 5) The Hierophant, 6) The Lovers, 7) The Chariot, 8) Justice, 9) The Hermit, 10) Fortune, 11) Strength, 12) The Hanged Man, 13) Death, 14) Temperance, 15) The Devil, 16) Lightning, 17) The Stars, 18) The Moon, 19) The Sun, 20) Judgement, 21) The World, and 22) The Fool.

The original designs were 'one way' which allowed them to be inversed when they were dealt. Usually, the inversed cards would lend an ominous cast to the reading. The full deck of 78 cards was used chiefly for predicting the outcome of future events or for reconstructing the past.

The advent of a 32-card pack was used exclusively by many cartomancers who followed Mademoiselle Lenormand, a famous cartomancer of the Napoleonic era

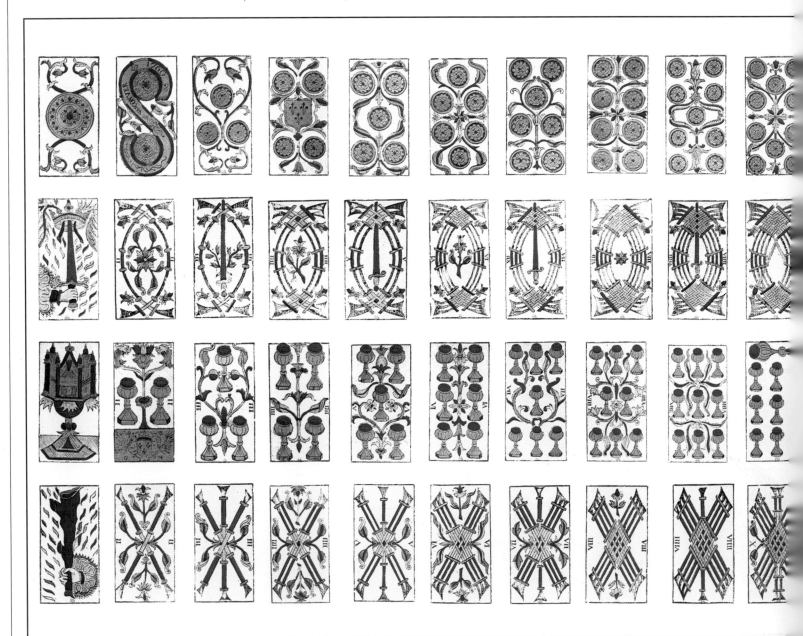

who greatly impressed Empress Josephine with her revelations. In response to questions over the direction of a drawn card, Mlle Lenormand and her followers adopted the practice of marking the cards to distinguish the tops from the bottoms. Using only aces to sevens, these 32-card packs were rendered obsolete as 52-card playing decks gained popularity.

As card games which used the lesser arcana grew in popularity, the decks were reduced to 56 cards. Eventually the knight was dropped from the court cards, and their designs were made 'double ended.' The suits were changed by the French to hearts, clubs, diamonds and spades. The 'spots' on the number cards were left 'one way' but the numbers were reproduced in both directions to facilitate group play. Of the remaining 52 cards that make up today's decks, the fool, or joker, is the only remnant of the greater arcana.

There are many systems, both known and obscure, for reading the cards. We will look at two of the more direct which have stood the test of time. The first uses the modern 52-card deck. The second uses the full 78 cards of the tarot. In both cases, certain guidelines must be followed in order to secure an accurate reading.

Each card bears a traditional meaning and various modified interpretations with which the reader should be familiar. Not only are there meanings associated with each card as it stands alone, but for each card as it relates to the layout as well. Knowing the impact of one card on another clarifies the suggestion of the first card. An inverted card will often carry subtle meanings beyond the opposite of the card's essential implications.

The person whose fortune is being told reflects on his or her question as the cards are drawn. The deck is first shuffled and

Below: **The entire 78-card deck of the Tarot de Marseille.**

Below: The circular spread provides a general forecast for the next 12 months. It uses 13 cards, but no significator. The first card represents the first month, the second card, the second month and so on. The thirteenth card gives a general impression of the entire year.

Opposite page: The Celtic cross is probably the most useful and versatile of all the tarot spreads and can be used to answer specific or general questions. The entire deck can be used, or the greater arcana can be used alone.

then laid out in the form of a cross, a square or a circle. The random order of the drawn cards will inevitably strike deep chords of wonder as they seem to illuminate and offer a solution to the person's situation. Just as the willingness of the participant to gain insight from the tarot will, without a doubt, enhance the reading, so will a skilled reader find the cards responsive. A knowledgeable reader who has spent time studying a wide range of medieval symbolism will be able to give a more accurate and complete reading on the relationship of the cards to the person's questions.

Most commonly seen are symbols of the Middle Ages such as the castle, chalice, tower, king, queen, knave and so on. The suits—rods, cups, swords and coins— represent different segments of medieval society: the peasantry, the clergy, the nobility and merchants, respectively.

These images are powerful archetypes that speak to the universal unconscious and are meant to shock the unconscious mind and unblock whatever psychic, emotional, physical block or confusion that exists.

Many modern occultists have modified the images on the cards to reflect contemporary concerns, personalizing the decks for women or men, and even omitting some cards or changing the nature of the decks.

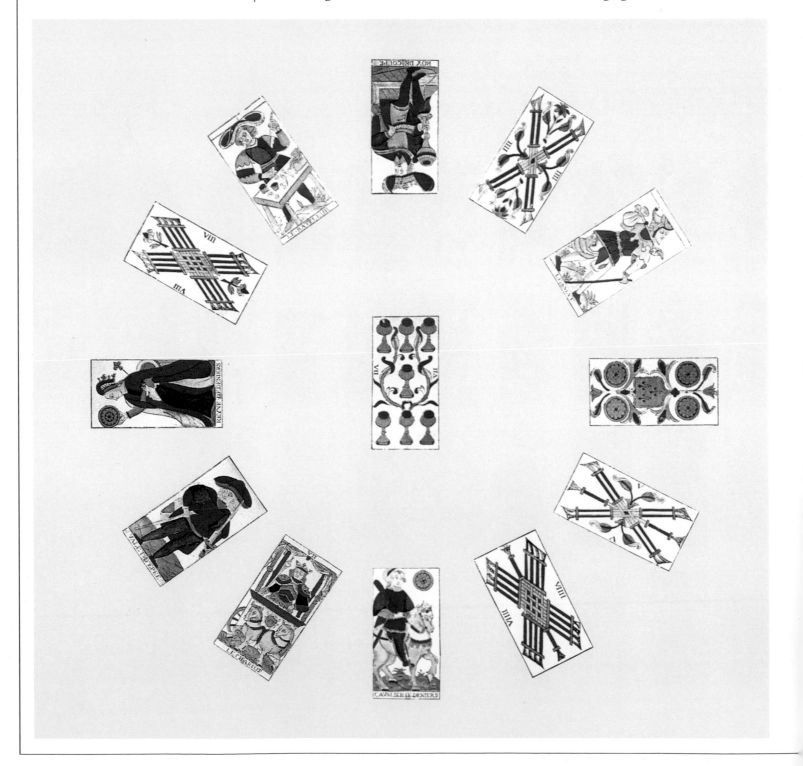

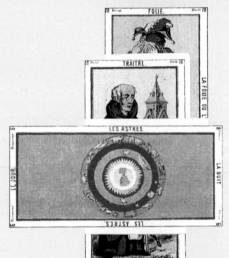

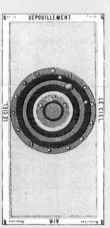

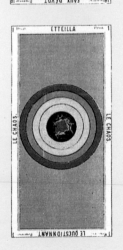

The Lesser Arcana

A general interpretation of each of the lesser arcana standing alone follows. The **aces** signify correspondence or news. **Twos** herald misunderstandings, quarrels or arguments. **Threes** imply improvement, progress, success, quietude and tranquility. **Fours** announce travel, outings, celebrations or sleepless nights due to overindulgence in alcohol. **Fives** are the cards of order, exactitude, resolutions and decisions taken with their inverse. **Sixes** reflect a state of prosperity, abundance, general well-being and ease at home or in the country residence. **Sevens** and **Eights** refer to male or female children.

Nines and **Tens** must be looked at by suit. The nine of swords signifies disaster, sickness with a strong possibility of death, troubles, sorrow, grief and mourning. The nine of rods predicts a delay for the good or bad. Nine of cups is a favorable card bringing pleasant and propitious things. The nine of coins brings festivities or outings. Ten of swords brings great suffering. The ten of rods implies the country, while the ten of cups, the city. The ten of coins connotes money.

The **Knaves** or **Jacks** represent young people, soldiers, lovers, seducers or rivals.

Below: **The seven-pointed star is used to predict events for the next seven days. The cards on the outside of the star are dealt face down, while the significator is placed face up in the center. The other cards are then turned up and interpreted.**

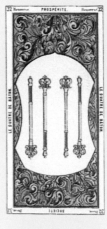

The **Knights** indicate gambling winnings will be greater than losses. The **Queens** are the intriguing women of mystery who are sometimes good, sometimes bad. The **Kings** represent the law, officials, persons in authority, parents or the elderly.

In addition to these isolated meanings, the cards are enhanced by their relative position to the other cards. A knowledgeable reader can illuminate these subtleties through a careful understanding of the consultant's question. Some authorities, however, point out that the reader does *not* have to know what the question is. The cards know!

The lesser arcana represent to many the stages in a person's life. The first 11 cards tend to be outward-looking as an innocent newborn (ie The Fool) moves into middle life. The Wheel of Fortune marks the midway point. The second 11 cards tend to be inward-looking and more contemplative as the individual approaches the end of his life and the symbol of The World.

Below: The 21 card spread provides an in-depth, yet easily interpreted response to a question. Each individual aspect of the reading is allocated three cards, which gives a more detailed picture of each area than does the simpler horseshoe spread.

The Greater Arcana

Below: **The horseshoe is the most straightforward of the tarot spreads. It is useful for answering specific questions and is typically used with the greater arcana alone. A significator is not required.**

Opposite page: **The mystic cross is traditionally used with regular playing cards rather than with tarot cards. In either case, the cards are quickly and easily interpreted.**

The greater arcana typically are used to tell fortunes. One of the easiest and most direct spreads for tarot reading is the horseshoe spread. First the deck should be put in order, with every card right side up. Then with both the reader and the querist concentrating on the cards, the deck should be shuffled and special attention should be paid to turning some cards at random so that there will be a chance for inverted cards to be cast. The querist should then shuffle the deck a final time and return the cards to the reader. At this point, the deck is ready to be dealt in any formation. Below is an example of the horseshoe spread.

```
        1                    7

   2                              6

      3                    5

              4
```

These positions refer to past influences (1), present circumstances (2), general future prospects (3), best course of action (4),

Below: **The fan is another layout that is used in cartomancy, divination with a modern deck of playing cards. This spread provides a general reading of the querist's future.**

the attitudes of others (5), possible obstacles (6), and final outcome (7).

Some layouts require that a significator be chosen. This card should represent the querist and correspond with the subject in complexion, sex and personality. The following traditional significators are appropriate: queen of cups for a fair-haired young woman; queen of coins for a fair, mature woman (especially if she is affluent); queen of rods for a dark woman with an air of danger about her; queen of swords for a dark and sad woman; knight of cups for a fair young man or any young man in love; knight of coins for a wealthy young man; knight of rods for a dark young man; knave

of rods for a young man who seems dangerous in character; king of cups for a fair-haired, mature man; king of coins for an affluent mature man; king of swords for a mature man in a position of power and influence; and king of rods for a dark or dangerous mature man. Some palm readers do not find it necessary for the significator to correspond *in appearance* with the querist as long as the significator card matches the querist's personality traits.

The seven-pointed star spread can be dealt on any day of the week and used to forecast the events of the next seven days. The circular spread gives a general prognostication of the next twelve months from

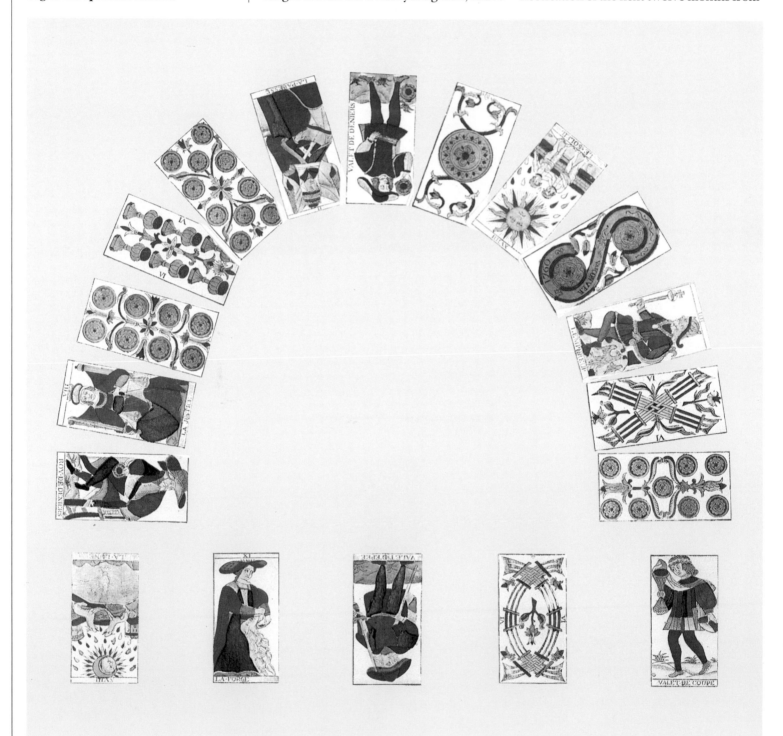

Below: **The fan is another layout that is used in cartomancy, divination with a modern deck of playing cards. This spread provides a general reading of the querist's future.**

the date of the reading. For the 21-card layout the cards are dealt in three lines of seven from right to left and top to bottom. The Celtic cross is perhaps the most useful spread for divination. It can be employed for specific or general questions or for giving an overview of the coming year. Either the whole deck or just the lesser arcana is suitable for this spread. Consulting the tarot in the Celtic cross layout gives a well-rounded response to the querist, because it takes into account the querist's present state of mind, external influences such as friends and family, the querist's own hopes and fears, and the final outcome based on the collective impression of the cards.

Overleaf: **On two occasions author T Wynne Griffin asked how this book would be received by the public. Both times the tarot cards predicted success and prosperity.**

Below: **The significator cards represent the querist and should correspond with him or her in sex, complexion and personality.**

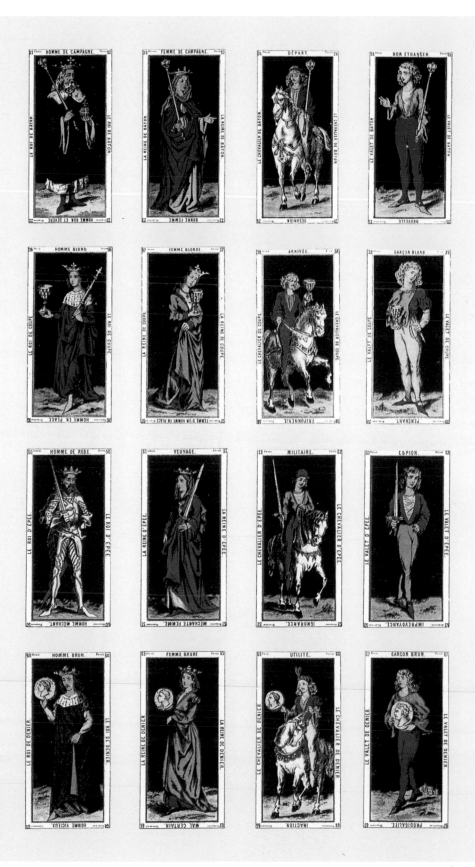

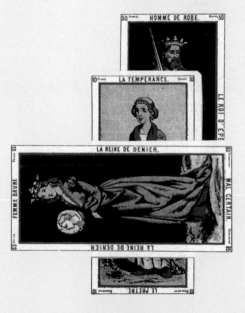

CRYSTALS

Crystals carry intrinsic powers that enhance one's physical, spiritual and mental well being. An amethyst quartz (*above*), for example, enhances mental clarity and strengthens one's will power, while a rose quartz (*opposite page*) promotes inner peace.

he popular fascination with crystals has its roots in the ancient art of crystal gazing, or divination using a crystal ball. Today, crystal balls are still used for telling fortunes, but crystals in and of themselves have gained a faithful following in members of the New Age movement.

The New Age movement grew out of a sense of spiritual emptiness shared by many people, including adult baby-boomers who had successfully or unsuccessfully made the transition to mainstream life. The New Ager is usually well-educated and affluent. Disillusioned with 'having it all,' these individuals looked inward and began private metaphysical journeys and searched for meaning and harmony through spiritual growth. Drawing from the wealth of spiritual and theological thought from both Eastern and Western religions, New Agers met others like themselves who shared the desire for enlightenment and true happiness.

Combining modern science and ancient wisdom, healing became a focal point of the movement. Spiritual healing, emotional healing, psycho-physical healing, self-awareness, creative visualization, meditation, astral projection, the discovery of past lives and purification are all part of the New Age agenda.

Developing crystal 'consciousness' plays a significant role in the New Age movement. Crystals are believed to bear intrinsic powers that can be transmitted and utilized to enhance meditation and spiritual growth, as well as develop latent psychic abilities such as clairvoyance and astral projection (the ability to leave one's body). New Agers contend that gaining an awareness of human potential in general and one's own potential in particular through crystal work rewards one with renewed energy, and new feelings of love, contentment, compassion, creativity and wisdom.

Crystals are formed naturally within the earth's crust by the powerful forces of heat and pressure. They are made from the elements silicon and water and are found in sandstone and often near gold. In nature, a quartz crystal forms six sides, or faces, that are identical and one pointed end or sometimes two. Those that have one pointed end are designated 'single-terminated,' whereas those with both ends pointed are designated 'double-terminated.'

Quartz crystals exist in nature in a variety of hues and colors. The most popular include clear quartz, amethyst quartz, blue quartz, rose quartz, citrine quartz, green quartz, rutilated quartz (which contain fine strands of gold or copper fibers) and quartz with black, blue, or green tourmaline rods inside.

A pioneer in the field of quartz crystal work and color stones, Uma Silbey gives a breakdown of the particular usefulness

Above: **A fortune teller gazes into her crystal ball.**

Below: **The power of the crystal begins in the base, flows up and out the top, its energy emanating through the crystal worker.**

Below right: **A New Age shop specializing in crystals.**

Opposite page: **This crystal ball cut from Burmese quartz can be used to induce an altered state of awareness, or trance. While in an altered state, an individual has access to information stored in the unconscious.**

of each type of crystal and the characteristics and powers particular to it in her ground-breaking book, *The Complete Crystal Guidebook.* According to Silbey, each crystal bears a known amount of energy that radiates, in the form of vibration, from it and creates a force field. This is recognized as the power of the crystal. The direction of the flow of energy starts or enters from the base and leaves through the point. If the crystal is double-terminated, energy flows in both directions, as in a battery.

Crystal workers emphasize the importance of proper storage and handling of the crystal, maintaining that the best way to store crystals while not in use is in natural fibers such as leather or silk. The color of the material is equally important because it influences the crystal. If the crystal has a special function, only the owner should handle it to avoid other residual influences that might detract from its power. Some people set aside a certain place or altar for their crystal where they store it and wrap and unwrap it.

Clearing a crystal is the first step before starting any kind of crystal work, and before and after any healing work, or when any negative influence has entered the crystal. However, there are times that the retrieval of the information stored in a crystal could be valuable. It is possible to program a crystal with the intent that the information be passed on to future generations, from mother to daughter for example. Crystals have been known to exist that were programmed by ancient civilizations. Silbey notes that only in a relaxed, recep-

tive mental state can one receive impressions of the stored information. A rational or logical approach will block the transmission of the images.

There are a number of methods for clearing a crystal, but the three described below are relatively simple and effective. The smudging method has been used by Native Americans for centuries. The crystal is cleared by passing it through the smoke of sage incense. Cedar, sweet grass or sandlewood incense may be substituted.

The breath method works better for clearing single crystals rather than crystal clusters. The proper position for the crystal is tip up, in the left hand between thumb and forefinger, with the thumb on the bottom. The right thumb is placed on any face of the crystal, and the right forefinger on the face opposite the right thumb, thereby representing all points of the compass. The crystal worker then inhales through the nose and exhales forcefully through the mouth onto the crystal, repeating this procedure two more times, each time rotating the right thumb and forefinger one face.

The salt or salt water method involves submerging the crystal in sea salt, either completely or partially, for a period of one to seven days. Soaking the crystal in a solution of salt water accomplishes the same effect.

The crystal and salt water solution is stored in a glass container and left in the sunlight for up to seven days. These methods depend on the smaller salt crystals drawing out the stored vibrations in the quartz and clearing it. The salt water solution is thrown out after the clearing process is completed.

THE HEALING POWERS OF CRYSTALS

Native American shamans, mystics, priests and healers all have known and used the power locked in crystals. There is a ritual to embarking on a path as a healer. The room or area, the person to be healed, the healer and the crystals must first be cleared by smudging or another method. Next, healers must ground themselves and balance their own energy. From a balanced and grounded position, the healer is better able to intuit the vibrations of the other person. It is not uncommon for healers to feel pain empathetically in the same spots as the person they are healing. Breathing and meditation exercises that sensitize the hands enable the healer to feel even the

slightest vibrations. The healer will find the negative energy or blockage that is affecting the individual and draw it out with the help of a crystal wand or other tool. Whenever healing work is completed, healers must rid themselves of the negative energy that they have pulled into themselves. The negative energy must be circled out of the troubled person, passing through the healer and circled out of the healer's body and into the earth where it can be transmuted.

Clearing of the body begins with washing the hands in cold water. Vigorous brushing of the body from head to toe may be followed by touching the ground with

Below: **A rhodochrosite crystal has the power to heal emotions, thereby strengthening one's self identity and the ability to function better.**

the hands. After the healer is cleared and grounded, the next step is to clear the room and the other person. Sometimes a feather is preferred when brushing the negative energy off the other person and into the ground.

Crystal work can be done on oneself or others and it can help program and radiate hidden energy reserves to stimulate intelligence, sexuality and digestion as well as help develop spiritual balance. Learning about the unlimited potential power in the body begins with an understanding of the kundalini. The kundalini is said to lie dormant and coiled three and one half times at the base of the spine. Many attempts to describe kundalini energy have yielded the following definitions: the life force of the universe, the supreme potential of human beings, the shakti or feminine creative force of the universe, Christ consciousness, and the nerve of the soul.

As the kundalini rises or awakens, it spirals upward and passes through and activates the seven energy centers in the body, called chakras, and passes out through the crown center at the top of the head. Chakra means a wheel or revolving disk. The chakras are thought to be swirling vortices where energy is transformed, absorbed, filtered and distributed to the incorporeal and physical body. The incorporeal, or etheric, body is said to be an exact replica of the physical body but projects an aura of about one quarter inch beyond the skin. This aura can be extended up to several feet through crystal work, increased vitality or special exercises. The etheric body functions as a filter and bridge between the physical forces of light, heat, sound and magnetic energy, among others. There is also an astral body where the collective cosmic consciousness resides and transmits dreams and awareness to the physical

Below: **Sapphires have the ability to calm the mind, improve memory and increase one's mental abilities and intuitive powers.**

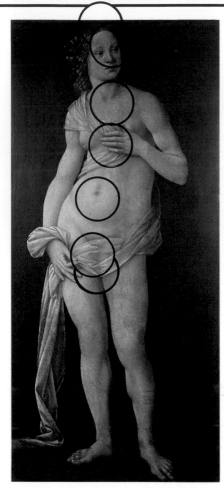

Above: **The circles represent the chakras, the areas in which energy is transformed as it flows from the base of the spine to the top of the head.**

Below: **Crystals can put us in touch with the past and the future by giving us access to the akashic records, an astral plane where all thoughts and actions are stored.**

Opposite page: **A diamond possesses the properties of any color crystal.**

brain and nervous system through the etheric bridge.

A channel corresponding to the spinal column connects the chakras. This is called the sushumna, and it lies between two other channels, the channel of receptive, feminine, Moon energy called the ida, and the channel of outward, masculine, Sun energy called the pingala.

Each chakra has certain qualities associated with it. The first chakra is called by its ancient name, Muladhara. It is sometimes referred to as the 'seat of the kundalini' and is located at the base of the spine.

The second chakra is located in the area of the sex organs and influences the spleen as well as sexual blockages or dysfunctions.

The third chakra is called Svadhisthana, or the navel center, and rests about two inches below the navel. It is believed that the will resides in the navel center and if it is not balanced the person is likely to become overly concerned with issues of power and control.

The fourth chakra is called Anahata and corresponds to the area in the chest between the two nipples. It is also called the heart center, and when this center is activated feelings of empathy and understanding toward others become apparent.

The fifth chakra is called Visuddha and controls the ability to hear and recognize sounds from the subtle etheric and astral planes. This exercise is known as clairaudience. The fifth chakra is located in the middle of the throat.

The sixth chakra is sometimes referred to as the third eye, and is positioned between the brows in the center of the forehead. It is called Ajna. The devel-

opment of this center stimulates clairvoyant and intuitive abilities. Opening this chakra leads to wisdom and all-knowing awareness.

The seventh chakra, or crown center, is located on the top of the head. It is slightly more forward on men than on women, but it is best visualized as a sunburst over the head. When this center is open the person is said to experience a feeling of gentle ecstacy or blissful harmony and connectedness with the universe. For many, describing their experiences of consciousness expansion are beyond words.

Crystal advocates assert that working with crystals allows one to develop the higher energy centers and learn to travel to the astral plane, a trance-like state. There, guides and teachers offer assistance and instruction that may prove useful later on the physical plane of day-to-day life. While on the astral plane, people are more attuned to what Jung termed the collective unconscious.

Crystal work expands reality in the narrow sense. Balance, meditation, visualization and healing all utilize an enormous amount of energy and require that a person maintain a strong, healthy body. One method of general health maintenance involves charging water with crystals or colored stones and drinking the charged water. A crystal that has a certain vibration associated with it, such as amethyst for any kind of healing or clear quartz for increased energy or preventative value, supposedly treats whatever ailments the individual is suffering from.

The properties of the water can allegedly be manipulated by concentration and the water will affect the body in ways inherent to the stone. The effect can be strengthened by letting the container stay in the sunlight for a minimum of one hour and a maximum of three days.

Crystal workers point out that the crystal may seem dull after extended use or serious healing work. Clearing by any of the methods mentioned above will give new brilliance to the crystal, but there are other ways to charge a crystal. A few powerful charging methods employ the forces of nature and include holding the crystal under a running stream or under a waterfall, letting the ocean waves invigorate it, or placing it on an altar under moonlight or sunlight. The Rainbow Light Box, a mechanized and commercially marketed charger, was developed by a company in Los Gatos, California and utilizes a motorized color wheel to charge crystals for specific healing purposes.

POWER OBJECTS

Above: **The Unicorn is a symbol of strength and purity. This is a channeled painting by New Age artist Marjosa Star.**

Below: **Crystals can be combined with other objects and materials, such as statuary, wands or jewelry to create a power object designed for a specific use.**

Power objects enhance the individual's capability to redirect subtle energy and empower the individual to do certain tasks. While quartz crystals themselves are very powerful, combinations of quartz crystals in statuary, wands and jewelry can add to their splendor and enlarge their energy field. The crystal generator, in particular, can be used when the influence of a large amount of energy is needed to displace negative or residual energy. The energy field released by the crystal generator is strong enough to flood a large room or even an entire house.

Certain symbology can be incorporated into the design of a piece of crystal jewelry. When symbology is used in conjunction with crystals, this causes the crystal to vibrate with the attributes of that symbol and similarly affect the wearer. Numbers, designs, pictures or any other object infused with personal meaning are acceptable in a power piece. Power pieces can be worn on the body or sewn into clothing, carried on the person, or used in ceremonial, healing or other significant occasions.

Examples of some of the more traditional power symbols that are often merged with crystal jewelry and their meanings follow.

Ankh This ancient symbol of fertility represents enduring life or procreation.

Circle The circle illustrates the principle of infinity, evinced by the life cycle and the seasons, for example.

Crescent moon with the horns up This is the sign of Isis, the Egyptian Goddess, and has come to embody the Goddess principle, a doctrine rooted in matriarchal religions, with emphasis on nature and love as a life force.

Cross An old symbol, the cross represents the Christ spirit and the four directions.

Dollar sign This symbolizes prosperity and can be combined with the Om sign for wisdom to form a desirable pair of attributes.

Dolphin A marine mammal with high intelligence and a gentle nature, the dolphin epitomizes the potentiality for cross species communication and symbolizes the joining of consciousness.

Eagle Long associated with power and spirituality, the eagle represents a union with the highest spirit.

Eye of Horus Offering protection from sickness, and promising new life, this is the sign of the solar male principle.

Fish The fish is the emblem of the spirit of Jesus Christ.

Hand with fingers extended with palm forward This is the sign of blessing.

Hand with thumb and first finger touching The ancient name for this sign is *gyan mudra*, which means wisdom and knowledge.

Heart The heart imparts and receives love.

Lotus flower The lotus flower symbolizes purity and realization.

Moon Denoting the female principle, the Moon symbolizes receptive energy and is a sign of great power and depth.

Om The Om is linked to cosmic wisdom and consciousness and symbolizes the highest realization.

Pentagram or five pointed star pointing up This sign represents a perfected

human being as well as the five ancient elements of air, fire, water, earth and spirit/ether. When pointing up, the pentagram is associated with white magic, but when it is pointing down it is associated with black magic or the devil.

Serpent The serpent is representative of Kundalini energy.

Solomon's seal or six-pointed star This seal illustrates the metaphysical union and interaction of matter and spirit or the form and the formless.

Square The square is a grounding shape recalling the four directions, the four seasons and a finite space.

Sun The Sun is associated with the male principle, activity, manifestation and light.

Triangle This is the sign of the trinity and infinity.

Trident The trident represents male cre-ative energy, or the realized Being. In Hindu symbology it is the sign of Shiva, while in Greek mythology it is Neptune's hallmark.

Unicorn This fanciful creature symbolizes purity and strength.

Yin Yang This Chinese symbol depicts the unity of opposites and the interaction of female and male energy.

These are just a few of the more commonly used symbols. Every object can have many meanings attached to it, and the descriptions above are in no way exhaustive or complete. Each religious group has its own powerful symbology, as do many other organizations. Each person has his or her own private world of symbology which should be respected and included when choosing power or special pieces. Consequently, there are myriad types of symbols.

Overleaf: **This jasper crystal has the ability to open the mind to new thinking and to balance the emotions.**

Below: **This sarcophagus provides examples of the symbology of the ancient Egyptians. Symbols like these are frequently seen in power objects.**

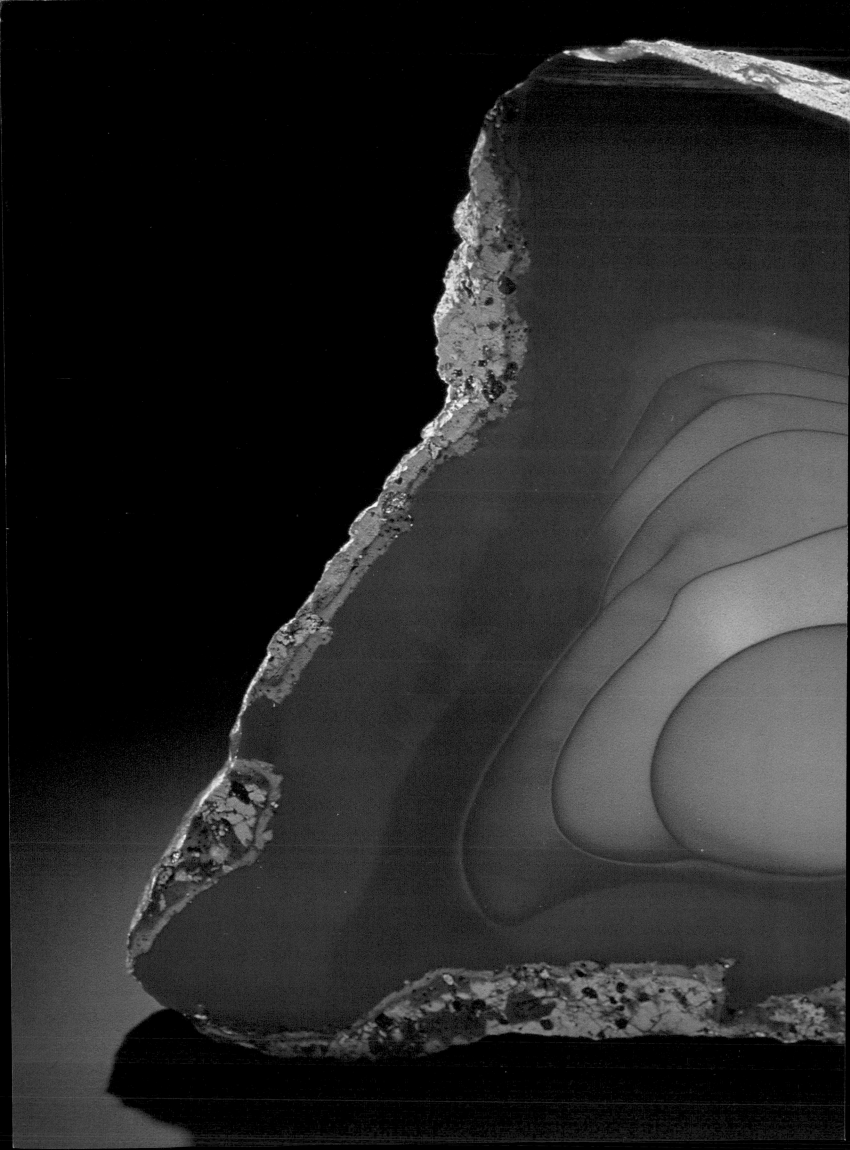

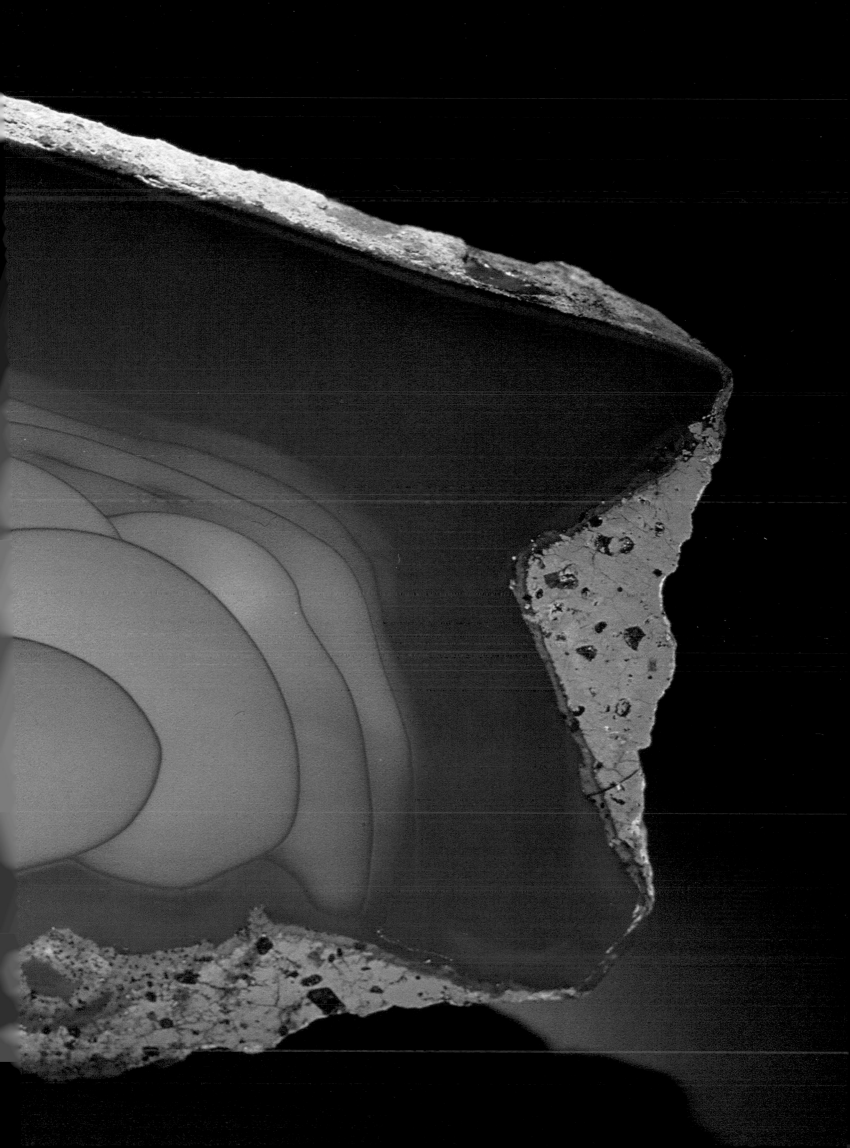

OUR DREAMS

e are such stuff as dreams are made of' wrote William Shakespeare almost 400 years ago. But what are dreams made of? Since the dawn of recorded time, man has been fascinated by dreams and what they signify. An ancient Egyptian papyrus dating back to 1350 BC contained explanations of the good and bad signs found in dreams. According to the Egyptians, a dream about losing one's teeth, for example, was an omen that the dreamer's relatives were plotting his death.

About 150 AD, Artemidorus, an oracle, offered his version of a 'dream dictionary,' a guide to interpreting and analyzing dreams. Artemidorus

Above: **Dreams with snakes are fraught with meaning. One snake warns of an argument, two snakes portend a deception, while many snakes represent numerous, difficult obstacles. Traditionally, the snake symbolizes man's sexuality, and therefore a dream involving a snake is often interpreted as fear of a man and his power.**

Opposite page: **During times of stress, a dream with a watch or a clock signifies that the dreamer fears the loss of time.**

divided dreams into two categories: those that dealt with everyday life and those that foretold the future. His interpretations were passed down to succeeding generations for the next 1000 years.

About the time of the Renaissance, dream analysis fell into disfavor, although segments of the population remained followers of Artemidorus. Despite the disregard of the general populace, his opus was published in Greek in 1518, in Latin in 1539, in French in 1546 and in English in 1644, where it continued to be published for the next 96 years in 24 editions.

The interpretation of dreams gained credence once again in the nineteenth century with the theories of Sigmund Freud. Freud argued that dreams held the key to our subconscious sexual desires that had been suppressed since childhood. Through psychoanalysis, a patient could come to understand the meaning of his or her dreams and thus come to terms with unresolved emotional issues.

Though Freud's theories gave the study

of dreams the stamp of approval from the scientific community, Freud was not without his detractors. Other psychiatrists criticized Freud's work because it was based on only his patients, who represented only a narrow segment of the population.

Carl G Jung, the noted Swiss psychiatrist, differed with Freud on various points. While Jung too believed that dreams offered a wealth of information once analyzed, he questioned Freud's emphasis on sexuality, which Jung believed was only one theme that might emerge from dream analysis. Jung proposed that the images in dreams were symbols that belonged to what he termed the collective unconscious. In his work, Jung had noticed that certain symbols and images, such as the wise old man or the evil serpent, appeared in many people's dreams. Moreover, these symbols transcended cultural barriers. In short, there seemed to be common symbolism even though there did not appear to be any sort of common denominator — apart from the human psyche. This is not to

say that a dream about a key, for example, will always have sexual connotations, for no individual symbolic image can be said to have a dogmatically fixed, generalized meaning.

Today, popular theory holds that dreams can be classified into seven archetypal categories. Some authorities, however, add an eighth type.

1. Dreams of affluence: In a dream of this sort, the dreamer acquires a prize of some sort. This could take the form of becoming a business tycoon or winning the lottery. In some cases, the dream involves fame rather than fortune.

2. Dreams of frustration: In this type of dream, the dreamer is never able to accomplish a seemingly simple goal, such as trying to pack a trunk or suitcase or locate a parked car. In other examples, the dreamer may need money but have no way of obtaining it, or may be trying to catch a plane or a train.

3. Dreams of travel: Dreams of this sort can be concrete, as in going someplace, or abstract, as in simply flying through the air or drifting through space. They generally indicate a need for freedom or the desire to possess something.

4. Dreams of falling: The dreamer is falling from a skyscraper, a bridge, an airplane and so on. Many people have dreamed of falling over Niagara Falls, and the sensation of simply falling has been experienced by numerous dreamers. People typically wake up, usually with a start, before they land. These dreams often represent a situation the dreamer has been worrying about.

5. Dreams of being chased: The dreamer is pursued by another person, an animal or the forces of nature, such as a flood or an avalanche. The menacing force is symbolic of a hidden fear.

6. Dreams of being trapped: In these dreams, the dreamer is in a cellar, cave or prison and unable to escape. A similar type of dream involves a dangerous situation in which the dreamer is likely to experience physical harm, such as an explosion or the collapse of a building. These dreams are interpreted as a hidden fear.

7. Dreams of lacking clothing: Dreams of this sort are often an indication that the dreamer is going through a period of frustration or is suffering from feelings of inadequacy. Dreams involving forgotten appointments or other examples of personal negligence, such as failing an exam, can be interpreted in a similar manner.

8. Dreams of violence: The dreamer is responsible for physically harming another individual. In extreme cases, the dreamer kills someone else. Such dreams are indicative of suppressed anger on the part of the dreamer.

For both Jung and Freud, dreams were triggered by the individual's internal struggles and desires, and if analyzed could provide therapeutic value. Neither, however, completely discounted the possibility that dreams may be caused by forces outside the dreamer's own mind, such as another individual sending a message to the dreamer telepathically. Freud rejected the notion of precognitive dreams—dreams that foretold the future—but he was will-

Below: **The bizarre imagery in dreams may seem incomprehensible on the surface, but our dreams hold the key to our subconscious desires and fears.**

ing to concede that telepathic dreams were a possibility, concluding that sleep might be a state that would permit the transference of thought between people.

Even as Freud was formulating his thesis, several prominent British scientists were studying the possibility of telepathic dreams at the Society for Psychical Research (SPR). Founded in 1882, the SPR was created to research all kinds of paranormal events, including telepathy, clairvoyance and spiritualism. The SPR's dream research disclosed 149 dreams in which the dreamer seemed to have received a message from an outside source. Of added interest to the researchers was the fact that a majority of the dreams dealt with the death of someone known to the dreamer. To further investigate this phenomenon, the SPR researchers sent out over 5000 questionnaires asking people if they had dreamed of the death of someone they knew in the last few years. The results convinced the SPR that something more than chance was a work.

But what was that something else? Throughout the ages, people have had dreams that foretold the future, oftentimes of tragedy and death. Samuel Clemens, better known to the world as Mark Twain, foresaw the death of his brother, Henry, in a dream. The year was 1858 and Sam Clemens was an apprentice pilot on a Mississippi River steamboat, the *Pennsylvania*. Henry worked as a clerk aboard the same boat. One night in a dream Sam saw the body of his brother laid out in a metal coffin resting on two chairs. On his chest lay a bouquet of white flowers with a single red flower in the center.

The *Pennsylvania* continued on its way down the Mississippi and the two brothers parted company when Sam joined the crew of the *Lacey*. A few days later, Sam heard the news that the *Pennsylvania* had blown up near Memphis. There, he found Henry, dying from the burns he had sustained in the accident.

Though Henry was a stranger to the people of Memphis, several women of the city had collected money to purchase a coffin for him, a metal one rather than the typical pine. When Sam went to pay his final respects to his brother, he found Henry laid out just as he had seen him in his dream—except for the flowers. And then an elderly woman entered the room and placed a bouquet like the one Sam had seen in his dream on Henry's chest.

In a dream, Abraham Lincoln heard the sounds of people crying in grief. He followed the sound of the mourners to the

East Room of the White House, where he saw a body lying in state. When he asked the mourners who died, the eerie reply came: 'The president. He was killed by an assassin.' Not long afterward, the president's dream became a horrible reality.

Likewise, the assassination of the Archduke Francis Ferdinand of Austria-Hungary was foreseen in a dream by his tutor, Bishop Joseph Lanyi. Lanyi dreamed that the Archduke was shot while driving in a car at Sarajevo. As fate would have it, the Archduke was in Sarajevo at the time, but Lanyi's warning came too late and Francis Ferdinand was killed, just as his tutor had foreseen.

J W Dunne, a British aviator and aeronautical engineer, experienced several dreams that he believed were prophetic. During the Boer War in South Africa, Dunne dreamed of a volcano about to erupt. He saw himself on a neighboring island, pleading with French officials to send ships to rescue the 4000 people stranded on the island. Soon afterward,

Above: A mask represents a deception. If the dreamer encounters a person wearing a mask, that person wishes to hide something from the dreamer. On the other hand, if the dreamer is wearing a mask, then he is the one hiding the truth.

Above and below: **One of the most intriguing aspects of dreams is that they do not conform to reality as we know it. A patient of a New Jersey psychologist found herself transported back to the Wild West, though she herself was dressed for work in a modern day, urban setting.**

Dunne saw a newspaper account in the *Daily Telegraph* of a volcanic eruption on the French-governed isle of Martinique. The report was eerily reminiscent of Dunne's dream: The survivors were removed by ship, and the number of victims reached 40,000—Dunne's dream was off by a tragic zero.

In another dream, Dunne encountered three men in Khartoum, in the Sudan. They told him they had just come all the way from the southern tip of Africa. The next morning, Dunne read in the morning paper that the 'Cape to Cairo' expedition had just arrived in Khartoum. Prior to that morning, Dunne had never heard of the expedition. On another occasion, Dunne dreamed of a train plummeting off an embankment near the Forth Bridge in Scotland. Several months later Dunne's dream became reality as the *Flying Scotsman* crashed not 15 miles from the Forth Bridge.

Dunne was a well-educated man, not the sort to invent the stories, but some people wondered if he hadn't simply imagined the dreams after reading about them. Others suggested that perhaps his dreams were the product of mental telepathy with the reporters on the *Daily Telegraph*. Dunne concluded that some dreams are simply prophetic.

Scientists continued to be intrigued by the possibility of dream telepathy, and in the 1940s Wilfred Daim, a Viennese psychologist, conducted the first series of dream telepathy experiments. Unfortunately, Daim's research encountered a major stumbling block. Even if the dreamer had received a telepathic message, it was virtually impossible to pinpoint the precise moment the dreamer had received the message. To complicate matters further, upon awakening, the dreamers often had only vague memories of their dreams, rendering them useless from a scientific perspective.

It wasn't until 1953, when Dr Nathaniel Kleitman discovered REM sleep, that researchers could come closer to understanding the nature of dreams. Kleitman and his team of researchers at the University of Chicago determined that sleep consists of two separate phases. In the first phase, physical and mental activity subsides, but in the second phase the sleeper's breathing is irregular, his brain activity is similar to a waking state, and his eyes move rapidly under closed lids. When sleepers were awakened during the first stage, they generally did not recall dreaming. In the second stage, dubbed REM for rapid-eye-movement, sleepers reported that they were dreaming. Researchers discovered that these REM phases occur about every 90 minutes, lasting roughly an hour. Additional research suggested that REM sleep is essential for sleepers, for when they are deprived of REM sleep the tendency is to dream more the following night.

Kleitman's research provided a major breakthrough in the study of dreams. Researchers could now determine when a subject was dreaming and could thus wake him up to question him about his dream. When awakened in the midst of a dream, the subjects could vividly recall their dreams.

With the previous obstacles to studying dream telepathy removed, research began in earnest. In 1965, landmark work was conducted at the Maimonides Medical Center in Brooklyn, New York under the direction of Dr Montague Ullman. In a series of now famous experiments, subjects were awakened during the REM phases of sleep and asked to describe their dreams. While they had been sleeping, other participants in the experiment had been asked to concentrate on a painting in an effort to transmit the image of the painting to the sleeper telepathically.

Ullman's research was the subject of great debate in the scientific community, with many scientists regarding Ullman's findings as inconclusive. The number of dreamers reporting a dream like the image that had been sent telepathically was relatively small. The Maimonides team was nevertheless so impressed by the accuracy

of those dreams that they concluded that telepathy had to be the only explanation.

One type of dream that has defied scientific explanation is known as the creative dream—a dream which inspires. After waking from a dream, the English poet Samuel Taylor Coleridge penned these words, the opening lines to his masterful poem 'Kubla Khan':

'In Xanadu did Kubla Khan
a stately pleasure dome decree:
Where Alph, the sacred river ran
Through caverns measureless to man
Down to a sunless sea.'

The writer Robert Louis Stevenson credited 'The Strange Case of Dr Jekyll and Mr Hyde' to a dream. Stevenson claimed that many of his works originated in a dream and that he could, in fact, dream stories on demand. He also professed the ability to dream in sequence, continuing a story where it had left off the night before.

Giuseppe Tartini, an eighteenth century composer, attributed his masterpiece to a dream in which he made a Faustian pact with the devil. When he handed his violin to the devil, Satan played a 'sonata of exquisite beauty.' Upon waking, Tartini composed 'The Devil's Trill,' though he said that his composition fell far short of the music he heard in his dream.

Creative dreams are not limited to the arts. The German chemist Fredrich August Kekulé determined the molecular structure of the compound benzene after dreaming of atoms that suddenly transformed themselves into a snake biting its own tail. Kekulé awoke immediately with the realization that the structure he needed, like the snake, formed a ring.

Extensive research has been done on dreams that foretell disasters, such as a plane or train crash. In many cases, the dreamers had no connection to anyone involved in the disaster, and researchers have concluded that these people have stronger psychic abilities than the general population. In other instances, however, the dream serves as a warning to the dreamer.

A woman (*below*) cancelled her trip to Italy following a recurring dream about a menacing stranger who followed her throughout the airport. On 9 October 1963, two days after her planned arrival, a landslide into the Vaiont Dam in Italy caused a flood, killing 2000 people.

DICTIONARY OF DREAM SYMBOLS AND IMAGES

Above: **Throughout the world, the bat evokes an image of badness, of decay and evil.**

Below: **Angels, a bear and an automobile—each of these can carry a subconscious meaning that comes to the forefront of our consciousness in a dream.**

Accordion Dreams featuring accordions are less common today than they were in the past. Hearing an accordion is interpreted as a sign that the dreamer is disappointed. An out of tune accordion represents an unhappy state of mind. Playing an accordion betokens marital bliss.

Acrobat An acrobat is an omen of a dangerous scheme. If the acrobat falls, the scheme should be avoided. A person dreaming that he is an acrobat is expressing a need for appreciation.

Actor, actress Dreaming about an actor or actress represents a desire for fame and recognition.

Airplane A plane taking off can be interpreted as a sign of high hopes for the future. However, if the plane is still on the ground, the dreamer seeks to avoid a troublesome situation.

Alligator An alligator or crocodile represents danger.

Anchor An anchor indicates a need for permanence in one's personal or professional life. An anchor tied to a ship symbolizes the desire to break free from an unpleasant situation.

Angel An angel is the traditional symbol of glad tidings, representing good news or protection from evil.

Animals A wild animal or one that is out of control represents a lust for sex. However, a pet signifies contentment and companionship.

Ants Ants represent minor irritants.

Apples Dating back to the legend of Adam and Eve, apples are said to represent sex. Ripe apples denote good luck, while fallen apples signify failed plans.

Automobiles Dreaming of an automobile represents the desire for financial gain, while a moving car is traditionally interpreted as sexual desire. A car accident is said to be a warning of a complication in one's life.

Ax An ax is the symbol of happiness after a struggle. A sharp ax is an assurance of financial success, while a dull one represents a downturn of economic conditions. A broken ax stands for a disappointment.

Baby A baby has various meanings. A crying baby represents disappointment, while a happy baby signifies friendship. A sleeping baby is interpreted as the desire for a mate, and to *have* a baby is thought to be the need to prove one's fertility.

Ballet A ballet signifies infidelity and jealousy.

Banana According to ancient lore, a banana represents a minor illness. An overripe banana indicates boredom, either with work or a partner.

Bath, bathing Taking a bath, especially more than one, denotes an interest in the opposite sex. For the person who has previously been married, a bath is a sign of remarriage. A psychological interpretation suggests feelings of guilt, while a physiological one indicates a physical problem.

Bats Bats signify bad news and sadness.

Beach Dreaming of a beach denotes the need for relaxation and pleasure. Dreams of this type often have sexual connotations.

Bear Bears are said to foretell a situation in which the odds are against the dreamer. A bear can also represent a rival, either personally or professionally.

Bells The tolling of bells augurs the death of a friend or a loved one.

Bicycle Riding a bike uphill betokens good news, while riding a bike downhill forewarns of misfortune.

Birds A dream of a bird perched in a tree signifies unexpected happiness, a flying bird symbolizes prosperity, a wounded bird denotes depression caused by a family member, and talking birds are a warning of gossip.

Blindness Dreaming of a blind person indicates a person in distress. If the dreamer is the blind person, that is a sign that he is not seeing his own faults.

Blindfold A blindfold signifies a temporary setback.

Bomb A bomb represents a situation that will be a source of great distress for the dreamer.

Books Books indicate intellectual pursuits. Shelves of books signify the need for more discipline where work is concerned, while empty shelves point to losses caused by a lack of knowledge.

Bridge A dream of crossing a bridge signifies overcoming an obstacle, while passing under a bridge denotes a burdensome problem that will take some thought to solve. A long bridge that seems to vanish in the distance indicates a loss or a disappointment in love.

Canoe Paddling a canoe in still waters is interpreted as being able to run a business successfully. However, a canoe in rough waters is the sign of discontent, either personally or professionally.

Cat Legend holds that a cat is symbolic of a woman. An angry cat denotes a female enemy, while a thin cat signifies bad news about a friend. A white cat is a sign of a youthful indiscretion. A white cat has also been interpreted as a loss for an adult.

Cemetery A dream about a cemetery represents news from someone from the past.

To the person who has lost a spouse, a cemetery betokens a remarriage or other major life change.

Cherries Cherries are a traditional symbol of good luck.

Children A dream of children playing and laughing is a sign of happiness. Conversely, unhappy children represent a disappointment. A sick child betokens monetary problems.

Below: Hieronymus Bosch's *Garden of Earthly Delights* transports us to a dreamlike world, replete with imagery of love, lust and death. The central panel of this famous triptych is a veritable catalogue of dream symbols, containing birds, strawberries, bears, unicorns, people flying, people drowning and, of course, the very insignia of the modern New Age movement—crystals.

Below: According to traditional dream interpretations, a lock and key represents the desire to reach or understand that which is inaccessible; a mouse symbolizes duplicity; and a snake denotes male sexuality.

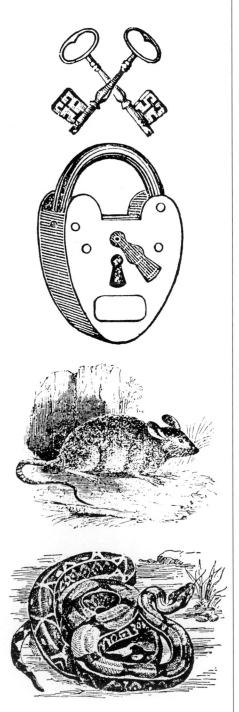

Church A dream of a church represents a wish come true. However, if the church is in the distance, it represents a disappointment. Entering a church is said to signify marriage. According to some authorities, a church symbolizes the nurturing, protective characteristics of women.

Clock A clock or a watch indicates that the dreamer is obsessed with time. A striking clock portends the death of a friend or loved one, or even oneself.

Clouds Dark clouds warn of dark times ahead.

Dancing According to traditional interpretations, dancing indicates happiness. Modern analysis, however, sees dancing as a sign of sexual desire.

Dogs Friendly dogs denote friendships, while angry, biting dogs signify anxiety. Freudian interpretations hold that mad dogs represent sexual desires. According to ancient dream lore, a white dog signified marriage for a woman and business sense for a man, a baying dog symbolized a death in the family, and a growling dog indicated depression.

Driving Driving a car in a dream expresses a desire for independence, while speeding signifies a need to escape. If the dreamer is the passenger, he has faith in the driver.

Drowning Popular theory interprets a dream about drowning as the desire to be reborn.

Elephants Elephants are symbols of power, force and memory.

Fire Dreams of fire represent sexual desires. Traditional interpretations regard fires as good luck. A fire at home indicates a happy home life, while a fire at one's place of business signifies prosperity.

Gate A dream of a closed gate warns of problems to come, while a broken gate is a failed endeavor. Swinging on a gate indicates a light-hearted nature.

Goat A goat symbolizes virility.

Grass Dreams of grass are thought to be prophetic. A vast expanse of grass augurs fulfillment of goals, but if the dreamer should crush the grass, the completion of one's goals will be fraught with problems.

Gun The sound of a gunshot is interpreted as a warning. Shooting a person signifies dishonor. According to Freudian analysis, a gun, like a knife or dagger, symbolizes male sexuality and desires.

Hat A hat signifies a change of place. Losing a hat is seen as a bad omen.

Horse A white horse means prosperity, a black horse, deception. A runaway horse warns of financial difficulties. According to modern interpretations, horses are symbols of sexual passion.

House Building a house signifies a major life change. Dreaming of an elegant house indicates the desire to improve one's social status. A house that is falling apart is a sign that finances need to be attended to. An unpleasant house may be indicative of discontent at home.

Island An island is a symbol of happiness and comfort. However, if the dreamer is seeking refuge on the island, it represents a desire to escape. If the island is populated with many people, the dreamer desires friends.

Jewelry Fine jewels denote high ambitions, while broken jewelry signifies disappointments, and tarnished jewelry, business problems. A gift of jewelry is said to represent a happy married life.

Key Dreaming about a key indicates a change ahead. A key that is broken symbolizes grief, while lost keys signify an unpleasant situation. Finding a key is a good omen.

King A king signifies authority. Dreaming of being king indicates a desire to control others, while seeing a king shows a need for direction.

Lamb A lamb frolicking in a pasture is a sign of happiness, while a lost lamb signifies uncertainty. A dead lamb is a bad omen.

Lightning A dream of lightning represents love.

Lock A lock represents confusion. If the lock is on a door or a trunk, the dreamer desires to see what lies beyond the lock, but in order to understand the dream, it is necessary to analyze the meaning of the door or the trunk.

Mice Dreams of mice represent deception and insincerity. Ancient dream lore holds that a young girl dreaming about mice should be forewarned of a scandal. Modern interpretations regard mice as sexual symbols.

Mountains Mountains are symbolic of the desire to attain great heights. If the dreamer reaches the top of the mountain, his goal will be fulfilled. Hazards encountered along the way signify life's frustrations.

Music Hearing music is a sign of good luck. If the dreamer is disturbed by the music, the music portends emotional uncertainty.

Needle Dreaming of threading a needle signifies problems that can be solved only through patience. Breaking a needle represents the urge to be alone, and sewing with a needle indicates a friend in need.

Newspaper Reading a newspaper is a warning that one's reputation is in danger. If the dreamer is trying but cannot see the words, business difficulties follow.

Nuns Dreaming of nuns indicates a need for spiritual reflection. If a woman dreams that she is a nun, she is discontented with her situation in life.

Nurse Nurses signify good health, but to dream that one is a nurse signifies a need to have friends.

Oak An oak tree filled with acorns signifies a promotion and a raise, while a forest of oak trees betokens prosperity.

Ocean A calm ocean is a sign of good fortune, while a rough ocean signifies danger. Dreaming of being on a ship on the ocean denotes the urge to travel. Various other interpretations view the ocean as a sign of death, a desire to be reborn or the opportunity to start again.

Oranges According to traditional interpretations, an orange is a sign of lost love for a woman and unexpected business complications for a man.

Owl The owl is commonly regarded as a sign of wisdom. Other interpretations see the owl as representing gossip. The hoot of an owl signifies ill health or bad news about a friend.

Paralysis Dreams of paralysis are fairly common. In these dreams, the dreamer cannot move, walk, talk or scream. The paralysis signifies a difficult problem that the dreamer cannot solve during his waking hours.

Peaches Dreaming of eating peaches symbolizes unattained wealth or unrequited love. Peaches on a tree mean that hard work will be rewarded.

Pearls A gift of pearls symbolizes a celebration. Breaking a strand of pearls or losing pearls represents misfortune.

Pears Pears betoken surprises and good health, followed by disappointments and temporary illness.

Pebbles Pebbles in dreams stand for petty jealousies.

Pregnancy Dreaming of pregnancy represents anxiety and impatience.

Pyramids Pyramids symbolize the desire for new surroundings or new areas of interest.

Railroad A railroad with winding tracks represents the changes and complications that exist throughout life.

Rain Dreams of rain are prophetic. Watching rain from indoors augurs prosperity, while being in the rain warns of a slowing of plans. A rainstorm is a sign of mental turmoil.

Reptiles Reptiles of all kinds represent obstacles. One snake denotes an argument, two stand for two friends that will deceive the dreamer. The snake also symbolizes male sexuality.

Ring A ring is a symbol of friendship, love and marriage. Receiving a ring foretells of meeting a new friend, while a broken ring denotes a separation from a loved one.

Shoes Old, worn shoes have traditionally been interpreted as a message to the dreamer to be tolerant and respectful of others. Untied shoes warn of misfortune, while having shoes shined is a sign of important changes ahead.

Smoke Dreaming about smoke indicates a confused state of mind.

Snakes See Reptiles.

Snow A snowfall warns of a crisis that may be costly as well as emotionally distressing. A snowstorm represents frustration. Climbing a snow-covered mountain indicates a business disappointment.

Above: A dream about a nun is typically interpreted as a need to contemplate the spiritual world. For people who attended parochial school, a nun may also symbolize discipline and authority.

Below: Swiss psychologist Carl Jung believed that certain symbols transcend cultural barriers, forming part of our collective unconscious. The swan (*see also below right*), for example, is seen as a symbol of prosperity. Other images, such as the umbrella or the tennis rackets, may impart a message that relates solely to the individual.

Right: A dream about walking signifies distress or misunderstanding.

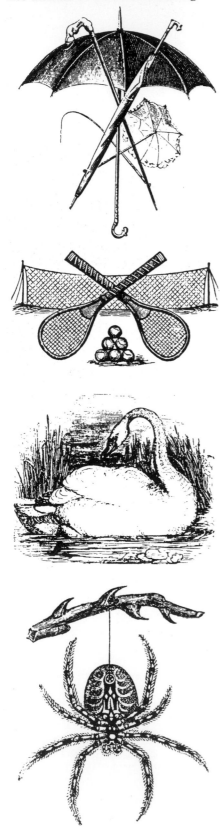

Spider A spider symbolizes a worrisome situation. This sort of dream is apt to recur until the dreamer has solved the situation.

Sports Dreams about baseball, football, soccer and other sports represent a need for harmony and teamwork. People who dream about sports generally expect others to act fairly.

Stairs According to some psychoanalysts, dreams about stairs reveal sexual desires. Traditional interpretations regard these dreams as signs of good fortune. However, walking down the stairs signifies bad luck in business and love, while falling down the stairs means that enemies will create obstacles.

Sun A sunrise is an omen of happy times, while a sunset warns the dreamer to be cautious where money and property are concerned. The sun showing through the clouds predicts prosperity.

Swan A white swan foretells of happiness and prosperity, while a black swan is a warning to avoid immoral situations.

Swimming When the dreamer is enjoying the sensation of swimming, the dream indicates the desire to have fun and enjoy life. However, if swimming is a struggle, the dreamer is going through a distressing period. Swimming with others indicates a desire to make new friends.

Thief A thief in a dream means that someone has usurped the dreamer's rights. However, if the dreamer is the thief, he has has usurped the rights of another.

Tiger A tiger is a sign of fear.

Tomato Dreaming of a tomato indicates a desire to socialize. Ripe tomatoes are symbolic of a happy marriage.

Torture Dreaming about torture reveals a conflict concerning love or money.

Trees Trees are symbolic of pleasure and success. Dead trees, however, portend losses. Cutting down a tree is a sign to avoid quarrels.

Trunk Dreaming of packing, opening or closing a truck or suitcase reveals a desire for change. A trunk that is never packed or closed symbolizes a frustrating situation.

Tunnels Tunnels are symbolic of insecurity. Being trapped in a tunnel reveals a desire to escape. Modern psychoanalysis interprets tunnels as a symbol of sexual interests.

Umbrella Dreaming about umbrellas reveals personal misunderstandings.

Valentine A valentine is symbolic of a marriage proposal.

Violin A violin represents esteem, possibly awards. A broken violin betokens separation from a loved one.

Volcano Volcanoes symbolize emotions and act as a warning to those who are quick to lose their temper.

Walking Walking on a rough or winding path indicates a distressing situation. Walking at night reveals fear or caution.

Walls Walls are symbols of frustration or the inability to attain a goal. Breaking through a wall signifies overcoming obstacles to reach one's goal.

Wallet Dreaming about a wallet indicates financial concerns.

War Dreaming of war during times of peace symbolizes family problems.

Watch Watches are omens of prosperity. Looking at a watch reveals a desire to use time more efficiently.

Water Clear water is a sign of wealth and happiness, while muddy water signifies illness. Playing in water indicates a desire to be loved, and rough water symbolizes difficult times leading to success. Jumping into water represents a desire for a second chance. Dreaming of drinking water often means that the dreamer is actually thirsty.

Window A closed window is a sign of frustration, while a broken window signifies a broken heart. Crawling through a window reveals bad intent.

Wolf Like the old adage about a wolf in sheep's clothing, a dream about a wolf signifies a friend who is really an enemy.

Above: **Rod Serling—the dream weaver. Each week from 1959 to 1965, Serling introduced a new mythical tale on his renowned television show, *The Twilight Zone*, with the words: 'There is a fifth dimension beyond that which is known to man. It is a dimension as vast as space and as timeless as infinity. It is the middle ground between light and shadow, between science and superstition, and it lies between the pit of man's fears and the summit of his knowledge.'**

Left: **Cupid, the cherubic god of love, is said to visit people in their dreams.**

REINCARNATION

Opposite page: **Based on dreams that she had in 1924, Lydia Davis Hucheson of Oakland, California became aware that in a previous life she had lived in India and had known the Hindu teacher Caitanyu Mahaprabhu. A trip to India in 1925 is said to have confirmed this, and Ms Hucheson, thereafter known as Sister Rana, devoted the rest of her life to the study of the Vedas.**

Below: **Reports of reincarnation are common among tribal people.**

 ultures around the world share a belief in reincarnation—the idea that a being can leave its body after death and return to the world in a new and different body. During the Stone Age, some 12,000 years ago, ancient peoples buried their dead in the fetal position, prompting archaeologists to speculate that they were literally readying the dead for a rebirth into the next life.

The concept of reincarnation as a formalized belief probably originated around the sixth century BC in India as part of the Hindu religion. One of the central tenets of Hinduism is transmigration, which holds that a person's soul passes on to another creature, either human or animal, at the time of death. The new life, which is seen as a reward or as a punishment based on the deeds of one's past life, is one's karma. Ultimately, after passing through many lives on the way to perfection, the soul reaches a divine world.

Belief in reincarnation spread from India to Greece. Pythagoras, the Greek mathematician of the sixth century BC, supposedly stopped a man from beating a puppy when he heard the puppy cry out in the voice of a dead friend. In the fifth century BC, Plato proposed his theory that the soul passed through various stages, or degrees. According to Plato, when the soul has reached a stage of enlightenment and is divorced from the material world, it may be born onto the body of an artist, a philosopher, a musician or a lover. After this final stage, the soul is ready to end its quest and to find peace in a heavenly realm.

It is likely that the Indian influence also spread throughout Asia and across the Bering Strait to the Indian tribes along the northwestern coast of North America. The beliefs of the Tlingit Indians of south-

Above and right: The ancient Egyptians buried their dead with books extolling the virtues of the deceased so that the god Osiris would grant them other lives. The Egyptians believed that it could take up to 3000 years for an individual to go through his entire cycle of lives.

Opposite page: Buddhists believe that human beings may be reborn into any of the five classes of living things: gods, human beings, animals, hungry ghosts or the damned. The process of rebirth ends when the individual has squelched the three fires—craving, ill will and ignorance—and thus has reached a state of Nirvana.

eastern Alaska share certain similarities to the Hindu karma.

Like Hinduism, Buddhism teaches reincarnation, as does Lamaism, the religion of the people of Tibet. Tibet's spiritual and temporal leader is the Dalai Lama, and when he dies, he is reincarnated, continuing a line of leaders that has existed since 1391. At the death of the Dalai Lama, the high lamas (monks) must conduct a search for their new leader. Prayer, meditation and various omens lead the way to a new Dalai Lama. Once the high lamas have located the young boy they believe to be the new Dalai Lama, the boy must prove that he is the true Dalai Lama by selecting articles—a rosary, a bell and so on—that belonged to the Dalai Lama in his previous incarnation.

In contrast to the Eastern belief that a soul is purified as it passes through various lives, Western Christian thought holds that a soul cannot be reborn and after death awaits Judgement Day. Even though the doctrine of reincarnation is seemingly in conflict with Christianity, church members throughout history have argued in its favor, from Origen, a third century theologian, who cited John 1:19-28 as evidence that John the Baptist was the reincarnation of Elijah, to New Agers of the 1990s, who base their arguments on several passages from the New Testament.

REINCARNATION RESEARCH

While on a trip to Egypt in 1912, Katherine O'Rourke Keating (*opposite page*) became aware of a series of nine past lives including that of an Egyptian slave girl (*above*) who lived during the reign of Ramses II. She informed her husband, the Philadelphia industrialist Charles Farris Keating, and an excursion was arranged to Ramses' palace at Abu Simbel.

To the amazement of Mr Keating and their traveling companions, Mrs Keating was able to describe the layout and contents of several rooms in the palace before entering them.

Upon return to America, the Keatings contacted researcher Paul Norwood Blaine. Together they visited the village of Bethlehem Junction, New Hampshire, where Mrs Keating claimed to have lived in 1841 when she was Mary Scott. Although she was able to describe in advance many of the details of the road between Twin Mountain, New Hampshire and the Connecticut River some 25 miles distant, Dr Blaine found the experiment to be, in *his* words, 'inconclusive.'

At the time of Mrs Keating's untimely death in 1921, a further experiment was being arranged in Arkansas.

Examples of reincarnation are found in all countries and cultures, with a particularly high incidence in India, where it is an accepted part of mainstream beliefs. Researchers in the field of reincarnation have noted various commonalities among all cultures. Typically, a person expresses feelings about a past life at an early age, from two to four years. Around the age of five to eight years, the person loses the sense of identification with the previous personality and stops talking about the past life. Another common feature is that the memories regarding the death of the previous personality are particularly intense.

Many of the alleged rebirths experienced a violent death, but the percentage varies by country. In Sri Lanka 40 percent of the cases claimed to have died a violent death in their previous life, while in Syria and Lebanon the figure increased to 80 percent. Thus, while there are certainly common features that transcend cultural barriers, researchers have also noted differences between cultures. Dr Ian Stevenson, a professor of psychiatry at the University of Virginia Medical School and a leader in the field of reincarnation research, discovered the lapse between death and rebirth varies by culture. In Turkey, the average time period is only nine months, but in Sri Lanka it is 21 months, in India, 45 months, and among the Tlingit Indians of Alaska, 48 months.

As additional evidence in support of reincarnation, Stevenson cites cases of people who seem to possess skills from a previous life, such as singing, dancing, an aptitude for working with machinery or weaving thatch roofs. Other authorities in the field have taken these examples one step further, speculating that reincarnation explains the child prodigy phenomenon. Children who exhibit talents that normally would take a lifetime to achieve are simply remembering the skills of a past life. Frequently cited examples are Wolfgang Amadeus Mozart, who composed music when he was four, and Blaise Pascal, the seventeenth-century mathematician, who proposed a new geometric system by the time he was 11. However, as Dr Stevenson pointed out, a major flaw in this theory is that there is no record of a child prodigy reporting memories of a past life.

Some researchers have suggested that the sensation of *déjà vu*—the feeling that one has been in a certain locale before—is the memory from a previous incarnation.

Once a potential case is discovered, researchers go back to historical records to confirm the details of the subject's past life. If the previous incarnation lived in the recent past, there are frequently friends and relatives who can corroborate the data.

In spite of innumerable stumbling blocks and evidence that is circumstantial at best, research in the field of reincarnation has persisted since the early twentieth century. One of the most dramatic cases of the twentieth century is the story of Shanti Devi of India. In 1929, when Shanti was three years old, she began telling her mother about her husband, a man named Kendarnath, their children and their home in Muttra. Shanti spoke of a difficult pregnancy and the breach birth that led to her death. After four years of listening to Shanti's tales of her previous life, her uncle decided to write to the man who had supposedly been Shanti's husband—Kendarnath. Kendarnath sent his cousin as an emissary. Shanti knew the man at once and was able to report trivial details of his life. Kendarnath was then compelled to visit Shanti himself.

By this time, Shanti had become a news sensation and an investigation was launched. Accompanied by a group of experts, Shanti arrived at the village of Muttra and led the group from the train station to the home where she had once lived as the wife of Kendarnath.

An intriguing case of reincarnation involved a Tlingit Indian who *predicted* his own rebirth. William George Sr, a fisherman of some renown, told his son and daughter-in-law, 'If there is anything to this rebirth business, I will come back and be your son.'

While on a fishing trip in 1949, William George disappeared, never to be seen again. Shortly after the elder George's disappearance and presumed death, his daughter in-law became pregnant and in due time had a son who, as his grandfather had predicted, had birthmarks similar to those of William George. His parents named the boy William George, Jr. As the boy grew up, his personality, as well as some physical characteristics, bore an uncanny resemblance to George William, Sr. He limped, for example, had a tendency to fret and worry, and was quite an expert on fishing and boats.

In addition, George William, Jr strongly

Above: **One of the most celebrated cases of reincarnation in the twentieth century involved an Ohio woman, Dolores Jay, who believed she had lived a previous life as Gretchen Gottlieb, a German girl in the nineteenth century.**

Opposite page: **Numerous cases of reincarnation have been reported among the Tlingit Indians of Alaska.**

identified with a watch that belonged to his grandfather. George William, Jr saw the watch, which George William, Sr had passed on to his son, the boy's father, and cried, 'That's my watch.'

In 1956, reincarnation came to the forefront of public attention with *The Search for Bridey Murphy*, a book by Morey Bernstein that detailed the amazing story of Virginia Tighe, a Colorado housewife, who claimed that she had lived a century earlier in Ireland as a woman named Bridey Murphy. While under hypnosis, Tighe reported the facts of her previous life. Bridey was born on 20 December 1798, the daughter of Kathleen and Duncan Murphy. As a child, she lived in a farmhouse called the Meadows in County Cork and attended Mrs Strayne's Day School.

Bridey married Brian McCarthy when she was 20 years old and settled in a small cottage in Belfast. Her husband, like her father, practiced law. Brian McCarthy taught at Queen's University and wrote articles for the Belfast *News-Letter*. The couple danced the sorcerer's jig, and Bridey frequently prepared boiled beef and onions, her husband's favorite dinner.

When she was 66, Bridey fell and broke her hip. She grew depressed, feeling she had become a 'burden' and one Sunday while her husband was at church, she 'sort of withered away' and died. Virginia Tighe's story of Bridey was so filled with detail that several investigators traveled to Ireland to confirm the particulars of Bridey's life. In spite of the wealth of detail, little hard evidence of Bridey Murphy McCarthy could be found. In the end, the intriguing case only served to reinforce the opinion of those who already believed in reincarnation and did nothing to convince those who did not believe.

In 1970, the Reverend Carroll E Jay of Ohio used hypnotherapy to treat the back pains his wife, Dolores, was suffering from. One evening, when she was hypnotized, Mrs Jay began to speak in German. Over the course of several sessions, Dolores Jay described the personality of her previous incarnation, Gretchen Gottlieb.

Gretchen had lived in the town of Eberswalde, Germany in the nineteenth century. Her father had been the mayor of the town at a time of political upheaval and Gretchen, consequently, had been murdered.

Mrs Jay's ability to speak German fluently—a language she did not know—while under hypnosis provided researchers with a compelling piece of evidence, and a trip to Germany was undertaken to confirm Gretchen's existence. Several towns with a name similar to Eberswalde were located but none had any records of a mayor Hermann Gottlieb. Researchers did uncover some correlation with Gretchen's story, but no exact proof of dates or places. While initial circumstances pointed to reincarnation, Reverend Jay later suggested that his wife may have been possessed by the spirit of Gretchen.

As the Bridey Murphy and Gretchen cases illustrate, hypnosis provides a primary method of investigation for the reincarnation researcher. While under hypnosis, a subject can regress to an earlier time of life and supposedly to a previous life. However, not all researchers, most notably Ian Stevenson, approve of this type of research. One shortcoming with evidence that emerges during hypnosis is that it may be purely the product of the subject's imagination. A person under a hypnotic suggestion is extremely pliable and eager to please the hypnotist and therefore does what he has been asked to do: tell the details of a past live.

In addition, hypnotized subjects may be prone to cryptomnesia, a type of abnormal memory. While under hypnosis, subjects may tap into memories that they are unaware of while in a normal, conscious state. The memories of what were presumed to be details of a previous life are, in reality, recollections of a book, movie or so on that were stored in the unconscious.

In the 1970s, Helen Wambach, a psychologist in California, conducted a detailed study of reincarnation. Her purpose was to demonstrate that remembrances of a previous existence were something more than just a creative fantasy.

Using hypnosis, she interviewed 1088 persons about their past lives. Roughly 90 percent had vivid memories of a past life. Wambach began her experiments by hypnotizing a group of people to see if anyone in the group had a strong reaction to a specific date. She would also have the subjects look at a map and pick a location that appealed to them. When a date or locale elicited a positive response, she had the subjects describe everything they saw, heard and felt. She was looking for details about a time and place that went beyond what is known by the general public, such as details concerning landscape, climate, personal appearance, eating utensils, clothing, money and home and community life.

As is to be expected from a hypnotized subject, the descriptions were ripe with detail. While some psychologists consider

such details to be little more than the subject's desire to please the hypnotist, Wambach found the information to be historically accurate and therefore highly significant from a statistical point of view.

Wambach also found that the description of past lives were an accurate reflection of the world's population and socioeconomic conditions. The past life recollections represented a roughly equal number of men and women, though Wambach's group of subjects was not equally composed of men and women. Depending on the time in which they had previously lived, most of the past lives belonged to the lower classes, and only 10 percent belonged to the upper class. The number belonging to the middle class increased as the centuries passed and the middle class became more prominent. Wambach found it significant that a high percentage of the past lives were from the twentieth century, which she interpreted as a reflection of the world's ever-increasing population.

Wambach's research included the period between incarnations. Close to 40 percent had no memories of this time, but most of the others believed that they had been reborn so that they would eventually attain spiritual perfection.

In agreement with other psychologists, Wambach concluded that the revelation of a past life trauma can help a patient overcome an emotional problem in this life. Despite the debate surrounding the merit of evidence obtained through hypnosis, many psychotherapists see hypnosis as a valuable tool for many of their patients, allowing them to learn about their past lives. Emotional problems and various neuroses may have their roots in a past life, and once a patient comes to terms with the past life incident, it becomes easier to deal with the problems of the present day. For example, one psychotherapist reported that a patient was afraid to leave the house. When the patient discovered that he had been a frontiersman whose family had died in a fire after he had left the house, he was able to deal with his fears. Likewise, a patient with a fear of heights can often trace that fear to a past life in which he died by falling from a bridge, building or other height, or a patient with a fear of water owes the fear to death by drowning in a previous life.

While past life regression therapy may prove to be an effective tool for many psychologists, they do not necessarily regard it as conclusive evidence in support of the existence of reincarnation—a view that is shared by most scientists. Indeed, many paranormal researchers scoff at the possibility of reincarnation and attribute the events to other paranormal phenomena, such as spirit possession, spirit-to-living telepathy or poltergeist activity. Though the doctrine of reincarnation lacks strong support on the academic front, it is a topic of interest to the general public in the United States. Weekly tabloids at the local supermarket frequently carry stories pertaining to reincarnation. According to a recent poll, one out of five Americans believe in reincarnation.

Some authorities have suggested that interest in reincarnation can be attributed to a certain extent to a desire to make life more interesting. The so-called average person may feel better about himself if he believes that he was a king or a great warrior in a previous life. In part, the public's recent fascination with the topic is a result of the growing popularity of the New Age movement, a pseudo-religion with connections to both Christianity and Eastern religions.

Marguerite La Fontaine Mather (*opposite page*) was a noted spiritualist and a prolific contributor to occult journals. Much of her writings in her later years were devoted to lengthy discussions of her past life in the early nineteenth century as a member of the Apache tribe in Arizona.

In the 1950s, some of Mrs Mather's followers decided that a US Army Signal Corps photograph (*below*) taken in the 1880s was actually a photograph of her in her previous incarnation as 'She who cries like the bird.'

Opposite page: 'Crystal Awakening,' a painting channeled through the subconsciousness of Marjosa Star. As the artist explains, 'My hand seems to be in tune with my subconscious rather than my conscious…. [The paintings] literally develop on their own, the conscious level becoming aware after the fact.'

The painting *below*, which was done when the artist was temporarily blind, illustrates how perfectly her hand is linked with her sub-conscious.

Above: Actress, writer and New Age advocate Shirley MacLaine.

THE NEW AGE MOVEMENT

The New Age movement is incredibly diverse, with proponents ranging from those who practice holistic medicine to those whose lives are directed by spirit guides. In essence, the New Age movement exhorts the need for a metaphysical search for meaning through personal growth and change.

Many New Agers believe that they can improve their lives by learning about past lives. To learn about their past lives, people have turned to channelers, the modern day version of a medium. Like mediums, channelers are in touch with a spirit guide from the past, and sometimes from another world.

One of the better known channelers is Jane Roberts, author of the Seth books. On 9 September 1963, Jane Roberts, a writer and a poet, first encountered the entity named Seth, a self-described 'energy personality essence no longer focused in physical reality.' For 20 years, until her death in 1984, Seth communicated through Jane in twice weekly sessions. The Seth books are compiled from Jane's transcripts of these sessions and discuss such topics as death, reincarnation, world religions, dreams, alternate states of awareness and human sexuality.

Neville Rowe, a New Zealander, speaks through the voice of Soli, 'an off-planet being.' While much of mainstream America tends to regard Rowe and his ilk as eccentrics and offshoots of the hippie era of the 1960s, many New Age proponents don't fit this profile.

Ruth Montgomery, for example, was a political reporter in Washington, DC for 25 years. A well-known syndicated columnist, she was also a panelist for 'Meet the Press' before she turned her investigative skills to psychic phenomena. Montgomery believes that reincarnation 'is the only explanation for the seeming inequities in life. We are treated by others according to how we have treated others in the past.'

Montgomery initially became interested in the paranormal when she attended a séance and communicated with her dead father and other relatives. On the advice of the well-known medium Arthur Ford, Montgomery tried automatic writing—written communications from the spirit world. To receive these messages, she sits in a relaxed state at her typewriter. Her first contact was from a spirit named Lily. Over the course of two decades, Lily, and then a group of 12 guides, communicated with Montgomery about 'the nature of everlasting life, the activity after death, and eternal evolution toward oneness with the Creator.' Arthur Ford, who died in 1971, later joined the group of spirit guides.

Montgomery did not believe in reincarnation at first, but the guides told her to investigate it and eventually the concept made sense to her. She later learned that in a previous life she had been a black washerwoman in Africa.

In one of her automatic writing sessions, Montgomery asked about King Juan Carlos of Spain and learned that in his previous lives he had often been born into the ruling class. At one time he had been a Pharaoh in Egypt, and at another, a member of the House of Savoy. He had also been a wandering friar in France and a lama in Tibet.

Jo Ann Karl, a former business executive, is another adherent of the New Age philosophy. Karl became interested in the paranormal when she had an out-of-body

Above: **Anna Lewis Montford and her two daughters, Genevieve and Louisa, were ardent disciples of Theosophy, a doctrine devised by Madame Helena Blavatsky in 1875. Mrs Montford became a convert to Theosophy when she read Madame Blavatsky's major treatise *The Secret Doctrine*, which asserted, among other things, that the individual undergoes a process of spiritual evolution through reincarnation.**

Since childhood, Mrs Montford had had the sense that she had lived before, but had never been willing to voice her feelings. With the publication of *The Secret Doctrine*, she announced that during a past life she had lived at the court of the Medici family in Florence, Italy during the early sixteenth century.

Madame Blavatsky's other followers included Thomas A Edison, Alfred Lord Tennyson and William Butler Yeats.

experience in 1980. She went on to explore her past lives, a lesson that has taught her about taking risks. 'I was married to St Peter,' she explains. 'We traveled widely with Jesus, teaching with him. After he was crucified, we continued to teach and travel for several more years, until we were caught by the Romans. Peter was crucified, and I was thrown to the lions after being raped and pilloried. Now I understand why I've always been afraid of big animals.' Today, Karl is a channeler herself, helping others get in touch with the spirit world through the archangel Gabriel and a spirit named Ashtar.

One highly successful channeler is J Z Knight, a former housewife from Yelm, Washington, who now speaks for Ramtha, a 35,000-year-old warrior from the lost continent of Lemuria. Ramtha's thoughts have been published in *I Am Ramtha* by Beyond Words Publishing. Zelm's detractors point out with sessions ranging in price from $150 to $400, she has a handsome income, supposedly earning millions of dollars.

In the late 1980s and early 1990s, numerous people turned to the Michael Channel. Michael is not a specific person, but rather a non-physical group of 1050 teachers who promote a philosophy of understanding one's essence and personality. According to Michael, learning to love and validate one's own truth is key in expressing love and truth to others. In part, this is accomplished by learning about one's past lives.

Perhaps the most famous advocate of the New Age philosophy is the actress Shirley MacLaine, whose search for meaning has been extensively recounted in several books. MacLaine relates that in past lives she was a Mongolian teenager, a court jester for Louis XV and a prostitute. 'I know I have lived past lives,' MacLaine asserts. 'I know there is life before birth. I can't prove that, but then I couldn't have proved that I had microbes on my arm until the microscope was invented.'

From a purely scientific point of view, it is unlikely that scientists will ever prove conclusively that reincarnation is a fact. Rather, they have compiled a large body of evidence that *suggests*, to use Dr Ian Stevenson's word, the possibility of reincarnation.

EDGAR CAYCE

Born in 1877, Edgar Cayce, the clairvoyant, did much to popularize reincarnation in the United States during the first half of the twentieth century. Cayce first became aware of his psychic gift when he was 13 years old.

One afternoon while he was reading the Bible in the woods, he looked up and saw a woman cloaked in sunlight. The woman said, 'Your prayers have been heard. Tell me what you would like most of all, so that I may give it to you.'

Stunned, young Cayce replied, 'Most of all I would like to be helpful to others, especially to children when they are sick.'

When the lady vanished, Cayce feared he was going crazy, but soon afterward he realized that he had been given a special gift. While studying his spelling lesson with his father, Cayce continually misspelled the words, as he was wont to do. Then, he heard the voice of the lady in the woods telling him to go to sleep. He asked his father for permission to take a nap, and when he awoke he was able to spell all the words correctly.

A short time later, Cayce was hit by a ball during recess. Though he seemed to be unhurt, he acted strangely for the rest of the day. Normally a quiet, well-behaved boy, he became loud and raucous, throwing things at his sisters. That night when he fell asleep, he began talking, telling his parents that he was in shock and to cure it, they should apply a poultice of cornmeal, onion and herbs, which they did. The next day, Cayce had no memory of these events, but his behavior had returned to normal.

Unwilling to believe he possessed psychic powers because they conflicted with his fundamentalist Christian beliefs, Cayce ignored these two strange events for the next decade. In 1900, he lost his voice, a condition that lasted into the new year. After consulting doctors who were unable to find a physical cause, he turned to Al C Layne, a hypnotist, out of desperation. Layne had heard of Cayce's poultice cure and proposed putting Edgar into a trance and letting him diagnose himself. Cayce agreed to try, and put himself to sleep without Layne's assistance. Layne then gave Cayce a hypnotic suggestion to look inside his body to find the cause of his problem.

Much to Layne's amazement, Cayce began to speak in authoritative terms about his throat problem, telling the hypnotist that the condition was a partial paralysis that was caused by a psychological condition. Still asleep, Cayce told Layne to give a hypnotic suggestion to increase the circulation in that part of the body. Layne did as he was told and then watched incredulously as Cayce's neck and chest turned red from the increased blood flow. When Cayce woke up, the condition was completely cured.

Layne persuaded Cayce that he had a gift and should use it for psychic healings. Reluctantly, Cayce embarked on a career that would eventually span 43 years. While in a deep sleep, Cayce could diagnose and prescribe a detailed treatment for an ailing individual. What made his readings all the more amazing was that he needed only a name and address—the patient did not need to be in Cayce's presence. His prescriptions were decidedly odd, a curious combination of diet, herbs, chiropractic massage, osteopathy and hydrotherapy.

Cayce's rate of success is not easy to pinpoint. Sherwood Eddy's study indicated a 90 percent rate of accuracy, but that was based on a very small sampling. While there were three instances of his providing cures for people who had already died, he did succeed at curing his wife of terminal tuberculosis. Successes and failures aside, his overwhelming popular appeal cannot be denied.

Edgar Cayce's career reached a turning point in 1923, when he was approached by Arthur Lammers. A wealthy printer from Dayton, Ohio, Lammers requested a reading, but not about health problems. Instead, Lammers wanted to explore the unknown—the mysteries of the soul, astrology, ancient religions, alchemy and the like. Cayce was averse to pursuing subjects that were in conflict with his fundamental beliefs, but he finally yielded to Lammer's request.

When he had concluded the reading, Cayce became a believer in reincarnation. After death, a soul could pass into a new body so that it could attain perfection, the ultimate goal being to join with God. Cayce added metaphysical readings to his physical readings, eventually developing what he called a life reading, which would begin with the astrological conditions of the subject's birth. Then, Cayce would turn to the subject's previous incarnations. The goal was to learn about the subject's past lives in order to enrich his present life.

Cayce established the Association for Research and Enlightenment (ARE) in 1931 as a vehicle for those who wished to develop their own psychic abilities. After his death in 1945, the ARE collected the written records of Cayce's 14,264 readings, most of which dealt with physical problems. Today, the ARE boasts a membership

of over 70,000 people, and many more belong to 'Search for God' study groups that follow Cayce's beliefs. Moreover, his work inspired the New Age psychics who provide deep-trance channeling.

Cayce's abilities are usually described as clairvoyance, but the man himself preferred to think of his talent as telepathy on a subconscious level. Indeed, Cayce believed he could tap into what he called 'God's book of remembrance or the universal consciousness,' an idea that is similar to Carl Jung's theory of the collective unconscious, a sort of shared universal psyche. In describing his abilities, Cayce used a term that would later be popularized by New Agers: the akashic records. The term comes from a Hindu theosophical word, *akasa*. According to *The Encyclopedia of Occultism and Parapsychology*, the akashic records are 'a central filtering system of all events, thoughts and actions impressed upon an astral plane, which may be consulted in certain conditions of consciousness.' Thus, when Cayce was in a deep sleep, he was able to connect with the akashic records.

The roots of present day holistic health can be traced to Edgar Cayce (*above*), a mystic who entered deep sleep trances and dictated a philosophy of life and healing called readings.

Cayce did over 14,000 readings, and succeeded in curing hundreds of people. According to Sherwood Eddy's study, which was based on interviews with physicians, Cayce achieved a 90-percent rate of accuracy.

PARAPSYCHOLOGY

Above and opposite page: Noted spiritualist Rosa duBois (born Rose Haydon Woodbridge in 1878) became aware of her powers at a young age and used it to great advantage throughout her life, foretelling both personal and business developments for some of the most powerful families in New York City and Newport, Rhode Island.

She is remembered today for her haunting beauty and for her uncanny predictions of the death of Franklin D Roosevelt and the dropping of the atomic bomb in 1945.

Right: Raphael's painting of the 'Vision of Ezekiel,' the archetypal apocalyptic dream. As explained in the Book of Revelation, the animals herald the end of time: Woe, woe, to the inhabitors of the earth' (Rev 8:13).

ince the dawn of recorded time, some people have possessed a special power, a sixth sense that allowed them to *see* or *know* things in ways that other people cannot. In ancient Greece, oracles foretold the death of kings. During the Middle Ages, Joan of Arc, a French peasant girl, heard voices telling her to lead the fight against the English invaders. Abraham Lincoln dreamed of his own assassination. Legions of other people have experienced events that were less spectacular but nonetheless beyond the pale of everyday existence.

Today scientists study these unusual events under the heading of parapsychology. The miracles and strange visions of old are now considered extrasensory perception.

Four types of extrasensory perception, or ESP, are commonly studied:

1. Telepathy, or mind reading, is the transference of thought between people without the use of words. Some parapsychologists believe that telepathy occurs most often between people with a close emotional bond, such as identical twins or mother and child.

2. Clairvoyance, or second sight, is the knowledge of distant events or objects through means other than the five senses. Clairvoyance can take the form of a prolonged vision, but it most often is a brief mental glimpse of the event or object.

3. Precognition is the ability to perceive the future. This knowledge can occur in a dream or while awake.

4. Psychokinesis is the ability to use the mind's powers to change external matter.

The word psi is an umbrella term used to describe any type of psychic ability. The term comes from the 23rd letter of the Greek alphabet and represents an unknown quantity.

THE SOCIETY FOR PSYCHICAL RESEARCH

In 1882, Henry Sedgwick, a prominent philosopher, formed the Society for Psychical Research (SPR) in London to study psychic phenomena and to rationalize them in both religious and scientific terms. The other founding members included physicists Sir William Barrett, Sir William Crookes and Sir Oliver Lodge, and philosophers Frederic W H Myers and Edmund Gurney—all respected members of the academic community.

The following year Sedgwick met with William James, the eminent Harvard psychologist and philosopher, who in turn founded the American Society for Psychical Research (ASPR) in 1885. James, along with several other psychologists, focused on studying the claims of various mediums.

Rather than trying to prove the truth of spiritualists and mediums, the ASPR and the SPR sought to understand the paranormal in logical, rational terms. The members' standing in the scientific community accorded psychic phenomena a new-found respectability. However, the ASPR and SPR were fraught with difficulties almost immediately. Though they were experts in their own fields, no one knew how to conduct research on the paranormal.

A major problem was separating frauds from the genuine article. One of the earliest investigations conducted by the SPR involved the thought-reading team of journalist Douglas Blackburn and hypnotist G A Smith. Blackburn supposedly transmitted an image such as drawing or a number to Smith, who was wrapped in blankets and wore a blindfold and earplugs. After Smith received the image via mental telepathy, he stuck his hand out from the blankets, asked for a pencil, drew a picture of the image, and then threw off the blankets, revealing a remarkable copy of the image.

Years later, after the scientists of SPR were dead, Blackburn revealed that the act had been a hoax and that he had made a drawing of the image on cigarette paper, which he then slipped to Smith, who in turn created his own drawing. Smith, however, denied that he and Blackburn had perpetrated a hoax. 'It was a bona fide experiment,' Smith insisted. 'The successful result was either due to chance or telepathy. I think it was most unlikely that it was due to chance.'

The ASPR, the American counterpart of

Opposite, from left to right: **The founding members of the Psychic Society of Chicago included Owen Paul Fuller, his wife Clara Willis Fuller, Davida Hillyard and Anne Wallenstein. They organized a systematic study of clairvoyant and telepathic phenomena that exposed several clever hoaxes including that perpetrated by Oscar Cruz Hoffman, who had astounded many members of Chicago society before he was unmasked in 1921. His hoax involved the use of a mirror placed across the street by an associate, and was eventually foiled by Ms Wallenstein's simply standing in front of the window!**

Many of the cases investigated by the PSC, such as the bizarre case of the four Freyberg sisters (*above*) who each possessed amazing psychic capabilities, were never fully explained, and this led in 1928 to Mrs Fuller and Ms Hillyard becoming believers in spiritualism themselves.

The Fullers were divorced in 1931 and Mrs Fuller became a clairvoyant who worked under the name Madame Clara for eight years before moving to St Louis. It is known that she was still alive in 1947, but the date of her death is not recorded.

Owen Paul Fuller remarried and became a successful real estate developer in California. Ms Wallenstein, who had married Everett Kuhn in 1942, continued the work of the PSC until her death in 1943.

Like the Great Houdini, magicians of the early twentieth century used their knowledge of the art of illusion to expose the frauds of the psychic world. 'Spirit' pictures were no more than manipulated photographs, the messages from the dead were phony, and ringing bells and flying tambourines were easy for anyone to use in a darkened room.

PT Selbit (Percy Thomas Tibbles, 1879-1939) (*below*) was a stage illusionist in Great Britain, Europe and America. One of the greatest inventors of stage illusions of all time, he was appearing at British music halls as 'The Wizard of the Sphinx' in 1905, when this poster was made.

Adelaide Hermann (*opposite page*), the foremost woman conjuror of the era, billed herself as 'The Queen of Magic.'

the SPR, had to contend with its share of hoaxes, but it also studied a number of interesting cases that appeared to be bona-fide examples of the paranormal at work.

One of the ASPR's most interesting studies involved Leonora Piper, a Boston homemaker. According to the ASPR, Mrs Piper was a mental medium, which meant she had the ability to bring a spoken or written message from the dead. At her sittings, Mrs Piper went into a trance to clear the way for spirit guides to speak in voices quite unlike her own. Mrs Piper's most famous spirit guide was named Phinuit. He spoke with a French accent and claimed to have been a physician in France, but no records of such a person ever having existed could be found and Phinuit's knowledge of French was limited. Nevertheless, after months of studying Mrs Piper, James

was convinced that she knew things while in a trance that she could not have possibly known in a waking state.

Over the course of her career, Mrs Piper supposedly was the host to a number of spirits, and she could even host two spirits at the same time—one would speak, while the other guided her hand to write a message.

In 1887 William James turned the research on Leonora Piper over to Dr Richard Hodgson, the representative of the London-based SPR. Hodgson, a rigorous and thorough investigator, moved Mrs Piper to London to ensure that the people who came to her seances were strangers to her. He also inspected her mail and had her followed by a detective. The accuracy of the information relayed during Mrs Piper's trances continued to amaze investigators, but Hodgson was never able to determine whether the information did indeed come from a spirit or whether Mrs Piper possessed incredible powers of clairvoyance and telepathy.

THE SCIENCE OF PSI

Research of psychic phenomena began in earnest in the late 1920s, with the work of Professor Joseph Banks Rhine at Duke University. A professor in the psychology department, Rhine believed that the potential for psychic abilities existed in the general public and thus concentrated his energies on 'everyday people' rather than on the avowed psychic. As subjects for his experiments, Rhine recruited students and faculty at Duke. He began his research with an experiment involving a shuffled deck of cards. Subjects were asked to guess the order of the cards. If they scored better than could be expected by chance, some unknown factor was believed to be responsible. Like other researchers of the day, Rhine used an ordinary deck of playing cards. However, he was worried that 52 cards was too large a number with which to work, reasoning that subjects might tend to pick favorite numbers or avoid numbers they associated with bad luck.

Rhine asked a colleague, Karl Zener, to design a new set of cards. The Zener cards, as Rhine promptly dubbed them, featured a total of 25 cards—five cards each of five different, yet simple, designs: a circle, a square, a star, a plus sign and a wavy line.

To test for telepathic powers, the sender (the person conducting the experiment) would concentrate on the card that he had turned up, while the subject recorded his impression of the card. Often the sender and subject were seated at the same table, but in some cases they were seated farther apart, sometimes even in different buildings. To test for clairvoyance, the subject tried to perceive the cards as they were being turned over, or he tried to predict the order of the cards in the shuffled deck. To test for precognition, the subject attempted to predict what the order of the cards would be after they were shuffled.

Below: The San Francisco home of parapsychologist Henry Neville Quinn. Many of his experiments were conducted here.

According to the laws of probability and averages, a person would guess the correct answer, or hit, five times. In just one run through the deck, he might hit only once or twice, but over several trials the average would be about five hits. An average of nine hits, however, would be considered more than just chance.

After two years of study, Rhine found eight subjects who regularly scored above chance. The most successful of Rhine's subjects was a shy divinity student named Hubert Pearce. When Pearce exhibited an incredible ability at predicting the cards, Rhine devised a further series of tests that are still regarded as milestones in paranormal research. The results were remarkable, especially considering that Pearce and his experimenter, J Gaither Pratt, were in separate buildings.

With Pearce situated in a cubicle at the Duke library, Pratt would take a card from the deck and place it down without looking at it. Pearce, meanwhile, would record his impression of each card. Since Pratt did not look at the cards, this was a test of Pierce's clairvoyant ability. The results were astounding. Over a period of eight months, 1850 trials were conducted, and in one series of 12 runs of the Zener cards, Pearce scored as high as 13 hits per deck.

Although Rhine and his associates could offer no explanations for the results, they began to understand the psychology behind the psychic process. They discovered, for example, that mood affected psychic ability. In general, subjects scored higher when they were motivated. Rhine once offered Pearce $100 for every hit — and Pearce hit every card in the deck. On the other hand, subjects' scores declined when they were depressed or fatigued. Pearce did poorly after his fiancee broke off their engagement.

In 1934, Rhine published the results of his research in a monograph entitled *Extra-Sensory Perception*. Rhine was the first to coin the term, and he selected it carefully, trying 'to make it sound as normal as may be.' As perception was a branch of psychology, Rhine hoped that ESP would be viewed as a serious science rather than as some strange, supernatural curiosity.

The general public was captivated by Rhine's treatise, and some members of the academic community were convinced of the validity of Rhine's work. *Extra-Sensory Perception*, however, was not without its detractors. Some psychologists criticized Rhine's statistical methodology, while others pointed out the possibility for a high margin of error. The biggest criticism was that Rhine's work could not be duplicated—which is the process by which experiments receive the seal of approval from the scientific community.

Most members of the scientific community did not accept ESP as a legitimate sci-

Henry Neville Quinn (*above*) was born Heinrich Neuenberg in Karlsruhe, Germany in 1891. He emigrated to New York at age 20 and later settled in California where he studied psychology and parapsychology at the University of California and Stanford University.

Already greatly influenced by Joseph Banks Rhine whose work in the field of ESP was first published in 1934. Using the work of Rhine and Karl Zener as a model, Quinn conducted many spectacular, if flamboyant experiments. One of these involved the use of Zener cards (*left*) in which one subject was aloft in an airplane. Amazingly the results of this investigation showed that Quinn's airborne associate achieved statistically better results than another one on the ground!

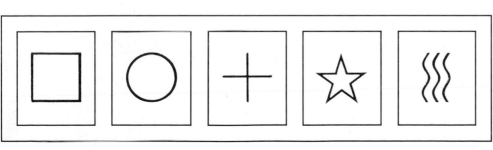

Below: **Since the groundbreaking work of JB Rhine at Duke University, the science of parapsychology has sought to unlock the mysteries of the human mind.**

Opposite page: **Magician Harry Kellar's popularity coincided with the rise of spiritualism and he had no hesitation with claiming that he had the power to communicate with the spirit world, albeit the devil. The implication that the magician was in league with the devil was a centuries-old concept, but Kellar was the first to use the image of the devil in his posters, letterhead and Christmas cards as a means of self-promotion.**

entific discipline. Even Duke University, which had established the country's first parapsychology laboratory with Rhine as its founding director, made a clear distinction between parapsychology and psychology and other established sciences.

Meanwhile, Gardner Murphy, a psychologist at Columbia University, was also studying psychic phenomena. Rhine referred his graduate students to Murphy, and in 1937 the two men founded *The Journal of Parapsychology*. The budding science soon attracted more students, and research centers were instituted at various universities. Rhine's book also came to the attention of the noted psychiatrist Carl Jung, who praised the work and encouraged Rhine to continue his research even though he would undoubtedly encounter criticism.

Jung had been fascinated by the paranormal since childhood, growing up in an environment that encouraged him to view psychic phenomena as a natural part of life. As an adult he studied astrology and the *I Ching*, and quite naturally followed Rhine's experiments with interest. Over the years Jung developed his theory of synchronicity to explain psychic events. According to Jung, synchronicity refers to a 'meaningful coincidence' of outer and inner events that are not themselves causally related. As an example of his theory, Jung referred to the pendulum clock in the palace of Frederick the Great at Sans Souci, which stopped when the emperor died. Jung noted that there are numerous other well-documented stories of this sort.

As Jung had predicted to Rhine, the science of parapsychology would be the subject of criticism for the next 25 years. In spite of the critics, Rhine and his colleagues persevered until 1965, when Rhine retired and the laboratory at Duke was closed. Elsewhere in the world, however, the study of parapsychology continued, and today parapsychology is studied at over 100 colleges and universities throughout the United States. One of the major centers of study is the University of Utrecht in the Netherlands.

Over the years the methods for testing psychic ability have become more technologically advanced. Hand-kept records have been replaced with computers, and Zener cards have been supplanted by Random Event Generators (REGs).

One of these first REGs was used by Dr Helmut Schmidt at Boeing Research Laboratory. The machine was driven by a piece of radioactive strontium 90. As the particle decayed, it emitted electrons that lit four colored lights at random. The subjects were asked to predict which light would be lit next. In one series of tests conducted with Schmidt's REG, subjects correctly predicted the light 26.7 percent of the time. The chance of correctly guessing would be about 25 percent, and while 26.7 percent seems only slightly higher, from a statistical point of view the difference is significant.

Free-response experiments are another method of psi testing. One of the best-known free response experiments was conducted by Harold Puthoff, Bonnar Cox and Russell Targ of the Stanford Research Institute (later SRI International) in 1974. Puthoff and Cox drove around for a half an hour, while the subject, Pat Price, a retired police commissioner from Burbank, California, was locked in an electrically shielded room.

The test was designed to study a phe-

Below: In a remote-viewing experiment conducted by SRI researchers Targ and Puthoff, subject Pat Price received an image of water and boats *before* the research team arrived at their destination—a marina in Redwood City, California.

nomenon known as remote viewing. After Puthoff and Cox had driven for half an hour, Price was to describe their location to Russell Targ, who was in the room with him to monitor the experiment. Price was able to describe the scene *before* Cox and Puthoff arrived—and they had no destination in mind as they were driving—with amazing accuracy: 'What I am looking at is a little boat jetty or a little boat dock along the bay. . . .I see some motor launches, some little sailing ships.' Price also noted 'a definite feeling of Oriental architecture that seems to be fairly adjacent to where they are.'

Twenty minutes later Cox and Puthoff arrived at the Redwood City Marina, a harbor and boat dock about five miles

away from SRI. Nearby was an Oriental restaurant.

Targ and Puthoff continued their experiments for the next several years, increasing the distance between subject and location. Their results were mixed, but one woman, Hella Hammid, described five out of nine sites correctly, prompting Targ and Puthoff to put her to a difficult test. From a submarine two miles off the California coast, Hammid was asked to identify a site somewhere in the San Francisco Bay area—a large oak tree on a cliff overlooking Stanford University. She correctly identified the tree and the cliff, and she reported that the experimenter, who was climbing the tree, was behaving in an 'unscientific manner.'

PSYCHIC PHENOMENA IN DAILY LIFE

Though virtually impossible to verify, evidence of psi ability is, of course, found beyond the confines of the laboratory. Researchers have attempted to document the reports of psychic experiences that often accompany stories of disasters such as earthquakes, plane crashes and so on. After studying rail accidents, W E Cox noted that the trains involved in accidents typically carried fewer passengers on the day of the accident than they did on other days. Cox hypothesized that many people may have had a premonition—perhaps unconscious—about the impending wreck and therefore stayed home.

One disaster that has been extensively studied is the 1912 sinking of the *Titanic*. Ian Stevenson, a psychiatrist and parapsychologist at the University of Virginia, studied psychic phenomenon associated with the *Titanic* and discovered 19 instances of apparent psi ability. The subjects ranged from people who had loved ones aboard the ocean liner to those who had no connection to the passengers or crew, and the psi experiences included dreams and hallucinations. An 11-year-old girl, whose mother was onboard, experienced a 'strange sense of doom.' Two days before the *Titanic* sank, a woman started screaming hysterically 'It's going to sink' as the great ocean liner passed by the waving crowds on the Isle of Wright.

Another catastrophe that was widely predicted was a coal-waste avalanche in the mining village of Aberfan, Wales. On the morning of 21 October 1966, a 600-foot mound of coal waste from the adjacent mountains shook and then roared down upon the village. Trees were uprooted, houses were swept away and the school was buried under the black mass—just as 10-year-old schoolgirl Eryl Mai Jones had seen in a dream the day before. 'I dreamed I went to school,' she told her mother, 'and there was no school there. Something black had come down all over it.'

Reports of visions of the tragedy at Aberfan were reported all over England. Prior to the disaster, an amateur artist in south-western England couldn't shake the feeling that a disaster involving coal dust was about to happen. Several other people had nightmares that they were suffocating in blackness, others dreamed of children running to escape an avalanche of black, and one man saw the word 'Aberfan' spelled out in a dream.

London psychiatrist J C Barker instigated a search for anyone who had experienced a premonition of the coal avalanche. Dr Barker investigated 76 people claiming to have foreseen the disaster. He immediately rejected 16 as inconclusive, but of the remaining 60 he discovered that more than half had experienced the sensation of impending disaster in a dream. In roughly a third of the cases, the people had documented the experience in a letter or diary before the coal slide occurred.

Convinced of the existence of psychic abilities, Dr Barker saw the need for a clearinghouse for predictions, and in 1967 established the British Premonitions Bureau to analyze and research predictions from known psychics as well as from the general public. Soon after, a similar agency, the Central Premonitions Registry, was formed in the United States.

Disasters are often associated with reports of precognition. Numerous psychic experiences were reported after the 1912 sinking of the *Titanic* (*above*), and were extensively studied by Dr Ian Stevenson of the University of Virginia. Similar, though not nearly as many, accounts were reported following the tragic crash of a circus train (*below*) in 1893.

ALTERED STATES

Because dreams were the channel in which so many people received information about the unknown, researchers began to explore a new area of study called Altered States Research (ASR). ASR examines the theory that when an individual is in a modified state of awareness—be it sleep or a trance—he is more sensitive to communication from deep within the mind.

Parapsychologists have long been aware that sleep improves psychic ability, and in 1965 an extensive study of dream telepathy was conducted by Drs Montague Ullman and Stanley Krippner at Maimonides Medical Center in Brooklyn, New York. In their experiments, the receiver slept in a sound-proofed room, while the sender in another room concentrated on a picture chosen at random.

Researchers used electroencephalographs to monitor the receivers' sleeping patterns. When the sleepers exhibited Rapid Eye Movement (REM), which signals that the sleeper is dreaming, they were awakened and asked what they were dreaming.

In many cases, the responses coincided with the picture the sender was concentrating on. One receiver, for example, described his dream as 'Something about posts. Just posts standing up from the ground and nothing else. There is some kind of feeling of movement.... Ah. Something about Madison Square Garden and a boxing fight.' The picture was George Bellow's *Dempsey and Firpo*, a painting of a prize fight at Madison Square Garden.

In addition to examining psi abilities during sleep, researchers have studied induced altered states of consciousness, such as hypnosis, drugs, meditation and biofeedback. One of the most successful experiments involving hypnotism was con-

Gertrude Wallingford Hamilton (*below*), a San Francisco socialite, had the ability to hypnotize herself and enter a deep-sleep trance. Once in this altered state, she experienced bizarre dreams and visions.

In her memoirs, she recalled a dream in which she saw her beloved city of San Francisco rising from flames and ashes like the mythical Phoenix. She interpreted the dream as a prophecy of the Great San Francisco fire and earthquake of 1906, which devastated the city and its subsequent rebirth with the Panama-Pacific International Exposition of 1915.

Left: The terrifying realization of Gertrude Hamilton's dream: the aftermath of the 1906 earthquake and fire. The dream ended with a vision of the Phoenix—a symbol for the Panama-Pacific International Exposition of 1915 (*below*).

Below: During an experiment in ganzfeld research at Princeton's Psychophysical Research, a subject reported an image of flames. In another room, the sender was concentrating on fire-eaters appearing on television. However, at that same moment, the subject's husband was taking photographs (including the one seen here) of a gas fire near the subject's home over 20 miles away.

Opposite page: Subjects at the Marin Psychic Center report that they can change their level of consciousness by concentrating on a candle flame. Once a higher level of consciousness is attained, an individual is more in tune with his or her psychic abilities.

ducted in the early 1960s by Milan Rylz, a Czechoslovakian biochemist. Rylz hypnotized Pavel Stepanek into believing that he had psychic powers. For more than a decade, Stepanek exhibited incredible psi ability. He was an especially high scorer at card guessing, sometimes at odds of 500,000 to one.

In the 1970s, a new area of research was developed called ganfeld, a German term that means 'total field.' Parapsychologist Charles Honorton was the first to conceive of the ganzfeld environment, which duplicates a highly relaxed dream state. Isolated from the external environment, the subject lies in a darkened room, his eyes covered

with halved table tennis balls and his ears filled with synthesized white noise. In this alert but relaxed state, he is deprived of outside stimulation and focuses on the images that come from within.

In one such experiment in 1984 at the Psychophysical Research Laboratories in Princeton, a sender concentrated on sending an image that appeared on a television screen to the subject. As the sender focused on projecting the image of two fire eaters, the subject reported 'This white noise, which ordinarily sounds like water, this time seems like flames... again hearing the rush of flames.... My images of flames didn't really include the feeling of heat.'

PSYCHICS AND CRIME

Some of the most sensational examples of psychic abilities are found in the headlines of grocery store tabloids proclaiming that a psychic has solved a crime that has baffled police for months. While these stories are frequently more fiction than fact, there have been numerous documented examples of people using psychic abilities to solve a crime.

Oddly enough, two of the best known psychics were from the Netherlands—Gerard Croiset and Peter Hurkos. Born in 1909, Croiset had established a name for himself by the late 1930s, but it was an uneasy existence. He found it difficult to hold down a job, and he was twice arrested by the Gestapo. Life finally turned around for him in 1945, when he met Willem Ten-

haeff, an unpaid lecturer in parapsychology at the University of Utrecht. Convinced that Croiset was the most talented psychic he had ever encountered, Tenhaeff eagerly ran the psychic through a series of tests.

For the next twenty years, Tenhaeff not only tested but also promoted Croiset's psychic abilities. Both men reached a level of prominence, with Tenhaeff becoming the world's first professor of parapsychology and the director of the University of Utrecht's renowned Parapsychology Institute and Croiset attaining international fame as a psychic.

As is often the case with psychics, Croiset's success rate for solving crimes was relatively small. Even so, some cases

Below: Psychic Gerard Croiset correctly predicted that the body of six-year-old Wimpje Slee would be found in a canal.

were remarkable for their accuracy, at least in certain details. Croiset is perhaps best known for the case involving four-year-old Edith Kiecorius of Brooklyn, New York, who had disappeared on 22 February 1961.

Croiset agreed to assist in the search for the missing girl, and before he had left Holland for New York, he had an image of the situation. The girl was dead. Her body would be found in a tall building with a billboard on top near an elevated railroad and a river. The murderer was a small, sharp-faced man, about 54 or 55, from southern Europe. He was wearing grey. Upon arriving in New York he had a clearer vision, declaring that the building had five floors and the body would be found on the second floor.

As Croiset had predicted, the body was found on the second floor of a building near the Hudson River and an elevated railroad. The police arrested and later convicted a small, sharp-nosed, swarthy man dressed in grey checks. Croiset did miss on a few accounts. The building was four stories, not five, and the suspect was from England, not southern Europe.

The irony of the case was that the police solved the case without the assistance of Croiset—they discovered the body in a search unrelated to the clues Croiset had provided.

Peter Hurkos was far more flamboyant and theatrical than his countryman Croiset. Hurkos' psychic abilities appeared in 1941 after he had fallen four floors from a building he had been painting. The thirty-year-old worker was taken to the hospital unconscious. When he awoke four days later he had amnesia and was suffering from a concussion and possible neurological damage. Shortly after regaining consciousness, he had a vision of his son, Benny, in a burning room. Five days later Benny was rescued from a fire.

After the accident, Hurkros' ability to concentrate was impaired to the point that he could not work or even read a book, but he suddenly seemed to have psychic abilities. He wasted no time in putting his new talents to use, giving shows for the public.

In 1947, he was asked to help solve the murder of a Dutch coal miner. Hurkos felt the dead man's coat, declaring that the man had been killed by his stepfather and the gun would be found on the roof of the dead man's house. Police did indeed find the gun where Hurkos had foreseen. Fingerprints on the gun led to the stepfather's conviction. Within a year Hurkos was famous throughout Europe and soon emigrated to the United States, where he became

equally well known as a physic advisor to Hollywood celebrities.

Though he didn't usually work on criminal cases, in 1964 Hurkos agreed to investigate the Boston Strangler case. For six days he studied two large boxes of items related to the case, eventually announcing that the Strangler would be found at Boston College. With Hurkos' pronouncement, the police showed him a letter to the Boston College School of Nursing from a man who wanted to interview—and perhaps marry—a typical nurse.

Upon seeing the letter, Hurkos declared that the letter writer was the killer. He described the man as a 52-year-old, homosexual, woman-hater who spoke with a French accent. He had a pointed nose, thin, receding hair and a prominent Adam's apple. Hurkos' dreams revealed even more details about the man: he slept on a cot, showered with his shoes on, and kept a diary that would reveal that he was the Boston Strangler.

Acting on Hurkos' clues, the police discovered a man they called Thomas P

Below: **Croiset's success as a psychic took him to New York City to solve the disappearance of the four-year-old Edith Kiecorius. Though he provided several clues that corresponded to where the girl's body was found, the police solved the case independently while investigating another matter.**

Below: While visiting a cousin in Sandpoint, Idaho, Donald Sandifer of Normal, Illinois volunteered to use his psychic powers to help the local authorities find Mikey Rosewall, a five-year-old boy who had been missing for two days in the fall of 1960.

When Sandifer told the police he saw water, the search was concentrated around the Pend Oreille River, and Mikey was found, dirty, hungry and tired but otherwise unharmed.

O'Brien (his real name was withheld from the public). In appearance and habits, O'Brien matched the description given by Hurkos, but the police had no evidence with which they could arrest him. They were, however, able to have O'Brien temporarily committed to a mental hospital for observation. In turn, O'Brien had himself voluntarily committed, making it impossible for him to tried for murder.

Several months later, Albert DeSalvo was arrested for rape, diagnosed as schizophrenic and committed to the same institution as O'Brien. DeSalvo began to boast that he was the Boston Strangler, and he spoke with enough knowledge of the crimes that police were convinced that he

truly was the killer. However, since he had been declared legally insane, DeSalvo, like O'Brien, could not be tried for murder, and the case of the Boston Strangler was closed without a trial.

The fact that Hurkos apparently had identified the wrong man tended to obscure his psychic accomplishments in the case. From simply examining evidence he had an amazing knowledge of the crimes, and his dreams of O'Brien and his surroundings were incredibly accurate.

Several years later Hurkos was again called upon to assist with a heinous crime—the 1969 murder of actress Sharon Tate by Charles Manson. Hurkos claimed to have played an important part in solving

the case, but police investigators minimized his significance.

Hurkos and Croiset typify the problems with using psychics to solve crimes. The details seldom lead to solving the crime and often are way off base. Dorothy Allison, a New Jersey psychic, has worked on over 4000 cases but claims to have solved less than 100. What cannot be ignored, however, is that in some instances, the psychics' predictions are correct, albeit grim, portraits of reality.

Allison first attracted public attention in December 1967, when she announced that she knew the whereabouts of five-year-old Michael Kurcsics. The boy was dead, she said, and his body would be found in a drainpipe. His shoes were on the wrong feet and he was wearing a green snowsuit. In the distance she saw a gray building, gold letters and the number eight.

Two months later, the boy's body was found in a drainpipe in Clifton, New Jersey. As Allison had predicted, he was wearing a green snowsuit and, under his boots, his sneakers were on the wrong feet. Nearby were a grey building, a factory with gold lettering and P S 8 elementary school.

In 1975, Dorothy Allison, among other psychics, assisted in the Patty Hearst kidnapping case. Her results were mixed. Although she could never exactly pinpoint the missing heiress' location, Allison was able to provide general information about Hearst's whereabouts and activities.

The following year Allison once again solved a missing person case. Like the case of Michael Kurcsics nine years earlier, this case began with a missing person and ended in murder. As before, Allison's clues led to the discovery of the body of 18-year-old Deborah Sue Kline. In this instance, she predicted that the body would be found on a hill. She also saw the color yellow, a dump, a shoe and a plastic swimming pool. Allison made the startling prediction that the case would soon be solved: Two men had been involved in the crime; one would confess and implicate the other.

Allison's vision was correct. A man named Richard Lee Dodson confessed and led the police to Fannettsburg Mountain. All of Allison's clues were present: yellow signs marked the route, a dump was nearby, the shoe belonged to the victim and she was buried under a plastic swimming pool.

Below: **With the assistance of psychic Henry Mikeskell, the San Francisco police solved the mysterious shooting that took place at 1635 Ellis Street on 4 June 1930.**

Mikeskell's clues led the police to Dorthea Howard, the woman who had vanished from the scene of the crime.

PSYCHOKINESIS

Opposite page: **Magicians of old may have relied on sleight-of-hand to thrill their audiences, but many of today's conjurors, such as Uri Geller and the Amazing Kreskin, possess psychic powers that enable them to perform amazing feats.**

Below: **At a series of experiments at a New England college, Amanda Stewart exhibited amazing powers of tele-kinesis. While locked in the parapsychology laboratory, she was able to bend an entire drawer of silverware in a cafeteria halfway across the campus.**

After completing her degree in 1959, Miss Stewart turned her back on scientific research and became a homemaker, devoting herself to raising a family.

In addition to his experiments on telepathy, precognition and clairvoyance, J B Rhine of Duke University later pursued a fourth area of psi research—psychokinesis. Known simply as PK, psychokinesis is the mind's ability to control matter. According to legend, Rhine became interested in PK when a professional gambler visited him at his laboratory at Duke. The gambler claimed that he could influence the roll of the dice when he was in a 'hot' frame of mind. Intrigued, Rhine conducted a series of experiments in which subjects rolled a single die 24 times or a pair of dice 12 times. The subject attempted to turn up a designated face or combination of faces.

Rhine based his conclusions on statistical evidence and was therefore not expecting to see psychokinesis at work on every throw of the dice. Instead, the results were compared with probability tables to determine whether something other than chance was operating. Rhine noted that the best results were obtained when the subjects were highly motivated. In one noteworthy series of throws, Rhine staged a dice-rolling contest between a team of four divinity students who relied on the power of prayer to succeed and a team of four other students who had shown a high degree of success at dice rolling. Both teams did exceedingly well—far better than if mere chance were operating. From the teams' points of view the contest was a draw, but from a statistical point of view Rhine came up the big winner.

In spite of such successes, much of Rhine's research was inconclusive, and he was reluctant to publish his results. Psi research as a whole lacked the support of the scientific community, and psychokinesis in particular was regarded in an even less favorable light. He was therefore hesitant to jeopardize his credibility.

By the 1960s, however, parapsychologists believed that the existence of psychokinesis had been sufficiently demonstrated in the laboratory, and thus turned their attention to the more sensational displays of psychokinesis that were to be found in the outside world.

Ingo Swann had demonstrated psychic ability as a young child. When he was only two years old, Ingo experienced the sensation of leaving his body and watching his own tonsillectomy. By the time he was an adult, his psychic powers were well developed and he agreed to be tested by the world's leading parapsychologists. Gertrude Schmeidler of City College in New York devised a series of experiments to test Swann's psychokinetic abilities. From a distance of four to 24 feet, Swann was able to change the temperature of a thermometer, some of which were sealed inside an insulated bottle. In some instances, Swann's own temperature also fluctuated.

One of the best known—and most controversial—psychics was Uri Geller, an Israeli nightclub performer. Geller was known for his sensational television performances in which he seemed to have the power to bend and even break metal by sheer concentration, or with just a few strokes of his fingers. After Geller's television appearances, the stations were flooded with reports from hundreds of viewers claiming that *their* own keys, silverware and other metal objects had bent during Geller's performance.

When meeting with parapsychologists,

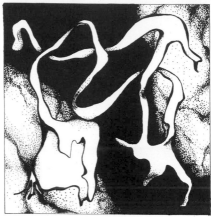

A spoon (*at top*) in its normal state and an artist's rendering of the psychokinetic energy (*above*) that flows through the spoon as it is bent.

Right: A before and after view of a fork used in an experiment testing the psychokinetic abilities of Jonathan Kemmerle. Kemmerle, an accountant in Cincinnati, Ohio, first became aware of his abilities when he was in high school. After a period of extensive testing, he experienced what psychologists term the decline effect and, discouraged, withdrew from further testing.

Geller liked to play little tricks on them, such as starting a stopped watch, but once in the laboratory Geller's abilities were difficult to assess. He proved to be an unwilling subject for the researchers at Stanford Research Institute and insisted on doing things his way.

When the results of the experiments were published, critics pointed out that the experiments lacked control and likened the situation to a circus. In fact, some of Geller's strongest critics were magicians who pointed out how Gellers' supposed psychokinetic powers could easily have been sleight-of-hand.

In contrast to Uri Geller, Nina Kulagina, a Russian housewife, proved to be a willing and able subject. Under supposedly controlled laboratory conditions, Kulagina has demonstrated the ability to move objects toward her, away from her and in a circular pattern.

Her PK powers affect fabric, metal and plastic, and she can work through plexiglass. She has reportedly separated an egg white from the yolk and moved the two parts in different directions.

Kulagina undergoes physical changes herself during her PK sessions. Her pulse rate climbs to over 200 beats per minute (75 to 80 is normal), brain activity at the rear of her head increases four times, and a magnetic field surrounds her body. She may also lose up to two pounds and suffer from insomnia, dizzy spells and muscle aches.

ESP THEORIES

The first challenge confronting the parapsychologists is to prove that psychic phenomena do indeed exist, and even as they work to document the existence of paranormal events, researchers must also attempt to explain *how* these events occur, for they contradict the laws of physics. Some researchers, however, contend that scientific theory can be used to explain the paranormal and have pointed to physical descriptions of the universe as models for paranormal activity.

One of the earliest models for ESP was found in the laws of electromagnetism, which describe how some signals for light, x-rays and so on travel in waves from a source to a receiver. At one end of the electromagnetic spectrum are short, high-frequency waves and at the other end are long, low-frequency waves, such as radio signals from a distant galaxy. Some parapsychologists hypothesized that psi waves were part of the spectrum, and like most electromagnetic waves cannot be sensed by human beings, except for those who can tune in their psychic receivers.

This model has been rejected by most parapsychologists today because psi waves were never found and the model failed to explain the faster-than-light speeds and undiminished power associated with precognition and telepathy.

A more recent model is based on multi-dimensional geometry. In this model, the paranormal exists outside, but interacts with, the four dimensions of time and space (height, width, depth). Some mathematicians have postulated that there are more than the four known dimensions, possibly as many as 26, and that the psi world belongs to one of these dimensions. The problem with this theory is that there is no *physical* evidence to support it.

A current model for psychic phenomena has its roots in quantum mechanics. According to the laws of quantum mechanics, units of matter at the subatomic level behave in a seemingly paradoxical manner, acting as neither particle nor wave. In fact, matter cannot even be said to exist; rather, matter is expressed in terms of mathematical probability and is said to have a 'tendency to exist.'

The paradoxical nature of quantum mechanics is demonstrated in the following famous example: When two particles— an electron and its antimatter equivalent, a positron, collide, the two particles are annihilated and two photons are created, each one speeding off in a different direction. Quantum mechanics states that photon A does not possess properties such as spin or velocity until it is noted by an observer. The moment that photon A is observed and takes on a spin, photon B acquires the opposite spin. In simple terms, photon B seems to know what photon A is doing, suggesting that the universe is connected in some hidden way.

The same concept is applied to psychic behavior, the implication being that human consciousness exists at the subatomic level, which explains why a psychic can know instantly of an event across the world.

As the study of parapsychology enters the 1990s, support from the academic world is mixed. Although some scientists see little value in continued research, the American Association of Science recently admitted the Parapsychology Association as an affiliated member society, and the National Institute of Mental Health, an American government body, has given grant support for the medical research of telepathic dreams. In Great Britain, intensive study of parapsychology is underway at Cambridge and a poll in *New Scientist* revealed keen interest in the subject. Worldwide, on the popular front, parapsychology continues to fascinate and amaze.

Below: Psychic energy—How does it happen? What form does it take? Researchers are constantly seeking the answers to questions like these, even as they work to persuade the skeptics that psychic phenomena occur.

INDEX

Page 176: From time immemorial, the human race has been fascinated by psychic occurrences. Since the era of the ghost hunters and the spiritualists, scientists have tried to unlock these mysteries of the universe, but the key is yet to be found.